Financial Globalization and the Emerging Market Economies

The whirlwind of financial globalization has descended upon emerging market economies and rapid change has brought both benefits and problems upon a dynamic group of nations.

This book examines the impact of ever-increasing financial globalization on emerging market economies, both in the developing economies and in the former socialist world. This impressive volume covers themes and issues such as:

- global capital flows and financial liberalization
- global financial architecture
- financial and macroeconomic instability.

Financial Globalization and the Emerging Market Economies will be of interest to students and academics in many areas including international economics, international finance and international political economy. It will also provide a useful source of information for those who work in the financial industry at large.

Dilip K. Das is a Toronto-based consultant to international organizations.

Routledge Studies in the Modern World Economy

Financial Globalization and the Emerging Market Economies

Dilip K. Das

Routledge
Taylor & Francis Group

LONDON AND NEW YORK

First published 2004
by Routledge
11 New Fetter Lane, London EC4P 4EE

Simultaneously published in the USA and Canada
by Routledge
29 West 35th Street, New York, NY 10001

Routledge is an imprint of the Taylor & Francis Group

Typeset in Sabon by Wearset Ltd, Boldon, Tyne & Wear
Printed and bound in Great Britain by MPG Books Ltd, Bodmin

British Library Cataloguing in Publication Data
A catalogue record for this book is available from the British Library

Library of Congress Cataloging in Publication Data
A catalog record for this book has been requested

ISBN 0-415-32876-4

For Vasanti,
who stood by me

[In the global financial system] capital is free to go where it is best rewarded, which in turn has led to the rapid growth of global financial markets. The result is a gigantic circulatory system, sucking up capital into the financial markets and institutions at the center and then pumping it out to the periphery either directly in the form of credits and portfolio investments, or indirectly through multinational corporations.

George Soros in *The Crisis of Global Capitalism*, 1998

Contents

Illustrations

Figures

Table

Preface

From an economic point of view, globalization represents a process of increasing international division of labor on the one hand and growing integration of national economies through trade in goods and services, cross-border corporate investment, and capital flows on the other. There is serendipity in globalization. As globalization, particularly financial globalization, progressed over the preceding quarter-century a new group of economies made its presence felt in the global economy. It was christened the emerging market economies. Several of them discernibly and measurably benefited from globalization during the preceding quarter-century. These economies tried to establish a framework for long-term economic growth which requires changes that, among other things, reduce government spending, lower trade barriers, and make the economy and financial markets more attractive to global investment. The liberalization, deregulation and reform-related gains in these economies were at the cost of at least some reform-induced pain. Presently, the emerging market economies are better integrated in the global economy than the rest of the developing world. Therefore, they have succeeded in benefiting from the synergy that the onward march of globalization provides.

This dynamic group of transitioning economies is endeavoring to seek a firmer foothold in the contemporary global economy than it had in the past. Chapter 1 shows that it is a medium-sized group of heterogeneous economies that is endeavoring to go down the matured economy path at a rapid clip, so that members are able to "emerge" as fully-fledged matured market economies in the foreseeable future. The industrial economies perceive them as a group of liberalizing and reforming economies that, by adopting liberalization and reform strategies, are creating opportunities for investment of surplus capital from the industrial economies, as well as markets for exporting goods and services. In their view, this country group represents *inter alia* the "emergence" of additional demand and new markets.

With liberalization, deregulation and reforms, global capital flow to the emerging market economies strengthened. Although in the 1970s they were limited to the emerging market economies of the western hemisphere, in the 1980s and the 1990s they spread to the emerging markets all over the globe. As Chapter 2 demonstrates, the emerging markets of Asia and Europe became important destinations for the private capital flows. After peaking at an unprecedented historical level in 1996, net capital flow from the global financial markets declined precipitously. The decade of the 1990s also saw a shift in the composition of global capital flows. The non-debt creating capital inflows and direct investment became the principal sources of new global capital available to the emerging market economies. After the Asian crisis of 1997, equity and bond investments and bank lending went into reverse gear. Banks and other institutional investors began cutting their exposure to the emerging market economies. However, the crisis failed to dampen the flow of the foreign direct investment (FDI) to this group of economies, although the catch was that the FDI flows were highly skewed and were heavily concentrated on a small group of emerging economies.

Chapter 3 indicates that liberalization and deregulation provided one cogent reason behind increased capital flows to emerging market economies during the 1990s. These flows were also boosted by apparently sound macroeconomic policies and explicit and implicit guarantees by the governments. Expectancy of higher returns on investment underlay the rise in private capital flows to this country group. These flows were stimulated by two recent trends: the first was toward globalization of markets for emerging market securities, while the second was toward broadening of the investor base. Latin American securities were increasingly being sold in European and Asian stock markets. Similarly, with the growing involve-ment of mainstream institutional investors, the range of investors became more diverse. The market pricing of emerging market securities was working reasonably well; consequently new investors were attracted toward them.

In a globalizing economy, financial liberalization does lead to tangible rewards. When emerging market economies enact policies to liberalize and deregulate equity markets to foreign investors and try to attract foreign direct investment, their endeavors for a healthy economic growth are strengthened. Although there is no evidence of a direct cause and effect relationship between financial liberalization and growth, if one formally examines economic growth before and after financial market liberaliza-tion, the results suggest that the liberalization is associated with higher real GDP growth. A reduction in the cost of capital, an increase in productive investment and improvement in growth opportunities are the most obvious channels through which financial liberalization can increase GDP growth. Economies with higher quality human resources, an improved physical infrastructure, a higher level of institutional development and proper regu-latory structure and market supervision benefit more from financial liberal-ization, which a priori stands to reason.

Over the last quarter century, particularly during the decade of the

1990s, the structure of the global financial markets as well as that in the emerging market economies evolved and underwent a dramatic transformation. As Chapter 4 delineates, noteworthy changes took place both in qualitative and quantitative aspects of global financial markets, and in the financial services industry, which includes equity and bond markets and the banking sector. Notwithstanding the recent decline in capital flows, the evidence of the preceding quarter century suggests that the financial markets in the emerging market economies have become increasingly deep and resilient. Not only are the financial flows more geographically diversified than in the past, but so too are the lenders and instruments used to direct capital to the emerging market economies.

If the emerging market economies benefited from the synergy that the onward march of globalization provided, they have also suffered from a well-known downside of financial globalization, namely macroeconomic and financial instability, which was frequently followed by the contagion effect. As analyzed in Chapter 5, premature and poorly sequenced, liberalization of the capital account and excessive reliance by some economies that were ill prepared to cope with large capital flows on global capital inflows created problems leading to financial crises. They caused large losses of output, serious economic dislocation, and had high social costs.

Chapter 6 focuses on the contagion effect, which became a defining feature of the emerging market economies during the 1990s and early 2000s. During this period capital flows to the emerging market economies became increasingly correlated. During the periods of financial crisis, bond spreads in the emerging market economies became increasingly (or even excessively) correlated. With increased integration in the global financial markets, some degree of correlation is normal. However, often co-movements appear to have been exaggerated, even *prima facie* illogical. They could be explained with the help of trade, banking, financial, linkages and macroeconomic similarities among the emerging markets. Non-economic factors such as herding and momentum trading are also known to be behind the contagion effect.

The focus of Chapter 7 is "global financial architecture" and financial and regulatory infrastructure. Global financial architecture is a multifaceted phenomenon. The chapter deals with several facets or components of the global financial system. It provides an exposition on crisis prevention and crisis resolution mechanisms, and also deals with weaknesses in the international financial system that contribute to the propensity for global financial instability. A discussion on the reforms needed in the global financial system follows. Various facets of global financial system are closely intertwined, and therefore putting one or some of them in place in isolation would not work, or would have a limited impact at best. This chapter provides the readers with a small illustration that is selective and relevant to the title of this book. To be sure, this treatment is far from exhaustive and complete.

An important strength of the book is the chosen theme. While there is a vast and growing literature on separate (although related) issues, such as globalization of finance, idiosyncrasies of the emerging market economies, financial crises, global capital flows, international banking, global financial architecture, and globalization, there is no book that brings these important and germane issues together within one common framework. The picture of both static and dynamic aspects of financial globalization and the emerging market economies has been painted in this book with a broad brush. The latest knowledge, the newest concepts and analyses of these topics have been covered. The unique feature that distinguishes it from the competition is its succinct coverage of numerous, carefully selected, thematic issues. The book is easy to access for the target readership because of its descriptive analysis style, which stops short of mathematical formulations and econometric modeling. It makes the book accessible to a larger number of readers. Many students and other readers who have good analytical minds and sound knowledge of economics and finance feel lost in mathematical formulations. Equations, technicalities and econometric modeling discourage many potential readers. They find overly technical works rather off-putting.

This subject is widely taught at both graduate and undergraduate levels. The theme is included in general courses such as International Economics, International Financial Economics, and International Political Economy. There is an increasing demand for a book on this topic from MBA, economics and finance students, who address issues pertaining to emerging market economies. Knowledge of emerging market economies is considered important for many jobs in the banking and finance sector, and a glance at the job advertisements in the *Financial Times* confirms this. The target readership for this volume includes graduate students in business, economics, finance, and international political economy, and senior level undergraduates as well as researchers, professionals and policymakers. It must also be clarified that this book is not rigorous and is not intended for academic specialists in this area.

Toronto   Dilip K. Das
June 2003

Acknowledgments

I take this opportunity to thank my son, Siddharth, for providing prompt and efficient research assistance and three anonymous referees for providing detailed comments on the manuscript. I am grateful to Robert Langham and Terry Clague of Routledge, London, for handling the publication of this book in an exceedingly efficient manner. I have been in the business of researching, writing and publishing for over three decades now. Their level of efficiency is an absolutely rare commodity in the publishing industry. To nurture excellence in any area of human endeavor, credit should be given where it is deserved. One neither needs a sword nor a gun to kill excellence in any society. Ignore and it will wilt away.

Toronto   Dilip K. Das
June 2003

1 The emergence of emerging market economies

1 Financial globalization

Neither the concept nor the phenomenon of globalization, or financial globalization, can be considered novel. Although the contemporary era of globalization is around a quarter of a century old, during the last decade the concept of globalization has acquired a great deal of currency, relevance, acceptance, and emotive force. From an economic point of view, globalization represents a process of increasing international division of labor on the one hand and growing integration of national economies through trade in goods and services, cross-border corporate investment, and capital flows on the other. There is serendipity in globalization, and several emerging market economies discernibly and measurably benefited from it during the preceding quarter-century. According to Horst Kohler, Managing Director of the International Monetary Fund: "This process led average global per capita income to more than triple in the second half of the last century."[1] That said, there is an imperative need for globalization to be handled in a pragmatic, knowledgeable, clairvoyant and sagacious manner, otherwise its negative effects can seriously destabilize an economy.

Within the neo-classical paradigm, capital flows where its marginal product is higher. As a result, the allocation of capital is more efficient and global welfare is higher when capital flows freely across national borders. As trans-border capital flows increase, economies are progressively integrating globally. The financial structures of economies as well as the world of finance are *pari passu* changing. This applies to both domestic and global financial markets. A quarter century ago, a businesswoman was restricted to borrowing from her domestic market. However, if she operates in an emerging market economy, several options are presently open to her. For instance, she can choose between issuing stocks and bonds in the domestic or foreign financial markets. She can reduce her cost of capital if foreign currency loans are available at more attractive terms than the domestic loans, and these loans can be hedged by using a variety of financial products. She can also consider selling equity at foreign Bourses, which are far more liquid than the domestic ones.

A functional definition of financial globalization is the integration of the domestic financial system of an economy with the global financial markets and institutions. The enabling framework of financial globalization essentially includes liberalization and deregulation of the domestic financial sector as well as liberalization of the capital account. In a globalized financial environment domestic lenders and borrowers participate in the global markets, and utilize global financial intermediaries for borrowing and lending. Trans-border capital flows tend to integrate the domestic and global financial markets and systems (Das, 2003a). One of the most significant aspects of financial globalization is the rapid expansion of international liquidity. There has been an enormous increase in liquid assets available to global market participants.

Section 2 of this chapter describes the characteristics of an emerging market economy, followed by definitional issues in Section 3. Section 4 focuses on what could be called an absolute pre-condition for the creation of an emerging market economy. Section 5 delves into the domestic and global economic and financial environment affecting the emergence of an economy. The next section explores the macroeconomic factors in the emerging market and industrial economies that shaped the global financial scenario of the 1990s, particularly the events after July 1997.[2] Section 7 pulls these strands together and is followed by the conclusion.

2   What are emerging market economies?

Although the term "emerging market" is of recent vintage, the phenomenon itself is centuries old. Were all the industrial economies of today not the emerging markets in one period of their economic history or the other? Countries like Argentina, Australia, Britain, Japan, and the United States (US) were all emerging market economies at one point in time. Each of these countries was also among the richest, in terms of *per capita* income. In the emerging market sense, the US emerged around two centuries ago. After that it did suffer some reversals, yet the US has stood as economic history's premier example of the successful emergence of a market economy to attain the status of a matured industrial economy, having highly developed economic and financial institutions. Argentina is a diametrically opposite case. Around a century ago, when Argentina, Australia, and Japan were emerging market economies, Argentina was the richest of the three by a good measure. However, unlike the other two economies, Argentina failed to complete its emergence process. Australia and Japan did so in the twentieth century. Of the two, Japan emerged as the second largest global economy and has maintained this status to the contemporary period.

First under the sponsorship of the General Agreement on Tariffs and Trade (GATT), and subsequently due to the concerted endeavors of the World Trade Organization (WTO), tariff and non-tariff barriers to global trade have fallen dramatically over the preceding half-century and global trade has expanded. A large number of developing economies launched into liberalizing and deregulating their economies of their own accord in the mid-1980s, during the Uruguay Round period (1986–1994). The Doha round of multilateral trade negotiations (MTNs) is presently (2001–2005) working toward the objective of further liberalizing world trade. Likewise, barriers to global financial flows fell under the direction of the International Monetary Fund (IMF) and the World Bank, as well as because of unilateral measures taken by several developing economies over the last quarter-century. Consequently global trade in goods and services has expanded many-fold, benefiting many new dynamic developing-country traders, and financial globalization has expanded to this sub-group of developing economies. In this macroeconomic and financial *mise-en-scène* a sub-group of developing economies was able to integrate with the global financial markets, and emerged to join the ranks of the so-called emerging market economies.

The sub-group of developing economies that was able to integrate with the global economy *inter alia* stood to benefit from well-managed financial integration with the global economy. Financial integration needs to be well managed, because poorly managed integration can result in myriad problems for the integrating emerging economies. The benefits of well-managed financial integration tend to accrue on both the production and consumption sides. Global financial integration provides possibilities for accelerating real GDP growth rate by creating opportunities for better diversification and shifting to riskier but more productive investments. Global financial integration also enables inflows of global capital, including that of foreign direct investment (FDI). FDI is known to augment the total volume of investment in the recipient economy.

Global financial integration successfully severs the bond between domestic saving and investment. Domestic saving no longer acts as a constraint on investment, and larger investment in more productive endeavors becomes feasible. Even when FDI merely substitutes for (rather than augments) capital, it may be more productive than the capital for which it substitutes. FDI has many spillover effects, one of which is to raise the productivity of existing domestic capital. It also allows creation of an improved global pool of risks, making it feasible to shift the investment mix to projects with higher *ex ante* returns. Global financial integration reduces volatility in consumption patterns by creating opportunities for borrowing from and lending to the global markets, as well as by enabling better diversification of portfolios (cf. Chapter 5).

For the emerging market economies to emerge, a rapid growth rate with an endogenous character is a vitally important condition. Emergence takes a conscious and calculated phased approach. By building the foundation of continued growth in the first phase for expansion in the second, an economy can engender the self-sustaining character of growth. The creation of the necessary institutional infrastructure and its subsequent attainment of maturity will *pari passu* develop with the sustainable growth endeavors. Second, it is indispensable for the economy to have a high propensity to save and invest for a sustained period. Together these factors ensure a reasonable level of capital accumulation and its efficient allocation. As these economies integrate globally, it will eventually be feasible for them to emerge and qualify for the epithet "emerging market economy."

3   Challenge of defining

The emerging markets – a transitioning group of economies – are somewhat vaguely and imprecisely defined. That there is a degree of vagueness regarding the concept of emerging market economies has caused amusement in some scholars.[3] The countries that coined this expression attach one set of meanings to the concept, while it has different implications in the set of countries for which the term was intended. The latter group thinks of the emerging market economies as a large, if heterogeneous, group with "a well-defined center but a hazy periphery." These economies are seeking a firmer foothold in the global economy than they presently have. They are endeavoring to go down the matured economy path at a rapid clip, so that they are able to "emerge" as fully-fledged matured market economies in the foreseeable future. As opposed to this, the industrial economies think of the emerging market economies as a country group that is liberalizing its economies, and in the process creating opportunities for the investment of surplus capital from the industrial economies as well as markets for the export of goods and services. In their view, this country group represents the "emergence" of additional demand and new markets.

Kolodko (2002) believes that it is easier to determine which countries are not emerging market economies than it is to determine those that are. Accordingly, the industrial economies do not qualify for the emerging market status, because for them the emergence stage of growth has been crossed and now they are economies with matured market institutions. That excludes all the members of the Organization for Economic Cooperation and Development (OECD) – except for Korea and Turkey.[4] These are highly developed market economies with matured institutions. The second country-group that is a candidate for exclusion comprises those economies that have not as yet developed as market economies. Should the residual economies be called the emerging market economies? Decidedly not. Of this residual group, the countries that can be classified as emerging market economies are those whose economies are gradually developing and approaching an advanced stage in structural reforms. These countries have been liberalizing their economies for so long that a qualitative transformation in their economies is either about to take place or has already taken place. This qualitative transformation in turn enables them to integrate with the global economy and to take advantage of global factors (particularly capital) and trade flows. Determining the emerging market status of an economy is a matter of establishing the openness and maturity of its institutions, as well as whether the economy in question adheres to the rules, laws and culture of an open-market economy. These considerations make a diverse group of developing and transition economies, with substantial differences in economic histories, candidates for the emerging market economy status.

So far there is little agreement on the country count. In the industrial economies the emerging market economies are thought of as the newly industrialized economies[5] (NIEs) and some middle-income developing countries. The latter group includes those countries in which governments and firms are creditworthy enough, from the perspective of global investors, to borrow successfully from the global capital markets and/or attract institutional portfolio investment.[6] Different international institutions include slightly different sets of countries in this category. For example, the Institute of International Finance (IIF) includes 29 countries; five from Africa and the Middle East, seven from the Asia-Pacific region, eight from Europe, and nine from Latin America.[7]

The IMF defines emerging markets as the developing countries' financial markets that are less than fully developed, but are nonetheless broadly accessible to foreign investors. According to the IMF, the term "emerging market economies" refers to "a group of countries comprising developing economies, countries in transition and the advanced economies."[8] Since 1997, the following five countries have been classified as advanced economies: Hong Kong SAR, Israel, Korea (the Republic of), Singapore, and Taiwan. Thus, this is a significantly broad interpretation of the term emerging market economies. A glance at various statistical appendices and tables of the IMF publications reveals that 20 countries are generally included in these tables as the emerging market economies. Their geographical division is as follows: one in Africa, ten in Asia, three in Europe, five in the Western hemisphere, and one in the Middle East.[9]

The Economist (2003a) is much more precise, and has classified 25 developing and transitional economies as emerging market economies for reporting its standard weekly tables of emerging market indicators. This classification includes ten Asian economies, seven in the Western hemisphere, four in the Middle East and Africa, and four in Eastern Europe.[10] Only 18 countries are common to *The Economist* and the IIF categorizations, implying a good deal of diversity in their concepts.

4   The *sine qua non* for an emerging market

Other than the rapid endogenous growth endeavors noted in Section 2, Sylla (1999) identified respect of property rights and respect of human rights as the basic prerequisites for becoming an emerging market economy. The national government should offer protection to property and human rights of both the citizens of the country and the non-residents alike. An indispensable condition for an emerging market economy is its sustained ability to attract global capital inflows, and only an assurance of protection of property rights will attract global investors. Thus, protection of property rights is a fundamental, non-negotiable condition that an economy must meet before embarking on the road to becoming an emerging market economy.

When an economy has the required quantity and quality of human and natural resources but lacks the third vital ingredient for economic growth, namely capital, it can wait until capital is domestically generated and accumulated with advancing growth. The alternative course is to convince global investors of its dormant economic potential. If it succeeds in doing so, the global capital infusion will help to realize the economic potential of the country in a shorter time span than it would take by striking out on its own. Thus, the concept of an emerging market is basically tied up with "arbitraging the difference between a country's current economic reality and its future economic potential" (see Sylla, 1999). However, the recipient economy needs to ensure that global capital infusion results in the mutual benefit of the global investors and the recipient economy. Global investors are rational economic agents and market participants. Only a reasonable certainty of a regular (if not handsome) rate of return on their investment would attract global investors to the potential emerging market economy.

First and foremost, to fulfill the above-mentioned pre-condition, a country needs to have political stability, a structure of credible legal institutions that protect property rights and human rights, and a progressively open and liberal economic system. Statist economic systems are anathema to emerging market economies. Second, a stable currency and a credible public finance system are the basic infrastructure for an emerging market economy. Together they provide a trustworthy means of servicing public debt and make these economies attractive to domestic and global investors, resulting in higher investment rates in the economy. Third, the government should assist its private sector to develop attractive financial asset markets and secondary markets where public and private securities can be traded at market value. Determining and maintaining high regulatory and supervisory norms is also the task of the financial authorities.

When an economy embarks on its goal to be an emerging market economy, in the initial phases assistance from the financial and monetary authorities may also be required in the development of banking and financial institutions. Initiatives by the central banks are generally needed in developing a system of supervision and regulation. Experiences of the preceding quarter-century reveal that once these financial, regulatory, and legal objectives have been achieved and a basic financial infrastructure established, governments should leave the arena for the private sector to get on with the development of the financial sector and, in turn, the economy. Markets should be allowed free play, although on specific occasions governments may take a corrective measure or two. This needs to be done when market failure becomes obvious. Governments must be cautious in not pursuing their own objectives that are incompatible with economic growth. If the market perception of the role of the government is that of an unwarranted interventionist, it will be highly detrimental to the cause of developing an emerging market economy.

Being able to attract global capital and becoming an emerging market economy can be a great advantage to an economy.[11] Although there are some limitations and dangers, on balance becoming an emerging market economy is far more advantageous than not becoming one. Laying down a robust foundation of domestic financial institutions – and maintaining their strength – can maximize the advantages of acquiring the emerging market status for an economy. This is an important lesson for the potential emerging market economies of the present era.

5   Environmental determinants of global capital flows

Domestic or country-specific economic and financial factors on the one hand and the external (or regional and global) economic and financial environment on the other are among the two most important determinants of global capital market inflows to, or outflows from, the emerging market economies (Fernandez-Arias and Montiel, 1996; Taylor and Sarno, 1997; Eichengreen and Mody, 1998). Until financial crisis struck the five Asian economies[12] in mid-1997, net global capital flow into emerging market economies had continued to rise in an almost monotonic manner (see Chapter 2). In the rising volume of financial flows lay another valuable lesson for the emerging market economies: that markets reward strong fundamentals, sound financial and macroeconomic policies, and commitment to liberalization and structural reforms. Incompatible and short-sighted macroeconomic and financial policies destabilize economies, and global financial markets are highly sensitive to policy inconsistencies and their outcome. Market disapproval is forthwith reflected in the reversal of the direction of capital inflows into the emerging market economies. Furthermore, a crisis-free and upbeat financial and economic external environment also stimulates capital flows to this group of economies. Conversely, a depressed external environment retards, even reverses, capital market flows to the emerging market economies (see Chapter 2, Sections 5 and 6).

The domestic macroeconomic environment is a crucial variable impinging upon domestic investment, foreign investment, and productivity growth at the micro level. It is one of the most significant variables that go to make up the "investment climate" of an economy. Being a broader term, "investment climate" envelops entry and exit laws for firms, regulations regarding expansion of production, and the quality of the support infrastructure. The latter includes financial services, power, transport, and telecommunications services. The overall economic governance in the domestic economy, which entails contract enforcement laws, rational taxation laws, and control over corruption, seriously influences investment climate. If an economy with poor domestic macroeconomic environment and investment climate liberalizes its trade and investment policy structure, the likely outcome will be increased imports and little growth in investment.

A recent study of the investment climate in India, which launched its economic liberalization program belatedly in mid-1991, provides many notable insights and is worth citing in this context.[13] It revealed substantial differences in investment climate across the country because many investment policies and the quality of economic governance are determined at the state level. During a structured survey, entrepreneurs were asked to rank the Indian states from the point of view of their investment climate. They were asked to identify the two extremes, the best and the worst states, and give estimates of the cost savings possible by setting up an enterprise in different states. Maharashtra was widely recognized as the state with the best investment climate, while West Bengal and Uttar Pradesh were ranked by the entrepreneurs at the other extreme. According to the survey results, owing to its good investment climate the cost advantage of operating an enterprise in Maharashtra was 30 percent compared to the two states at the other extreme. This was indeed a large competitive advantage for the entrepreneurs.

The study found that a poor investment climate adversely affected both value added and factor productivity. Little wonder that there has been a large interstate variation in the mean rate of net fixed investment in India. States with a superior investment climate, namely Maharashtra, Gujarat, and Andhra Pradesh, have been successfully attracting far more global and domestic investment than the ones that were rated poorly in terms of investment climate. Although this was an intra-country study, the same tendency is reflected at the global level. The economies that are now the emerging market economies have paid a great deal of attention to and focused policy thinking on improving their investment climate.

The global financial market perception of the economic and financial environment – also referred to as market sentiment or market confidence – is of vital significance because most decisions are based on this subjective reading of the emerging markets. If the financial markets detect an environment of unsound fundamentals, exchange rate inflexibility at an unsustainable level, or other financial and systemic limitations, the impact is generally pernicious. For market perceptions, perception is reality. A change in market sentiment can lead to the drying up of global financial flows, recession, exchange rate depreciation, and interest rate hikes.[14] The decade of the 1990s suffered a spate of speculative attacks on emerging markets as well as matured industrial economies. Speculative attacks are squarely based on market perceptions and the presence of imperfections in the global financial markets. Several speculative attacks were launched on the European economies (France, Italy, Spain, and the United Kingdom) during the 1992–1993 period. The Mexican peso came under speculative attack in 1994. The Czech koruna, Thai baht, Indonesian rupiah, and several other Asian currencies came under speculative attacks during 1997 and 1998.

The presence of institutional investors in the global financial markets exposed the emerging market economies to further vulnerability. Institutional investors and currency speculators could potentially take substantial short positions in a weak currency. It was observed during the recent emerging market crises that as soon as an inflexible exchange rate and other financial sector weaknesses became apparent in an economy, institutional investors and currency speculators were attracted toward it, making a currency crisis imminent. The well-known "herding" behavior of investors immediately made this situation worse.[15] The impact of momentum trading, noise trading, and bandwagon effects is the same,[16] and these were typical and endemic market imperfections. Information asymmetry exacerbates this kind of market behavior. In addition, the currency and stock markets tended to over-react because it is the financial agents who manage investment, not the principals. Economies having inflexible exchange rate regimes are considered to be more vulnerable by speculators (Das, 2001a). However, this is not to say that the flexible exchange rate regimes are completely free of problems.

The expression "external environment" represents both regional and global environments. The contemporary period of financial globalization has witnessed several instances of national, regional, and global economic turbulence. Between 1992 and 1998, three major regional currency crises and two major country defaults took place. They were the European monetary crisis of 1992–1993,[17] the Latin American crisis of 1994–1995, and the Asian crisis of 1997–1998. Two of these three regional crises jolted the emerging market economies and affected global economic performance.

The litany of problems did not end there. There was a spate of individual economy crises, which also cannot be ignored. The 1998 sovereign default by the Russian Federation and sharp depression of the ruble had serious ramifications for the global financial markets.[18] Serious financial and currency problems followed in Brazil and Ecuador (1998–1999) as well as Turkey (2000–2001).[19] The Argentinian economy not only suffered a crisis (2000–2002) but also a sovereign defaulted, and Venezuela suffered a crisis (2002–2003) (see Chapter 5). This was caused by persisting with a fixed and overvalued exchange rate arrangement, proving that fixed exchange rate regimes are vulnerable to asymmetric shocks. Recent experiences have demonstrated that together they contribute negatively to the macroeconomic environment of the economy, and act as a serious destabilizing factor.

Disentangling the country-specific and global factors

Evidence of domestic or country-specific economic and financial factors on the one hand and of the external (or regional and global) economic and financial environment on the other determining the volume and price of the global capital inflows into the emerging markets is provided by the recent variations in the capital flows. The Asian crisis of mid-1997 and the Russian, Brazilian and LTCM[20] crises of 1998 impacted upon the capital flows to the emerging market economies in a negative manner, causing a sharp decline in them. This fall was general and was caused by underlying global driving forces. Various explanations have been provided for it (Calvo and Reinhart, 1999). Several emerging market economies received only a trickle of global capital after these crises, while in others they virtually stopped. Recovery in and after 1999 was uneven, indicating that the country-specific factors played a greater role than the external factors. While capital flows reached pre-crisis levels in Brazil and Mexico in 1999, capital flows in Argentina and Venezuela continued to fall until 2000. They became outflows in 2001, particularly in the emerging markets of Eastern Europe. An empirical framework is available for disentangling the relative weights of country-specific and external factors in determining capital flows, using data from Argentina, Brazil, Mexico, and Venezuela during the 1990s (Fiess, 2003).

Using this approach, the common component of the emerging market economy's country credit spreads is separated from its country-specific components. It is logical to believe that country spreads reflect global conditions and, therefore, capture the systemic or global risks. As opposed to this, the country-specific components reflect an emerging market economy's economic fundamentals or, more correctly, the financial market's perception regarding the fundamentals. The latter provides an emerging market economy's pure risk premium. The pure country risk and global risk components are then used as explanatory variables to account for the observed pattern of capital flows in the emerging markets under analysis. To this end, multivariate co-integration models have been used.

When the co-movements in sovereign bond spreads are large and when they increase they are considered to be common emerging market-wide events – that is, they are viewed as being systemic or external shocks. As opposed to this, when the co-movements are small and declining they are regarded as pointing to more idiosyncratic or country-specific shocks. Therefore, it is important that shocks are split into idiosyncratic, or country-specific and global. Mauro *et al.* (2000) and Dungey *et al.* (2000) use factor analysis to divide international interest rate spreads into these two categories. Following these earlier studies, and using principal component analysis, Fiess (2003) constructed an indicator of global co-movement. He argued that only the idiosyncratic or country-specific (residual of a regression of the spread on the first principal component) is a country risk. As opposed to this, the first principal component itself (systemic component of the spread) is driven by external factors.

The results of this study can be summarized as follows. First, global capital flows to emerging market economies can be driven by internal, country-specific factors, or external, global factors. The first set of factors (or pull factors) reflects domestic investment opportunities as well as domestic risk. The second set of factors (or push factors) reflects the level of economic activity and alternative investment opportunities in the emerging market economies. Second, capital flows were found to be a negative function of country risk, global co-movement and long-term US interest rates. Capital flows to emerging markets increase when country risk, systemic risk, and US interest rates go down. This result is consistent with the theoretical argument regarding the pull and push factor approach, where capital flows to the recipient emerging market increase if the perceived country risk is low, and if the interest rates in the creditor country are low. Third, as regards global capital flows to the sample countries, Fiess (2003) concluded that idiosyncratic or country-specific factors played a significant role in the observed capital flows in Brazil, Mexico and Venezuela. Conversely, external global factors played a domineering role in capital flows to Argentina. Fourth, during the decade of the 1990s the contribution of country-specific and external factors was far from uniform. Before 1996, strong evidence of the influence of both types of determinants was found in Argentina. However, after the crisis struck in the Russian Federation, only country-specific factors reached statistical significance, while the influence of external factors became insignificant. In Brazil, the country-specific factors lost significance after the real depreciation in 1999, while the external factors remained dominant in determining the capital flow through the period under consideration (1990–2001). The story for Mexico was different to that of Argentina and Brazil. Country-specific risk remained a dominant factor until only the 1994 *Tequila* crisis. The influence of the US interest rate remained strong over the capital flows for Mexico, reflecting its close ties and integration with the US economy.

Building up market sentiment: the Brazilian case

In the preceding section, I focused on the significance of financial market sentiments for the emerging market economies. A short case study of Brazil demonstrates how such economies assign a great deal of importance to the quest for market confidence. Brazil went through a cycle of ups and down in the financial markets' confidence. It was strongly favorable at first, then it weakened and had a deleterious impact on the economy before it improved again. The policy-makers had constantly and thoughtfully to work toward the often elusive target of building up strong financial market confidence in the Brazilian economy.

When Brazil introduced a new currency (the real) in 1994 and adopted a crawling-peg regime *vis-à-vis* the dollar, the economy turned a corner. Several other thoughtful structural reforms were made and macroeconomic measures taken, and these were reflected in a tight rein on inflation and rapid GDP growth rate in 1995. Financial reforms and liberalization measures were part of the new policy package. The economy enjoyed strong financial market sentiment, and its level of public debt rose from 21 percent of the GDP in 1994 to 30 percent in 1997.

The Asian crisis, the Russian sovereign default and the LTCM implosion took place during 1997 and 1998. These were not years of favorable financial market sentiment for the emerging market economies. The real came under growing pressure in late 1998, and in mid-January 1999 the Brazilian stock market crashed.[21] The contagious effect of the Russian crisis was blamed for the crash. The Brazilian authorities chose to defend the crawling-peg regime by raising interest rates, substituting fixed-rate debt with dollar-linked indexed debts, and tightening fiscal policy. Fiscal institutional reforms were also implemented, which strengthened the management of public finances. In response to the crisis, the Brazilian economy had adopted a sound package of macroeconomic policies. As regards the currency management, first the exchange rate band was widened, and then the real was floated in January 1999. These endeavors were also supported by a $18 billion stand-by facility from the IMF. The result was that the currency stabilized, although at a depreciated level, and financial outflows stopped. The rate of inflation began to fall by 2000, and real GDP growth resumed after the stagnation of 1998–1999. These post-crisis developments resulted in a favorable financial market sentiment for the Brazilian economy.

In mid-2002, although Brazil resisted the contagious effect of the Argentinian crisis, it did face deterioration in financial market sentiment. The principal cause of deterioration was the sharp depreciation in the real, which in turn was caused by the prospects of uncertainties in the forthcoming (in October 2002) presidential election. The high level of Brazil's public debt, which had nearly doubled between 1996 and 2002, added to this feeling of market uncertainty and weakened the market confidence level. Given the high level of external financial requirement and the fact that Brazil was a large and important emerging market economy, the IMF had to agree to a $30 billion stand-by arrangement, to be disbursed during 2003. The IMF agreement was followed by public commitment by all the presidential candidates to follow prudent macroeconomic policies. This was accompanied by an expression of support by foreign banks active in Brazil, "to sustain their general level of business in Brazil, including trade credit lines." All these measures added up, and the cumulative impact was that financial market sentiment improved toward the end of 2002. Market participants saw these measures supporting stability and growth in the Brazilian economy. Consequently, a significant decline in bond spread was noticed, although it remained high. Thus the cycle of high and low market confidence levels continued with variations in the economic circumstances and policy responses to changing circumstances.[22]

6   Macroeconomics of global capital flows

Domestic and global macroeconomic factors have played a meaningful role in the recent growth and development of emerging market economies. The general global macroeconomic environment has improved markedly over the last two decades, particularly during the 1990s. In an improved environment, many developing and transition economies succeeded in upgrading their status and became emerging market economies. Several factors were responsible for the improvement in the global economic performance during the 1990s, up until mid-1997. One of the principal factors was the general macroeconomic improvements in both the emerging market and industrial economies. These two sub-groups performed markedly better in the 1990s than in the 1980s. The institution of the Brady Plan in 1989 helped those emerging market economies that were struggling with the debt-servicing problems of the early 1980s (see Chapter 4, Section 3). This group essentially comprised the emerging markets of the Western hemisphere. Thus, the emergence of the emerging market economies during the 1980s and 1990s was not merely a fortuitous accident; it was significantly aided and abetted by the domestic and global macroeconomic and financial environment of this period.

According to the statistics compiled by the International Monetary Fund (IMF, 1997), fiscal deficits for the emerging market economies fell from an average of 6 percent of the GDP in 1983–1989 to 3 percent of the GDP in 1990–1996. Likewise, the average rate of inflation for this country group also declined, slowly at first and sharply later. The rate of real GDP growth, which had declined to 2.2 percent during the 1979–1989 period, soared to 6 percent during the 1990–1996 period. The rate of export growth was down to 6 percent for the former period, while it soared to 11 percent for the latter. The export surge facilitated debt servicing, and therefore the ratio of external debt service payment to exports fell sharply between 1990 and 1996. Also, the ratio of external public debt to GDP fell from 54 percent in 1990 to 37 percent in 1996. A marked improvement in the macroeconomic performance was one of the fundamental reasons behind the improved access of this country group to international financial markets. The number of economies having investment grade rating went on increasing, and the number of emerging market countries with Moody's credit rating rose from 11 in 1989 to 52 in 1997. In addition, extensive privatization took place in these economies during the 1990s. This single measure further opened these economies for the inflow of global finance.

Likewise, evidence of macroeconomic improvements in the industrial economies abounds. For instance, the average inflation rate fell from a little above 4 percent to less than 2 percent during the period under consideration. This resulted in a fall in both short- and long-term nominal interest rates. The former declined from an average of 7.3 percent during 1987–1990 to 4.3 percent during 1994–1996. The long-term interest rates, fell from an average of 8 percent to 6.3 percent during the same periods. A declining interest rate in one set of economies and stronger fundamentals in the other has been alluded to while discussing the so-called push and pull factors. There was a well-publicized earlier view that it was the downward interest rate movement alone in the industrial economies that was sufficient to trigger greater capital movement toward emerging market economies. However, this does not seem to be correct because it was the foreign direct investment (FDI) flows that increased more during the 1990s as compared to the other categories of private capital flows. These flows are largely unresponsive to small interest rate changes. Therefore, a pull factor was as important as the push factor.

This optimistic view cannot possibly be of the "Pollyanna" variety, because industrial economies are known to go through business cycles. As demonstrated in Chapter 2 (Section 6), when the cycle takes a downward turn the favorable capital market environment changes and so does the much-vaunted investor sentiment, and markets become risk averse and liquidity is scarce. The other possibility is that economic conditions in emerging market economies may deteriorate, which may cost them access to the international financial markets. Under both these sets of circumstances, the financial flows may be slowed, stopped or even reversed. Therefore, sustainability of global financial inflows must not be taken for granted by the policy mandarins in the emerging market economies.

In principle, two basic forces tend to drive global investors toward the emerging market economies. The first is the expectation of a high long-term rate of return, which is largely based on liberalization and macroeconomic policy reforms undertaken by the emerging market economies. This improves the creditworthiness of this sub-group of economies. Second, by investing in the emerging markets, global investors see that they are exploiting an opportunity for risk diversification. Improvements in the enabling environment over this period, in the emerging markets as well as in the matured industrial economies, further abetted these two factors. The macroeconomic and regulatory environment on the one hand and the techno-economic conditions that govern production and operation of the financial markets on the other had markedly improved during this period. Consequently, as noted above, large financial flows took place from the global capital market to the emerging market economies during the 1980s and 1990s.

However, hindsight reveals that the quantum of these capital flows was large relative to the size of the GDP of many of the recipient emerging market economies. Therefore, a risk of macroeconomic overheating was a distinct possibility. Most emerging markets succeeded in warding off overheating by relying on sterilized intervention in their foreign exchange markets. Capital controls were used by only a small number of those that received the largest capital flows relative to the size of the GDP. The nominal exchange rate management varied from country to country, and some resisted real appreciation of the currency more than others. The same observation applied to fiscal belt-tightening – some tightened belts more than others.

Global capital inflows can also have negative short- and medium-term repercussions. If they finance current account deficits and higher domestic investment rates in the recipient emerging markets, they also tend to inflate real exchange rates (see Chapter 5, Section 1). An inflated exchange rate undermines export competitiveness and distorts resource allocation. It encourages excess investment in the non-traded goods sectors, such as domestic services sectors, retailing, and real estate, which appear more competitive than investment in export and import competing sectors. Excessive investment in real estate has been observed in many crisis-affected economies, particularly those of Asia, during their pre-crisis periods. Capital inflows also inflate equity prices and create an equity market boom. Inflated exchange rates weaken the confidence of the global investors, who prepare for exit. When the capital inflows reverse, both real estate and equity prices fall sharply.

Another important development in this regard was that the composition of the financial flows to the emerging market economies underwent a discernible transformation in the 1990s. Short-term flows in the form of bonds, equities, and short-term instruments like certificates of deposit and commercial papers became popular instruments and accounted for a substantial proportion of total financial flows to emerging market economies. Due to their short maturities these flows are inherently unsustainable, and the "hot money" argument became popular. It should, however, be noted that the composition of inflows varied considerably among economies. High relative volatility is one of the notions that has been associated with hot money – that is, hot money is likely to disappear or reverse its flow as soon as the perception of investors regarding the emerging market concerned changes or the economy receives an external shock.

However, on the basis of a statistical time series for ten countries, Claessens *et al.* (1995) established that this distinction between hot and cold money is spurious. They concluded that long-term capital flows are as volatile as short-term flows. The time it takes between an unexpected shock to the economy and capital inflow dying out is similar across a variety of flows. There was also little evidence that information about the composition of capital flows is useful in forecasting the overall level of flows, and this suggests that the overall capital account inflow is independent of the type of flow. Thus, sustainability is neutral to the temperature of the flow, hot or cold. This evidence is consistent with the view that capital flows are fungible with respect to external shocks.

Among other factors, the sustainability of financial flows is also influenced by the exchange rate regime. A flexible and pragmatic management of the exchange rate regime contributes directly to sustainability. During the post-Bretton Woods period, most countries adopted one kind of floating exchange rate system or another. However, not all the regimes were prudent, carefully contrived and successful. Some emerging market economies mismanaged them and allowed their flexible exchange rate regimes to become *de facto* fixed exchange rate systems. Perhaps "overmanaged" is the more correct expression. When the financial markets perceive such inconsistencies or policy weaknesses, speculative attacks are the result. Speculators perceive those economies that have exchange rate flexibility as being most vulnerable. The Asian emerging market economies fell into this category during 1997–1998, making their currencies vulnerable to speculative runs by inadvertently making their currency regimes inflexible. When the trend became obvious they took much too long to correct the policy error, in the process opening their currency markets to speculative runs and depleting their foreign exchange reserves.

7   Global capital inflows and domestic investment

As the emerging market economies liberalized and eased restrictions on the capital account, the soaring global capital inflow was celebrated as a font for investable capital to accelerate GDP growth in these economies (see Chapter 2). As an emerging market economy begins to access the global capital markets, the supply curve of capital becomes perfectly elastic for it. However, in many cases the surge in global capital inflows was not followed by commensurate GDP growth (Easterly, 2000), and therefore, the long-term impact of global capital inflows on GDP growth was called into question (Rodrik, 1998). However, recent, more nuanced, studies have concluded that global capital inflows do stimulate GDP growth. That said, the cause of doubt and distrust is the non-linearity in the relationship between capital flows and GDP growth. Also, this relationship was found to be conditional and to have a threshold effect. For instance, Edwards (2000) concluded that capital account liberalization and global capital inflows hardly have any impact on the low-income developing economies. When the correlation coefficients were calculated, they were negligible or even negative for this country group. However, for the emerging market economies, which was a higher-income group of economies, this relationship was found to be found to be positive. Similarly, Borensztein *et al.* (1998) found a positive relationship between global capital inflows and GDP growth, but only in the emerging economies where the development of human capital was sufficiently high. In the economies where human capital was not well developed, this relationship did not exist. Another empirical study found that global capital inflows stimulate GDP growth rate only in those emerging market economies where policy measures for promoting macroeconomic stability are in place. Achieving macroeconomic stability was found to be a pre-condition of the capital flow–GDP growth link (Arteta *et al.*, 2001).

Mody and Murshid (2002) took this investigation one logical step further, and found that over the decade of the 1990s a substantial part of the global capital inflows found alternative uses in the recipient emerging market economies. According to them, the reason behind this was that during the 1990s capital flows were driven more by "push" (or external) factors than by "pull" (or internal) factors. The latter reflect unmet domestic demand for investment financing. Augmenting reserves accumulation was one of the frequent alternative uses of the global capital inflows in many developing economies. Another interesting and striking alternative use was a large outflow of the capital from the recipient economies. This caused the relationship between global capital inflows and domestic investment to weaken in many recipient emerging market economies. This is *prima facie* irrational, if not paradoxical, because the very fact that these economies are developing implies that they suffer from capital scarcity. An important long-standing objective of the policy-makers at the national and international levels has been to alleviate capital constraints in a majority of these economies.

There were two essential reasons why global capital inflows became outflows in several emerging market economies. First, many of these emerging market economies did not suffer from an acute capital constraint (the emerging markets of Asia fall into this category). Second, some of the recipient economies had a limited capacity to absorb the global capital productively and profitably. The decade of the 1990s was a period of growing up for the emerging market economies. They had opened their doors wide for the inflow of global private capital. To be sure, learning to handle and harness this was a challenging task, and this country group worked hard at it. Creating a pragmatic macroeconomic environment and devising the institutional support needed for raising the marginal productivity of capital, including global capital, takes time, effort and knowledge. Once they are in place, the link between external capital inflows and domestic investment naturally strengthens.

Using the technique devised by Bosworth and Collins (1999), Mody and Murshid (2002) examined the relationship between long-term global capital inflows and domestic investment. They took 20-year data from 60 developing economies (including emerging market economies) for their study. There are both behavioral and econometric reasons for studying the external capital and domestic investment link. As scarcity of capital is one of the defining conditions of underdevelopment, any additional investment in the developing economies should have high marginal productivity (Summers, 2000). When capital account restrictions are removed external capital flows in, favorably influencing domestic investment directly and the GDP growth rate indirectly. Therefore the first link, that of external capital inflows and domestic investment, should be easier to trace than the second one, between external capital inflows and GDP growth rate. The latter relationship develops over a longer period. The result of this study was that a dollar's worth of global capital inflow was, on average, associated with "just under an additional dollar of domestic investment." However, this relationship takes time to evolve. Improvements in the macroeconomic framework not only increased global capital inflows, but also tended to strengthen the link between external capital inflows and domestic investment. Conversely, the factors that tended to cause weakness in this link included the changing composition of the global capital flows, offsetting outflows, and rising foreign currency reserve requirements.

The composition of capital inflows is of great relevance, because the impact on domestic investment varies with different types of flows. When they enter an emerging market economy as FDI, they result in a significant increase in domestic investment. As opposed to this, when external capital enters as portfolio investment, there is little impact on the domestic investment.[23] The former are generally the so-called greenfield projects, while the latter is sought by entrepreneurs either for sourcing lower-cost funds or to diversify risk. Therefore, portfolio flows typically go into financing ongoing projects. This also explains the weakening of the relationship between global capital inflows and domestic investment. According to World Bank data, the share of portfolio investment in total capital flows to the emerging market economies has increased from 5 percent in 1975–1979 to 29 percent during 1995–1998.[24]

8   Summary and conclusions

The emergence of economies is an age-old phenomenon, although the term "emerging market economies" has only recently become part of the economic lexicon. Each one of the contemporary matured economies was once an emerging market economy. As trade and financial barriers came down and macroeconomic and financial regimes became liberal, several developing economies benefited from this macroeconomic and financial ambiance and became the so-called emerging market economies.

A precise definition has so far eluded this group of countries. However, the newly industrialized economies (NIEs) and middle-income developing countries in which governments and corporations have access to private international capital markets, or can attract institutional portfolio investment, or both, are generally considered to be emerging market economies. Protection for property rights and human rights are indispensable for becoming an emerging market economy. Infusion of global capital is not possible without this condition being fulfilled.

For an emerging market economy to emerge, a rapid growth rate with an endogenous character is essential. These countries have been liberalizing so much and for so long that a qualitative transformation in their economies is either about to take place or has already taken place. This qualitative transformation enables them to integrate with the global economy and take advantage of global factors (particularly capital) and trade flows. In addition, determining the emerging market status of an economy is a matter of openness and the maturity of its institutions, as well as whether the economy in question adheres to the rules, laws and culture of an open market economy. These considerations make a diverse group of transitional and developing economies candidates for the emerging market status.

Other important prerequisites include political stability, a structure of credible legal institutions that protect property rights, and a liberal economic system. Laying down the foundation of domestic financial institutions and creation of a banking and financial infrastructure is of vital importance for joining the ranks of emerging market economies. In the initial stages, the development of banking and financial institutions may require assistance from the financial and monetary authorities. Being able to attract global capital and becoming an emerging economy can be a great advantage to a country's economic status.

Domestic and external economic and financial environments are among the two most important determinants of global capital market inflows to, or outflows from, the emerging market economies. So too is the market perception, because so many important decisions regarding capital flows are based on it. The presence of institutional investors and currency speculators in the global financial markets exposes emerging market economies to vulnerability. Domestic and global macroeconomic factors have played a meaningful role in the recent growth and development of emerging market economies. The investment climate is another important variable that determines the ability to attract global capital.

Thus the emergence of the emerging market economies during the 1980s and 1990s was not a fortuitous accident; it was significantly aided and abetted by the domestic and global macroeconomic and financial environment of this period. The macroeconomic performance of the industrial economies and most emerging market economies improved discernibly during this period. Fiscal deficits for the emerging market economies fell from an average of 6 percent of the GDP in 1983–1989 to 3 percent of the GDP in 1990–1996. Likewise, the average rate of inflation for this country group fell slowly initially and sharply later. The rate of real GDP growth, which had come down to 2.2 percent during the 1979–1989 period, soared to 6 percent during the 1990–1996 period. A marked improvement in the macroeconomic performance was one of the fundamental reasons behind the improved access of this country group to international financial markets. The number of emerging market countries with an investment-grade Moody's credit rating rose dramatically during the 1990s.

2 Global capital flows to emerging market economies

1 Introduction

As noted in Chapter 1, one of the most significant aspects of financial globalization is the extremely rapid expansion of international liquidity. There has been an enormous increase in liquid assets available to participants in the global financial markets. The objective of this chapter is to provide quantitative and qualitative details regarding capital flows from the global financial markets to the emerging market economies, and other closely related features. The constitution and geographical distribution of these flows has undergone significant transformation with the passage of time. The entry of institutional investors onto the global financial scene and their progressively increasing significance has ushered in many changes, as well as adding to the liquidity of the financial markets. Little wonder that they are considered heavyweights in the global financial markets and have enormous impact on the emerging market economies. However, their presence has exposed the emerging market economies to some vulnerabilities – for instance, institutional investors can take short positions in weak currencies, in the process destabilizing the economy of that emerging market economy.

Financial globalization caused, and was supported by, globalization of banking activity. During the debt crisis of the early 1980s it was the large money-centered American banks that were most active in global banking, while the European and Japanese banks took a back seat. During the 1990s this scenario did not hold. The European banks nudged the American banks off the top perch and became the most active global players, a position they still maintain. According to the BIS statistics, in 2000, European banks were responsible for 59 percent of the total lending to the emerging market economies. The share of North American banks was 17 percent, and that of Japan 12 percent.[1]

This chapter also focuses on the variables that are responsible for stimulating the global financial flows to the emerging market economies. Some of these factors are the so-called push factors, while others are pull factors. Also, the global financial markets reward certain kinds of economic and financial policy measures, and the opposite is also true. Financial markets are sensitive to policy inconsistencies and their outcomes, and are known to punish macroeconomic policy incongruities. The impact of both sets of measures has been investigated at length. Patterns of capital flows to an individual emerging market and their determinants is another issue discussed in this chapter. It has been observed that there was a downside of the entry of the institutional investors into the global financial markets: namely, the role they played in speculative activities. A large section of this chapter is devoted to this role, and ways have been proposed to defend against probable speculative runs. The global economic and financial milieu of the early 2000s has so far been fragile, and not conducive to large-scale capital flows to the emerging market economies. A realistic projection of the short-term future scenario cannot be optimistic.

Regarding the structure of the chapter, the global capital flows to emerging market economies are discussed in Section 2, while Section 3 concentrates on the patterns of capital flows into individual emerging markets. Section 4 focuses on stimulants to capital flows, while the factors that have a depressing impact on it are taken up in the next section. The role of institutional investors as speculators and defensive measures from speculative runs are dealt with in Sections 6 and 7, respectively. In Section 8 the current unsupportive global economic and financial environment is discussed at length, and Section 9 provides a summary and conclusion.

2   Capital flows to emerging market economies

Quantitative dimensions

This chapter begins with an examination of capital inflows into the emerging market economies. To put this analysis in perspective, a brief look at the financial scenario of the 1970s and 1980s is essential. Following the oil shock of 1973, many large commercial banks in the industrial economies found themselves holding large deposits of petrodollars. Part of this liquidity was loaned to the governments in the emerging market economies through syndicated loan arrangements on floating interest rates. Owing to rising commodity processes during this period and improvements in the terms of trade, the borrowing economies did not face any problems in servicing their bank credits. Net private capital flows steadily increased, peaking at $49.8 billion in 1981. This period was known for large borrowing by the Latin American emerging markets.

Three deleterious developments took place in the early 1980s: a softening of commodity prices, a spike in LIBOR rates to unprecedented levels, and recession in the industrial economies. Under this set of circumstances, the Latin American economies found themselves in dire financial difficulties. Beginning with Mexico in August 1982, several of them declared moratoriums on their sovereign obligations. After the Latin American debt crisis of 1982–1983 there was a sharp deterioration in the macroeconomic performance of many emerging market economies, and therefore net private capital inflows declined to a trickle.[2] Several emerging market economies, particularly those in Latin America, experienced severe debt-servicing difficulties, and their rate of inflation accelerated menacingly. In addition, the most heavily indebted emerging markets had a ratio of external debt to exports close to 375 percent in the latter half of the 1980s. Some market observers therefore argued that it could take several years before market access for the emerging market economies could be restored, despite several years of adjustment efforts (Powell, 1990; USS, 1990).

The average net private capital flows to emerging market economies were $17.8 billion per annum for the 1971–1979 period. They declined to $16.3 billion per annum for the 1980–1989 period.[3] Failure to revive private capital flows to the emerging market economies during the 1980s led some observers to qualify this period as the "lost decade." Notwithstanding the pessimism at the start of the 1990s, cumulative net private capital flows to emerging markets in the 1990–1996 period soared to $1,055 billion – more than seven times the amount they received over the 1973–1981 period. These flows were also more than nine times as large as net borrowings from official creditors during the same period.

A characteristic feature of the global financial market activity during the 1990s was a remarkable growth in international bank lending and investments from the non-bank financial institutions to emerging market economies, and its sharp retrenchment following the onset of the financial crisis in Asia in July 1997. Table 2.1 shows that total net capital inflows soared from $45.7 billion in 1990 to $228.3 billion in 1996, and net FDI from $18.8 billion to $109.5 billion over the same period – more than five-fold increases in net terms. Net capital flows peaked in 1996, but net FDI flows did not follow this trend and peaked at $170.5 in 2001 (see Table 2.1, Figures 2.1, 2.2).

The trend in portfolio investments (particularly bonds) was not so smooth. These rose from $17.0 billion to $113.0 billion between 1990 and 1994, but declined considerably to $48.8 billion in 1995. This was less than half the level of a year earlier. The financial crisis in Mexico had begun in late 1994, and the bond market was adversely affected by it. The net flows picked up again in 1996, reaching $94.6 billion, which was again much less than the peak reached in 1994. Likewise, the category of other net flows (which includes mostly bank lendings), after rising sharply during the early 1990s, became negative in 1994 – that is, withdrawals or repayments were larger than new lendings. However, 1995 again saw steep increases in net flows under this category, which reached $64.6 billion. It is worth pointing out that official capital flows during this period remained flat.[4]

After peaking in 1996, net capital flows to emerging market economies

Table 2.1 Net capital flows to emerging markets (1990–2004) ($ billions)

Year	1990	1991	1992	1993	1994	1995	1996	1997	1998	1999	2000	2001	2002	2003 (estimates)	2004 (projections)
Total net flows	45.7	118.1	120.6	176.3	151.5	208.3	228.3	75.5	53.4	96.0	51.1	38.8	85.9	90.5	113.2
Net foreign direct investment	18.8	31.5	35.3	57.9	80.6	95.0	109.5	136.0	148.8	156.8	149.0	170.5	139.2	147.6	146.7
Net portfolio investment	17.0	24.7	55.6	98.7	113.0	48.0	94.6	48.5	1.7	41.4	12.1	-38.5	-36.6	-3.5	10.3
Other net flows	9.9	62.0	29.7	19.6	-41.9	64.6	24.2	-108.8	-97.1	-102.2	-110.1	-93.2	-16.7	-53.6	-43.7
Asia	21.4	24.8	29.0	31.8	70.3	98.4	132.2	12.0	-44.9	6.3	-18.3	-15.5	69.5	18.4	13.8
Middle East and Europe	7.0	65.7	38.8	29.1	15.7	8.2	9.5	16.9	10.2	-3.9	-18.8	-38.3	-25.3	-6.0	1.9
Western hemisphere	10.3	24.1	55.7	61.4	47.1	39.1	65.3	58.7	63.3	50.0	50.5	34.7	2.1	27.6	59.4
Economies in transition	4.2	-9.9	3.1	19.7	4.3	51.4	20.2	-20.9	14.5	29.8	32.9	20.9	34.1	40.4	29.9

Sources: International Monetary Fund, 1999, Table 2.2, p. 52; 2002a, Table 1.4, p. 30; 2003a, Table 1.3, p. 9.

Note
Net capital flows comprise net foreign direct investment, net portfolio investment, and other long- and short-term net investment flows, including official and private borrowings from the global capital markets.

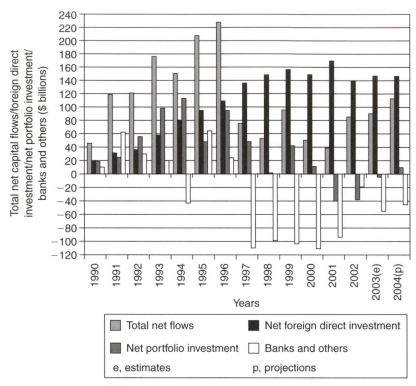

Figure 2.1 Net capital flows to emerging market economies (1990–2004).

never recovered. As seen in Table 2.1, considerable tightening in emerging market financial conditions took place after 1996. The principal reason was recurring crises in the emerging markets, which led to an increased perception of risk. Net capital flows rose somewhat in 1999 because of increased capital flows to the Western hemisphere, but declined again and weakness in flows continued. Volatility in the global equity markets has continued since 2000. Between 1997 and 2002, FDI flows remained strong and larger than the net inflows to the emerging market economies. The crises in emerging markets failed to affect them. In absolute terms, the FDI flows declined from $170.5 billion in 2001 to $139.2 billion in 2002. This decline was part of a global decline in FDI that reflected unsettled investor sentiment throughout much of 2002–2003 period. It also reflected falloff in privatization activity in the emerging markets and transactions involving mergers and acquisitions (M&As). The FDI continued to be heavily concentrated in a small number of host countries.

Net portfolio investment became negative in 2001, and stock markets continued to lose ground until 2003. Return on equity in the emerging markets followed the trend set by the matured industrial economies. However, in 2002, although emerging markets finished the year lower, they

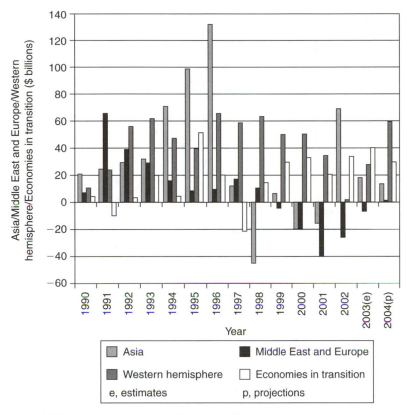

Figure 2.2 Regional distribution of capital flows to emerging market economies (1990–2004).

lost less than their matured market counterparts. The emerging markets of Asia were supported by improvements in macroeconomic fundamentals, and corporates had healthier balance sheets as a result of continued de-leveraging since the crisis of 1997–1998. Yet Asian equity markets performed poorly in 2002, although dollar returns were slightly inflated due to regional currency movements. Emerging markets in Europe were the only markets that generated positive returns in dollar terms. Stock markets in the Western hemisphere were the worst performers in dollar terms. This was largely due to sizable depreciation in the value of regional currencies, and reflected the dollar's decline *vis-à-vis* the euro (IMF, 2003b).

Bank and other capital flows turned negative in 1997, and have yet to become positive. Syndicated loan volumes have remained weak, although in 2002 there was a marginal improvement. Due to several high-profile bankruptcies of US and EU corporates and sovereign default in Argentina, banks have continued to tighten their lending standards. However, lending activity has remained buoyant in the high-grade sectors (IMF, 2003b).

The emerging markets of the Western hemisphere suffered a deep recession in 2001–2002. Following the sovereign default in Argentina and uncertainty due to the Brazilian presidential elections, there was a sharp decline of capital flows to the emerging markets of the Western hemisphere. Risk perception in the global financial markets regarding the emerging markets of the Middle East and Western hemisphere increased during this period, although in 2002 most emerging market economies of the Western hemisphere retained market access to the global capital markets. The saving grace is that, with some exceptions, flexible exchange rate regimes have facilitated a relatively smooth adjustment to the movement of funds in major currencies. As the net capital flows have continued to maintain a low level since 2000 (see Table 2.1, Figures 2.1, 2.2), prospects of widespread contagion in emerging markets has markedly declined (IMF, 2003a).

Net capital flows to emerging market economies in 2002 were $85.9 billion, close to the 1997 Asian crisis year level, and are expected to improve marginally in 2003. If problems in the emerging markets of the Western hemisphere worsen – especially with lackluster growth in major industrial economies – the potential for a more widespread impact on emerging market asset classes may increase significantly. The same observation applies to bank lending, which has remained negative since 1997.

Qualitative dimensions

Accumulation of large petrodollar deposits was the principal reason behind private capital flows to the emerging market economies in the 1970s. The bankers considered the recycling of these liquid resources to some of the better performing, creditworthy economies to be a productive and prudent investment. After the Mexican crisis unraveled, it was the multilateral capital flows from the International Financial Institutions (IFIs), particularly the International Monetary Fund (IMF), that took up the slack. Throughout the 1980s, the IMF introduced a number of new lending facilities aimed at assisting the highly indebted economies of the Western hemisphere. In 1989, the US Treasury took the initiative and launched the Brady Plan to allow the debt-ridden economies to restructure their debts by converting existing bank loans into collateralized bonds at a significant discount, or at below market interest rates. The Brady bonds were collateralized with zero-coupon US treasury bonds. The Brady Plan provided debt relief to the affected debtors, and the Brady bonds innovated under this plan were more liquid and therefore more tradable. This turned out to be the catalyst for the development of the emerging market bond market in the 1990s (see Chapter 4, Section 3).[5]

Following the Brady exchanges, when private capital flows to the emerging market economies resumed in the 1990s, there was a marked surge in capital flows to the emerging markets of Asia. These economies were basking in their newly acquired glory as the "Asian miracle." They were being extolled for the high quality of their human resources, sound macroeconomic policies, better institutional base, and market-friendly governments. Private capital flows to the emerging markets during the 1990s were stimulated by two new trends; the first was toward globalization of markets for emerging market securities, while the second was toward broadening of the investor base. Latin American securities were increasingly being sold in European and Asian stock markets. Similarly, with the growing involvement of mainstream institutional investors, the range of investors became more diverse. The market pricing of emerging market securities was working reasonably well, and consequently new investors were attracted toward them.

There are two interesting features regarding the capital flows to the emerging market economies. First, the surge in capital flow during the 1990s was far from uniform across the emerging market economies. Five major emerging market economies (namely Brazil, the People's Republic of China (hereinafter China), the Republic of Korea (hereinafter Korea), Mexico, and Thailand) accounted for over half of the total inflows. Furthermore, if this tally is extended to a dozen emerging markets, they accounted for almost 80 percent of total global capital inflows. As for the regional distribution, the growth in global capital flows to the emerging market economies of Asia during the 1990s was most pronounced. It increased sharply until 1996, but the retrenchment thereafter was equally dramatic (Table 2.1). In quantitative terms, the emerging market economies of Eastern Europe followed Asia during the 1990s, and the those from the Western hemisphere were right on the heels of this country group. Global capital flows to economies in transition, which started from a low base, recorded erratic increases and decreases, without any trend. In contrast, lendings to Africa and Middle Eastern regions almost stagnated.

Geographical distribution of these financial flows was, and continues to be, extremely uneven. In 1990, Asia received the largest proportion (46.8 percent of the total), followed by Latin America (22.5 percent; see Table 2.1). The emerging economies of the Middle East and Europe accounted for 15.3 percent of the total flows, while the economies in transition received 9.3 percent. In 1996, Asia's share of total private capital declined to 29.4 percent of the total. During the early 1990s, the bulk of the flows continued to be concentrated in a few Asian and European emerging markets that had avoided debt-servicing difficulties in the 1980s, and Latin American countries that were able to normalize their relations with global creditors. For a number of market re-entrants, the surge in capital flows complicated macroeconomic management. They had to face either excessive monetary growth or upward pressure on the exchange rate, which implied loss of external competitiveness. By 1996, flows to the Latin American emerging economies increased substantially, to 37.3 percent of the total net flows. This increase took place at the cost of other emerging market economies – particularly those in the Middle East and Europe, whose proportion declined to 10.5 percent. Global capital flows to Africa also stagnated during the period under consideration.

During the 2000s, Asian emerging markets not only continued their dominance over the proportion of net capital flows to the emerging market economies but also strengthened it. In 2002, Asian emerging markets accounted for 80.9 percent of the total net flows to the emerging market economies. The real GDP growth rate in the emerging markets of Asia, particularly China, exceeded expectations in 2002. The downside was the recent slowing of the information and communication technology (ICT) sector in the ASEAN-4 (Indonesia, Malaysia, the Philippines, and Thailand). There was a strong trend of reverse flow from the Middle East and Europe. Given their problems, the emerging markets of the Western hemisphere accounted for a mere 2.4 percent of the net capital flows. Although the GDP growth rate began to rise in 2003, serious vulnerabilities remained in Argentina, Brazil, and Uruguay. The political crisis in Venezuela continued to have its economic fallout. Between 1999 and 2002, the emerging economies in transition had built up their share considerably, accounting for 39.7 percent of the total flows in 2002. Foreign direct investment to these countries strengthened because several of them were on their way to signing the Treaty to join the European Union (EU) in April 2003. Net flows to Africa were weak, and during the 2000 they weakened further.

Composition of financial flows

Over the last two decades, the composition of the net flows has undergone a considerable transformation. Syndicated bank loans were a dominant instrument during the 1978–1982 period (large loans jointly made by a group of banks to one borrower are called syndicated loans; usually, one lead bank takes a small percentage of the loan and partitions or syndicates the rest to other banks). As opposed to this, portfolio investment (particularly bonds) and FDI became the most important instruments during the 1990s.

Direct capital investment was the principal source of capital available to emerging market economies. During the earlier years of the 1990s, FDI flows had maintained a higher profile than the capital flows of other kinds. In 1990 they were 41.1 percent of the total net inflows, while by 1995 this had risen to 45.6 percent. In 1996, the year net flows peaked, FDI flows were 48.0 percent of the total net flow. Thus, until this point in time almost half of the global financial flows to the emerging market economies were in the form of FDI. The United States was the largest FDI provider economy to the emerging markets. After the Asian crisis, international banks and institutional investors began cutting their exposure to the emerging market economies.

Bonds, equities, and short-term portfolio investments such as certificates of deposit and commercial paper became popular during the 1990s.

During the 1990–1996 period, portfolio investment accounted for 39 percent of the total capital flows into the emerging markets. Perhaps the most significant change was in portfolio equity flows, which rose from $17 billion in 1990 to $74 billion in 1996. In all, inflows of private capital rose from the equivalent of 3 percent of domestic investment in emerging market countries in 1990 to 13 percent in 1996. The financial institutions from the emerging markets participated increasingly in the international capital markets during the 1990s. This was the outcome of large foreign exchange reserves held by many, particularly China, Hong Kong SAR, Taiwan, and other East Asian economies.

During the period under review, much of the increase in lending to the emerging market economies resulted from a large increase in short-term claims (Jeanneau and Micu, 2002). The principal factors supporting this trend were growth in trade financing, the liberalization of financial sector in the recipient emerging market economies, and creation of several off-shore centers. In addition, there are advantages to the lending financial institutions in making short-term loans in terms of monitoring and management of international exposures. High local nominal interest rates and fixed or almost fixed exchange rates created arbitrage opportunities for institutional borrowing in foreign exchange.[6]

The short-term loans were the highest for the Asian emerging market economies, when they were measured as a proportion of total global borrowings of an individual economy. This was due to the rapid development and liberalization of the local banking system in Asia, and the creation of offshore markets. The proportion of short-term loans was initially low for the Latin American emerging market economies because they had a large proportion of long-term loans from the global banking system. These loans were taken by the public sector enterprises in these economies. However, the proportion of short-term claims has risen substantially (by around 20 percent) for the Latin American emerging market economies during the last two decades (Jeanneau and Micu, 2002).

The most harmful downside of increasing the proportion of short-term bank lending was that it became easy for the lending banks and non-bank financial institutions to retrench their exposure at short notice, or even without notice. When short-term credit lines were cut for an economy facing instability, the immediate impact was increased volatility, compounding the existing set of problems for the debtor economy. This has been observed during several recent emerging market crises, particularly those in Asia.

Globalization of banks

European banks have expanded their global lending activity at a rapid rate during the last two decades. Their traditionally favored areas of activity were limited to Eastern Europe, Africa, and the Middle East, where European banks dominated the global financial activity. Adopting a new globalization strategy, they started to diversify their exposure by expanding their activity to the Asian and Latin American emerging market economies. The diversification plan of European banks was born of the need for higher returns in traditional banking activities in the face of tepid European growth. In many European countries, particularly Germany, banks faced intense competition in the domestic market. Also, FDI flows and trade by European corporations were constantly growing in Asian and Latin American emerging economies. According to the statistics compiled by the Bank for International Settlements (BIS), European banks were the most globalized by 1997. They had not only the highest exposure to the emerging market economies, but also the largest geographical spread in terms of banking activity (BIS, 2002).

Unlike European banks, the global lending growth of American banks was slow and cautious. This was because their balance sheets had suffered serious losses during the 1982 debt crisis in the Western hemisphere. The so-called money-centered American Banks largely returned to global lending in the early 1990s, but were again stopped in their tracks by the Mexican crisis of 1994. They preferred to dispose of high-yielding Mexican short-term government debt securities. Since then, American banks have adopted a subdued position in global lending. Although they have steered clear of the emerging market economies in the Western hemisphere, they did involve themselves, in the same cautious and measured way, in Africa, Eastern Europe, and the Middle East.

The global assets accumulated by Japanese banks were substantial, and further increased in the early 1990s. However, since then their share of global bank claims has continued to decline owing to mounting losses on the domestic loan front. A large (almost $400 billion) overhang of domestic non-performing loans (NPLs) has led to a chronic crisis situation.[7] The pressing need to raise capital ratios further reduced the ability of Japanese banks to participate in global lending. Their global exposure was traditionally (and logically) focused on the Asian economies, and, of any single national group of banks, Japanese banks had the largest exposure to the Asian emerging market economies.[8]

Although firm statistical data are still not available, there is evidence of capital flows among the emerging market economies. The reason precise statistics are not available is that the capital account reporting systems of the emerging market economies provide relatively limited information about the country of origin of most capital flows. Asia has had a tradition of intra-regional flows since the mid-1980s (Das, 1996a). Apart from Japan, China, Korea, Hong Kong SAR, and Taiwan are substantial capital exporters in Asia.[9] Taiwan has come to acquire the sobriquet of "the banker" for the region. However, Hong Kong SAR is the single largest outward investor among the emerging markets. Firms in Hong Kong SAR invested a total of $78 billion overseas in 1996, a major proportion (65 percent) of which went to China.

While China remains a net importer of capital, its firms are beginning to invest abroad, with the financial services sector in the recipient countries attracting the largest share of these foreign investments. Chinese firms make large investments in Hong Kong SAR, Indonesia, Malaysia, Singapore, and Thailand. In Latin America, Chilean firms are known to make large intra-regional investments and acquisitions. Foreign acquisitions by them were worth $2.3 billion in 1996 (IMF, 1997), and most of these were state-owned assets of Argentina, Brazil, Colombia, and Peru. These assets could not be accumulated without the assistance of international financial markets. To finance these purchases, Chilean firms floated bonds in the international financial markets.

Changing global investor categories

With variations in the use of financial instruments, the global private investor categories also underwent a transformation. Development of bonds and equity markets in the emerging market economies attracted a different set of global investors to these countries. During the 1990s, two generic investor categories became active; crossover investors and dedicated investors (Perrault, 2002). For a given risk level, crossover investors move their investments about easily and frequently between investments. The present set of financial instruments facilitates this kind of movement of funds. Their objective is to maximize returns on their investments, and in following this objective they rapidly move capital from economy to economy, oblivious of the categories of instrument or the kind of economy. Therefore, financial flows of crossover investors tend to be volatile. The highly leveraged institutions (HLIs), such as hedge funds (HFs) and other net flows (which is mostly bank lending), come under this category. On the contrary, dedicated investors are "bound by self-imposed restrictions on either asset class (bonds and equities, for instance), or various definitions of location" of investment. They may direct their investments to a country group (say, the emerging market economies) or may adopt even narrower targets, like Argentinian and Korean equities. Dedicated investors, who focus on emerging markets, closely track various indexes of equities and bonds in these economies. The most frequently followed indexes are JP Morgan's Emerging Market Bond Index Plus (EMBI+), or the various Morgan Stanley Capital International Indexes.

Dedicated investors cannot be taken to be a passive or inactive category. For sure they are less volatile, but they have considerable latitude regarding their investment decisions. A series of important decisions depend upon their analytical capacities. Regional investors, for instance, must make decisions regarding which instrument and/or what country or countries of a particular region must be picked for investment. Investors in the emerging markets who follow various indexes must also take into account the sovereign risk of the economies of their focus, and whether these economies should be over-weighted or under-weighted in their portfolios. Other than the choice of instruments, they need to make clear decisions regarding the maturity period, which could seriously affect their returns. While dedicated investors can also liquidate their positions, it is the category of crossover investors that is associated with volatile portfolio capital flows in the emerging markets. The perspective of the crossover investors is generally short-term.

Diversification of risk is an essential characteristic of both kinds of investors. To this end, crossover investors invest a part of their portfolios in financial markets which show little co-movement. When portfolio investments in the emerging markets increase, it was observed that there was a synchronized movement in the sovereign credit spreads in the emerging market economies and high-risk investment indexes in advanced economies. That is, co-movement in these markets increased. Consequently, there was a narrowing of returns to investors in the emerging markets. Also, the risk–reward payoffs did not justify investment in the emerging markets by the crossover category of investors – that is, they soon found that their risk was not well diversified when they invested in emerging market assets. Owing to increased linkages between financial markets in industrial economies and the emerging market economies, and the resulting reduction in diversification of risk, some analysts believe that portfolio flows in future may well be low profile (Perrault, 2002).

3   Patterns of capital inflows

In the preceding exposition we saw that the pattern of private global capital inflows varies widely in individual emerging market economies. There are many factors that affect the pattern of capital flows to the emerging market economies. As seen in the preceding sections, these include interest rate variations, liberalization policies in the host emerging market, political risk and stage of economic development of the recipient emerging economy, the stage of the business cycle in the industrial economy, macroeconomic factors, external factors, regulatory controls, tax incentives, institutional investors' strategies, and other similar factors. Growth potential and the level of financial market development in the host country also affect the quantitative aspect as well as the composition of capital inflows. While myriad factors impact the capital flows, there is no widely accepted explanation regarding why the volume and composition of capital flows differ from one emerging market to another.

Chen and Khan (2003) developed a theoretical model and used the cost-of-financing argument to explain different patterns of capital inflows to emerging markets, including reversal of capital flows. They derived their results from the inefficiency of the domestic financial markets. They modeled financial market inefficiency as a result of asymmetric information between outside investors, who rely on information in the domestic financial markets, and insiders in the firms. Such information asymmetry is typical in an underdeveloped financial market where information is not properly disclosed and processed due to weak accounting and disclosure rules and poor financial market infrastructure.

Chen and Khan (2003) demonstrated that a rich variety of capital flow patterns could be generated by the interaction of the degree of financial market development in the recipient country, and the country's growth potential. These are two of the many consequential variables that have an impact over the patterns of capital flows.[10] By no stretch of the imagination can the explanation provided by variations in these two variables provide a complete answer regarding the variance in volume and composition patterns in individual emerging market economies, although it does suggest to some interesting and plausible conclusions. One of their conclusions is that an emerging market economy with high growth potential and less developed equity markets may be able to attract global portfolio equity investments from countries with high investment-making potential and efficient financial markets. However, if the financial market is extremely inefficient in the host country relative to its growth potential, the cost of attracting portfolio capital can also be exceedingly high. Under such circumstances, it pays for the host country to improve its financial market and infrastructure. Such improvements should be made quickly in order to avoid getting stuck in the slippery middle ground, as economies that do this run the risk of volatility of capital flows.

Another conclusion is that a catastrophic change in the financial costs, and therefore a sudden financial flow reversal, may occur in those emerging market economies that are experiencing perceived changes in their return potentials. Economies with moderate growth potential and semi-developed financial markets have a great tendency to suffer from financial flow reversals. Although Chen and Khan (2003) have focused only on portfolio equity flows to emerging markets, bonds and bank lending can be analyzed in a similar manner.

4   Stimulants to capital inflows

With the abandonment of the fixed exchange rate regime during the 1971–1973 period, better-performing middle-income developing economies were able to open up to greater capital mobility while maintaining autonomy over their monetary policy, which was essentially in keeping with the Mundellian trilemma.[11] Consequently, capital flows increased sharply during the latter half of the 1970s and early 1980s, leading to the debt crisis of 1982. As stated in Chapter 1 (Section 6), the Brady Plan was launched in 1989 to resolve the debt crisis of the developing countries. Investors in the industrial countries found that deregulation, privatization, merger and acquisitions (M&As), and advances in the information and communication technology (ICT) were making foreign direct investment

(FDI) and security investment in the emerging market more attractive and easier than before. The result was an FDI and equity investment spike in the emerging market economies in the 1990s (Mundell, 2000).

Of the factors enumerated in the preceding paragraph, advances in ICT and computer technology are widely regarded as one of the most important factors driving and supporting financial globalization and the flow of financial resources to the emerging market economies, and integrating them with the global economy. Technology has reduced the cost of communications, increased the power of computers, shrunk the globe, and made national boundaries less significant. New developments in ICT have facilitated the collection and processing of information for the market participants, as well as for monetary and banking authorities and banks. They have made it possible to measure, monitor, and manage financial risk for the market participants. Without computers, pricing and trading of complex new financial instruments is not feasible. Managing large and rapid transactions and then managing the books for these transactions, which are presently widely spread across continents and countries, cannot be accomplished without the support of ICT and computers.

Transnational corporations (TNCs) have played a proactive role in the trans-border flow of global capital, as well as that to the emerging market economies. They have expanded their networks by way of M&As with other national and international firms. TNCs have managed to "slice the value chain" and create production and distribution networks spanning the globe. As noted above, a good number of emerging market economies had begun liberalizing their domestic economies in a methodical manner in the mid-1980s by lowering barriers to trade and financial flows, and consequently increasing global trade in both goods and services. These developments facilitated the spread of TNC activities across the globe. The result was a heightened demand for trans-border financial flows. Therefore, an internationally mobile pool of capital and liquidity was created, which underpinned not only financial globalization, but also the flow of capital to emerging market economies.

Furthermore, liberalized and deregulated domestic economic strategies, advances in ICT, and globalizing emerging market economies combined to catalyze financial innovation. Responding to the increasing demand for trans-border financial flows, financial intermediation activity globalized. It was buttressed by declining barriers to trade in financial services as well as by deregulation and the removal of entry restrictions on foreign financial institutions into domestic markets in a large number of emerging market economies. Consequently, since the mid-1980s trans-border flows have increased at a rapid clip.

The regulatory authorities in the emerging market economies both modernized their structure and transformed their role. The new set of regulations facilitated the creation of a broader range of institutions to provide financial services. Additionally, new categories of non-bank institutions and institutional investors were launched, and far-reaching structural changes in the financial sector took place. Gradually, investment banks, securities firms, asset managers, mutual funds, insurance companies, specialty and trade finance companies, hedge funds, and even telecommunications, software, and food companies, began providing services similar to those traditionally provided by banks.

Several economic and political developments during the first half of the 1990s also led to an increase in financial flows from private capital markets to the emerging market economies. These developments included sweeping structural adjustments in the developing economies during the 1980s and 1990s, the increasing unpopularity of statist and protectionist policies, and the adoption of market-friendly strategies. Intellectual *zeitgeist* changed during this period, and the "Washington consensus" came to be widely accepted.[12] The acceptance and popularity of the Washington consensus among the policy-making community was on the rise. Free markets and sound money were accepted as being key to economic development. Some analysts believe that the rise of the Washington consensus was a turning point in world economic affairs (Krugman, 1995).

During this period, in the matured industrial economies savings were becoming increasingly institutionalized. Assets of pension funds, insurance companies and mutual funds in the 30 OECD (Organization for Economic Co-operation and Development) economies reached $29 trillion in 1995.[13] Such has been the scale of saving accumulation that by the end of 1998, the total assets of mutual funds in the United States were estimated to have overtaken those of banks, which had been the dominant financial intermediary for the past two centuries (*The Economist*, 1998). The same trend existed in Japan and the larger economies of Europe, namely Germany, France, and the United Kingdom (UK), where financial institutions became large reservoirs of savings.

Due to the implementation of structural adjustment programs in several emerging markets, as well as adoption of the sound macroeconomic and financial policies subsequently followed by them, these economies were far healthier in the 1990s than ever before. Their good economic health was reflected in their leading economic indicators. As international capital is attracted by improvements in economic fundamentals, these economies found that their strong fundamentals were stimulating private capital market inflows. In addition, institutional investors needed to diversify their portfolios and, in their quest for global diversification, could not overlook the promise of the emerging market economies. Thus, rising capital flows to emerging market economies provided large institutional investors with the risk-mitigation benefits that are associated with globally diversified portfolios. Tepid GDP growth in the European Union (EU) and Japan had reduced investment opportunities in these economies during the first half of the 1990s, which again stimulated a surge in capital flows into the emerging markets. The growing integration of emerging markets into the international financial system is viewed by a number of observers as a re-establishment of the type of relationships between capital-importing and capital-exporting countries that existed earlier in two periods of high capital mobility, that is 1880–1914 and the 1920s (Das, 1996b, 2003a; Obstfeld and Taylor, 1997).

Real interest rates declined during the early 1990s and there was a sharp fall in emerging market spreads. Since the financial markets in the industrial economies were highly liquid, it is often wondered whether compression in the emerging market credit spreads during this period was excessive. It is now sometimes believed that this compression reached a point where credit risk was being underpriced. Some market analysts believe that abundant global liquidity and the quest for higher returns in the emerging markets were the prime causal factors responsible for a sharp decline in the emerging market spreads and underpricing credit risk. Several empirical studies have analyzed the key pull (or internal) and push (or external) factors behind the large-scale capital flows to the emerging market economies during the 1990s.[14] The pull factors refer to the history of domestic structural adjustment measures taken by the emerging market economies, their macroeconomic management, and the political and non-economic factors that made them more creditworthy than ever before. As opposed to these, the push factors included both the structural and the cyclical developments in international financial markets (enumerated earlier in this paragraph) that led investors to globally diversify their portfolios and turn to emerging markets in search of higher yields.

Empirical evidence exists to show that two of the push factors, namely real GDP in the lending countries and real interest in the lending countries, have had the largest effect on capital flows into the emerging market economies during the period under consideration. In order to identify the broad determinants of global capital flows, Jeanneau and Micu (2002) selected a "baseline" equation that was applied to aggregate lending flows – that is, by all lending countries as a group to all borrowing countries as a group. Their baseline equation showed that while both push and pull factors have an impact on capital flows to emerging market economies, when real economic activity in lending countries is above the deterministic trend there is a tendency of expansion of lending to the emerging market economies. A large positive correlation between strong GDP growth in the lending countries and large capital flows to the emerging market economies existed during the 1990s, up until 1997, which reflected this fact.

The upswing of a business cycle is also associated with the tendency for higher profitability for banks in the lending countries, and they thus become disposed to take greater risks by lending to the emerging markets. A similar positive correlation was found to exist between real short-term interest rates in the lending countries and large capital flows to the emerging market economies (Jeanneau and Micu, 2002). Although it is normal for bankers in the lending countries to look for diversification of investable funds to high-yield countries when domestic real interest rates are plummeting, the need for such diversification was outweighed here by the improved confidence of lending banks in the matured industrial economies. This confidence was the result of the favorable impact of robust industrial country growth on the emerging market economies.

The structural adjustments and liberalization measures that were implemented in the international and domestic financial markets during the 1990s affected the scale, composition, and direction of the capital flows. Two of the most important developments were the liberalization of domestic financial markets, and capital account transactions. These two changes took place in both industrial and emerging market economies. Liberalization of capital account transactions is vital for financial globalization; without it no markets can emerge. One characteristic of these developments was that they were progressive and self-reinforcing and, therefore, once they were launched they continued to grow on their own.

Bartolini and Drazen (1997) prepared an index of capital control measures in emerging markets, and demonstrated how capital controls have been relaxed since the mid-1980s. Their index conclusively established that the decline in capital account restrictions facilitated the recent boom in capital flows to emerging markets. The correlation between the index and capital inflows for the 1982–1996 period was −0.3. This provided a simple corroboration for the assumption that the liberalization of external transactions is instrumental in attracting foreign capital. Another index, developed by the World Bank (1997a), demonstrated that while more and more emerging markets were better integrated into the international financial system, the process is still at an early stage. An empirical study conducted by Dooley *et al.* (1996) provided support for the premise that there is a growing degree of *de facto* integration of domestic and international financial markets. Also, it is becoming increasingly difficult to keep domestic financial market conditions isolated from developments in international markets.

The progressively increasing roles of institutional investors on the one hand and securitization on the other have been alluded to above. They resulted in an increased flow of global capital into portfolio investment, both bonds and equity, in the emerging market economies during the 1990s. Emerging market securities were increasingly bought by institutional investors such as mutual funds, insurance companies, pension funds, and of late, hedge funds.[15] Seeking higher returns and greater diversification, these institutional investors sent only a small part of their capital to emerging markets, but since their portfolios were mammoth in size, even a small part of these portfolios created a rising tide of capital flowing to emerging markets. Growing securitization became more or less a global trend, which in turn led to greater use of direct debt and equity markets. In the direct debt market, lenders or investors hold a tradable direct claim on the borrowers or borrowing firms. This works differently from indirect finance, where an intermediary holds a non-traded loan asset and the saver holds a liability. This liability may be tradable on the intermediary. Recent advances in information technology proved to be a facilitating factor, improving the capability of both investors and creditors to manage their portfolios and undertake better risk analysis of credit and market risks (Das, 1996b, 2003a).

5 Depressants to capital inflows

If financial markets reward sound fundamentals, they punish the opposite. Crises and other turbulence in the global economy, no matter what the causal factors, have an adverse impact on the volume of capital market flows to the emerging market economies. They affect the middle-income emerging markets particularly badly. In 1997, the economic climate, and with that the financial market scenario, underwent a dramatic transformation. The financial turmoil that started in July 1997 in Thailand rolled on to other emerging market economies within and outside Asia in 1998. Capital flows to emerging market economies fell from $213.8 billion to $148.8 billion in 1997 – a 30.4 percent fall, steep by any measure. After the substantial market disturbances in late 1997, the outlook for emerging markets appeared to have improved in 1998, creating an impression that the Asian crisis was coming to an end. However, these expectations proved to be wrong and the turmoil continued unabated. This was reflected in a slowing down of capital flows to the emerging markets to $65.4 billion in 1998, which was a precipitous fall from their 1996 level (see Table 2.1).

The depressed global economic environment was also reflected in a rise in bond yield spreads and a fall in equity prices. The sovereign default, devaluation and unilateral domestic debt restructuring by the Russian Federation worsened an already bad situation, and general apprehension regarding an all-round emerging market financial crisis began to raise its head. After Brazil devalued its currency, there was a small recovery in the emerging markets in the first half of 1999. Therefore, by mid-1999 market access for the higher-rated or investment-grade emerging market borrowers had improved. However, yield spreads continued to remain high, and international capital markets remained closed to many emerging market corporations.

Anemic flows during 1998 and 1999 *inter alia* reflected the persistence of a higher degree of aversion to risks associated with lending to emerging markets on the part of commercial banks and stock analysts. In addition, there was a weaker demand for credit in several emerging markets, where borrowing firms were endeavoring to reduce indebtedness following recent crises. Many of these firms had taken on substantial short-term external debts, which, they belatedly realized, was a crisis prone strategy.[16] Net private capital flows to Asia recovered temporarily in the last quarter of

1999 as portfolio equity flows increased and repayment obligations reduced significantly (IIF, 1999); however, on the whole this was a year of negative inflows for the Asian emerging market economies.

Although the global economy picked up some momentum in 2000, during 2001 it slipped into a mild recession. Emerging market economies saw their growth rate plunge. Growth in global trade underwent one of the most severe decelerations in modern times, from over 13 percent in 2000 to just 1 percent in 2001 (World Bank, 2002). Deteriorating growth prospects for the emerging market economies, the collapse in prices of technology stocks, the continuing crises in Turkey and Argentina, and increased concern over risk reduced the demand for capital from the emerging market economies. Speculative-grade borrowers saw a sharp fall in market access, faced much higher spreads, and sharply reduced capital flows. The majority of the emerging market borrowers from the private capital markets are speculative grade borrowers. In contrast, investment-grade borrowers enjoyed improved terms. A further fall in capital flows was recorded in 2000, and by 2001 net emerging market flows had been reduced dramatically to $3.3 billion (see Table 2.1).

Global causal factors played the predominant role in reducing the flow of external finances to a trickle in 2001. The slowdown in industrial economies led to a decline in export revenues of the emerging market economies, the impact of which was only in part mitigated by the drop in international interest rates. Slower growth and the collapse of technology stock prices increased uncertainty and sharply reduced the wealth of investors in high-risk assets, and thus reduced their appetite for risk. Net portfolio investments in emerging market economies had risen to $33.9 billion in 1999, but after that they became net outflows and shrank to minus $4.3 billion in 2000 and further to minus $30.2 billion in 2001. Portfolio investment flows are extremely sensitive to the external economic environment and, although the crises in Argentina and Turkey did not set in motion any contagion, the external economic environment was far from encouraging. Therefore, global investors lost confidence in the emerging market economies. Asian and Middle Eastern emerging market economies were found to record the largest outflows.

6 Institutional investors and speculative runs

There is a downside to emerging markets being well integrated into global financial markets. The presence of large institutional investors in the global financial markets acts as a stimulant for the emerging markets, as well as exposing them to some vulnerability. As they were large absorbers of emerging market securities, the emerging markets became vulnerable to their capability of intense speculative attacks. These institutional investors can take substantial short positions in a weak currency through spot, forward, and currency options markets. According to one estimate, the total assets of hedge funds, traders and speculative-type mutual funds grew to well over $100 billion in 1995 (*F&D*, 1997), and the current size of their assets could well be more than $200 billion. These institutions are known to create large leveraged positions, at times leveraging their capital by 10 times or more.[17] Thus the magnitude of financial resources controlled by speculative-type mutual funds is large, and therefore, compared to the past, more international reserves and more complex intervention strategies are needed to offset their speculative attacks.

One lesson of the 1990s is that the emerging markets with inflexible or less flexible exchange rate regimes are most vulnerable to speculative attacks. It needs to be clarified that when we say "speculators" there is no negative connotation intended; it is not used in a pejorative sense. Besides, in the financial markets any economic agent, whether a large domestic or foreign firm, an investment bank, a hedge fund, a domestic or foreign mutual fund, or a clairvoyant individual who keeps a discerning eye on the movements of the financial market and the economy, can turn to speculation at an opportune moment.

When financial sector weaknesses become apparent in an economy and its fundamentals begin to deteriorate, it will necessarily attract the attention of the institutional investors and currency speculators, and a currency crisis becomes predictable. It has, however, been noticed that a currency crisis is precipitated well before the deteriorating fundamentals have reached a point at which the exchange rate will collapse. The crisis precipitates as soon as a speculative run begins. To the uninformed onlooker this gives the impression that the currency crisis has been sparked by the speculative attack, and that weakness in fundamentals or the financial sector are not the basic causal factors. Once a currency crisis-like situation develops, "herd behavior" or the "bandwagon effect" soon aggravates it. There is evidence that foreign exchange markets are inefficient (Krugman, 1997a) and that they do not make the best use of available information, which leads to herd behavior.[18] The waves of market participants taking short positions, whatever the initial motivation, are magnified through sheer imitation. This develops almost into a stampede, causing a sharp depreciation in the value of the currency. This is what happened to the Czech koruna, the Thai baht, the Philippine peso, the Malaysian ringgit, the Indonesian rupiah, and the Korean won during their 1997–1998 crises. The bandwagon effect is also precipitated by awareness that other investors have "special information." Kehoe and Chari (1996) have argued that such bandwagon effects in markets with private information create a sort of "hot money effect," alluded to earlier, that at least sometimes causes foreign exchange markets to overreact to news about national economic prospects.

The currency markets also over-react because agents manage foreign investments in crisis-prone economies, rather than principals. These traders or money managers, whether from a mutual fund or a hedge fund, have a lot to lose from staying in a currency that is considered by their profession as "ripe for depreciation." They have little motivation to stay in that currency and prove their peers wrong. Since traders and money managers are compensated on the basis of comparison with other money managers, they have a strong incentive to act alike even if their personal instincts suggest that the judgment of the market is wrong. The trader's or money manager's thought line is as follows: "It'll be worse to lose money on the won depreciation when others do not than to lose the same amount in a general currency rout."

In the recent past, a strong tendency toward contagion has been observed in speculative runs on currencies. Empirical proof of this tendency was provided by Eichengreen *et al.* (1996). Their estimates, based on data from 20 countries spanning three decades, revealed that attacks on foreign currencies raise the probability of an attack on domestic currency by 8 percent. Contagion in foreign exchange markets essentially uses two channels of international transmission: the first is trade links, that is, the speculative runs spill over contagiously to other countries with which the subject country trades, and the second is macroeconomic similarities, where the speculative runs spread to other countries having similar economic conditions and policies. The effect of contagion operating through trade was found to be stronger than that of contagion spreading as a result of macroeconomic similarities.

One lesson of the 1990s is that inflexible or pegged exchange rate regimes *vide ut supra* tend to attract speculators.[19] A speculative attack requires the establishment of a net short position in the domestic currency. To attack a currency, say the peso, a speculator takes a short position in the peso. He sells it to a bank through relatively long-dated (at least a month) forward contracts. To balance this short position, the bank will immediately take a long position – that is, the bank will sell the peso on the spot market for, say, dollars for the conventional two-day settlement. In this process, the bank has balanced its currency mismatch. So far this is only one half of the balancing act, because it continues to face a maturity mismatch. In order to close this maturity mismatch the bank will transact a foreign exchange swap – that is, it will deliver dollars for pesos in 2 days and deliver pesos for dollars 30 days forward. This is a standard wholesale transaction in normal periods.

When an institutional investor or speculator takes a short position, the domestic central bank plays the role of a customer in the forward currency market, or it is the counter party for the speculating entity. It sells the required amount in hard currency (generally the dollar) to the speculator. The central bank's domestic currency receipt from the forward contract becomes a one-month loan to the speculator who is taking a short position. If the central bank does not provide the credit directly, it must come through its money market operations. From the above mechanics it is clear that if the central bank plans to dissuade the speculators, it should raise the cost of short positions. Short-term interest rates are allowed to rise, tightening conditions in financial markets and making it more costly for speculators to obtain a net short position by borrowing domestic currency.

7   Defending against a speculative run

The first defensive strategy that a central bank adopts against a speculative run is sterilized intervention, which may occur in both the foreign exchange markets – that is, spot and forward markets. In the spot market, the direct consequence is depletion of foreign exchange reserves. This also implies a reduction in the monetary base, resulting from the sale of foreign exchange by the central banking authority. Thus, the size of foreign exchange reserves works as a limiting factor, although borrowing from the international markets or multilateral financial institutions can augment the reserves. Intervention in the forward market is a different ball game, because it does not result in an immediate reduction in the foreign exchange reserves and the monetary base does not shrink. This is the reason why some central banks prefer the latter to the former. For instance, when the Korean won first came under a speculative attack in the months of October and November 1997, the government immediately responded by sterilizing intervention in the forward market because it wanted to preserve its foreign exchange reserves.

A speculative attack requires the establishment of a net short position in the domestic currency. Therefore, if speculators are to be dissuaded from making speculative runs short-term interest rates should be allowed to rise, tightening conditions in financial markets, which in turn makes it more costly for speculators to obtain a net short position by borrowing domestic currency. However, this defensive strategy cannot be sustained for an extended period because high short-term interest rates are detrimental for the real economy. If the economy is slowing down, high interest rates work in a pro-cyclical manner, causing a deeper downturn in the economy. To ward off such a situation countries create a two-tier system or interest rate; the two-tier system prevents speculators from getting domestic credit, but the non-speculative, productive, capital needs are met at the normal rates of interest.

The market manipulating capability of hedge funds has plagued the policy-makers for some time. It bears repeating that hedge funds are not large relative to financial markets as a whole, although they may be large relative to a particular emerging market. To reduce the volatility-creating activities of hedge funds, policy-makers can consider margin and collateral requirements for all financial market participants. Such measures would affect – and discourage – hedge funds more than other investors, because they are heavy users of credit. Governments can also undertake more fundamental reforms to deal with market volatility. A reduction in information asymmetry will discourage herd behavior in the currency and financial markets. If investors run with the herd, they do so to emulate the actions of other investors, assuming that the other investors know something they do not know themselves. Therefore, providing better information regarding market conditions helps to discourage herd behavior.

Markets are well aware that inflexible regimes are fragile in the face of adverse external or domestic shocks. Therefore, market participants are likely to speculate against pegged rates in the face of such shocks. Either the defense of pegged rates proves to be costly in the face of speculation (as in Argentina in 1995), or the market pressures lead to the abandonment of the pegged rate (as in several ERM countries in 1992,[20] in Mexico in 1994, and in several Asian economies in 1997). Thus to keep a crisis at bay, central banks should not – or only rarely – adopt inflexible pegs (Sachs, 1997). Perhaps less obviously, self-fulfilling panic is also much easier to handle by floating exchange rate regimes compared with pegged rate regimes. A pegged exchange rate regime can only be justified under special circumstances. For instance, it could be considered appropriate under an optimal currency union with one or more countries. In such a case, a common central bank can act as lender of last resort for the whole union. A second case for justifiable pegging could be an extremely open and diversified economy with a very flexible labor market. Such an economy can adjust to external shocks through internal deflation if necessary, rather than depreciation. Also, by virtue of diversification, such an economy may be less likely to be hit by serious external shocks than is an economy that is highly concentrated in a few export goods. Hong Kong SAR and Estonia both have currency boards, because they more or less meet the second condition.

The strongest defense against a speculative run on a currency is to have a macroeconomic environment that is sound, functional, and pragmatic, a currency peg that is realistic and flexible, and a financial sector with a sound framework of prudential norms. To attain these objectives, the macroeconomic policy must avoid inconstancies and the currency peg must be supportable. The adverse effects of inflation, large budget deficits or unsustainable exchange rates on the macroeconomy and the financial sector can be compounded by capital inflows – particularly short-term ones. If policy inconsistencies are not avoided and if the economic and currency value scenarios are perceived as weak and inflexible, the currency becomes a target for one-way bets for speculators.

Gradual liberalization as a defensive measure

Most (if not all) emerging market economies have liberalized and deregulated their financial markets in the recent past. Many a crisis has been related to financial market liberalization, especially the elimination of controls on international financial movements. Cautious, gradual, calculated and, therefore, prudent liberalization works as a defensive measure. This is a significant lesson from the crises of the 1990s. Several of these crises distinctively exhibited a boom–bust cycle – that is, a large but ephemeral wave of capital inflows accompanied by a pegged exchange rate. When the inflows stabilized the exchange rate needed to be devalued, and the subsequent devaluation was delayed until a serious macroeconomic crisis had developed.

The Asian crises and those before them in Argentina, Ecuador, Mexico, Venezuela, Israel, Sweden, and Norway have proved that it is dangerous to liberalize capital restrictions without a number of safety valves. These safety valves control the large and sudden inflows and outflows of capital that have become a common feature of global financial markets. Two entities can potentially work as safety valves: (1) the degree of exchange rate flexibility, and (2) strengthened domestic financial institutions, which are less vulnerable to fluctuations in the value of their assets. Other than these two safety valves, it might be pragmatic to have some prudential restrictions on short-term capital inflows as well. For instance, central banks can make commercial banks sterilize a stipulated part of their short-term capital inflows by keeping them in non-interest bearing deposits, or at least low-interest bearing deposits. This measure will defend the emerging market economies from the herd instinct of speculators, which drives them to seek safety in numbers.

Gradual liberalization is another way out. If the financial markets are liberalized gradually, as in Chile, domestic financial institutions are not able to take on foreign debt of large dimensions. Their borrowing limits are reached only gradually, which in turn dampens the boom–bust cycle. Also, gradual liberalization keeps the real exchange rate from appreciating rapidly. Therefore, the devaluation needed after the stabilization of the capital inflows is less dramatic. An optimal sequencing of the liberalization process may have to work through the following stages: free inflow of foreign direct investment, followed by liberalization of portfolio equity investment, long-term borrowing by non-financial institutions, short-term borrowing by non-financial institutions, and, finally, short-term borrowing by commercial banks. This sequence, operating gradually, will go a long way in eliminating the boom–bust cycle.

An amber signal is warranted here: the foregoing statements must not be seen as a stand against the liberalization of the financial sector. Rather, they are saying that rapid liberalization, in the absence of sound macroeconomic policies, adequate regulatory and prudential norms, and supervision and monitoring, can create problems in the financial sector. Liberalization reduces the ability of institutions to survive poor performance, as rising competition reduces the rents and profitability of the financial sector. If, on top of that, there is government intervention, the crisis situation develops earlier and the economy becomes an attractive proposition for speculators. Here, while casting a vote against the globalization of financial markets, I am also stressing the need for not allowing globalization to race ahead of national and/or international supervisory regimes.

A regulatory regime as a defensive measure

The financial crises of the 1990s, particularly those in the Asian economies, have called into question the ability of the global financial system to manage transnational financial flows of such large dimensions as are prevalent at present. The foundation of the current international financial system was laid in 1946, when the dimension of transnational capital flows (1) was tiny, and (2) was limited among the industrial economies, and (3) there were few short-term financial flows involved. The systemic needs of the present period differ widely from those of the past; this is well recognized in most quarters, and there are calls for "a new financial architecture." Various proposals were floated at the time of the Spring Meetings of the International Monetary Fund (IMF) and the World Bank in the third week of April 1998, when the world's economic rule-makers converged on Washington, DC. Although a consensus on the contours of the new financial architecture was far away, a great deal of thought was given to it. If the new global financial architecture is so devised that whenever a financial crisis breaks out due to short-term fund movements those who made mistakes share the losses, the emerging market economies will benefit. This will ensure that investors in short-term instruments will also be held responsible, and, will therefore, share part of the post-crisis cost with the recipient emerging market economy.

Capital controls in the form of quantitative restrictions and taxes are frequently resorted to as defensive measures, and some scholars (such as Rudigar Dornbusch, the famous MIT economist) support their utility for short periods. However, the experiences of the 1960s and early 1970s reveal that expectations of controls increase the probability and the frequency of speculative runs and balance of payments crises. It was also observed that transitory controls increased the volatility of exchange rates. Thus, controls prove to be counterproductive. A noteworthy characteristic of this period (known as the Bretton-Woods period) was the high frequency as well as the severity of speculative runs and balance of payments crises in both developing and industrial economies. Of these, the sterling crises of 1964–1967 and the dollar and French franc crises of 1967–1969 are well known. These experiences also vouch for the fact that capital controls create self-fulfilling expectations of currency depreciation.

The experience of the 1990s shows that financial crises are stirred up by (and feed on) undercapitalized banks. They are more vulnerable to self-fulfilling panic and more prone to excessively risky borrowings. Since most emerging market economies lack effective and efficacious supervising and monitoring institutions, the book value of their capital overstates the amount of shareholder equity. Bad assets are generally not written down expeditiously. Therefore, the regulatory regime for these economies should be stricter than that for the industrial economies. A minimum capital-to-asset ratio of 8 percent, the so-called BIS[21] norm, may be grossly inadequate for the emerging market economies. Therefore, BIS-plus prudential norms are recommended as a defensive strategy. Having a sound capital base and adopting higher prudential standards will make the banking sector less vulnerable at the time of a market panic.

8   Current unsupportive environment

Although a weak to moderate recovery in the US was on track during the first half of 2002, corporate malpractices and accounting fiddles had a devastating impact on the US and global bourses. Infectious greed took hold of corporate America, and led to a series of accounting scandals. The overall GDP growth estimates for 2002 were not encouraging, and during the second quarter of 2002 the US GDP grew by only 1.1 percent.[22] The global economic and financial environment was severely undermined by volatility in the stock markets, which in turn created an extremely high degree of uncertainty in the investment climate. In the first two weeks of July 2002, the Dow Jones Industrial Average and the S&P 500 index had lost 14.5 percent of their respective values. In mid-July, the FTSE 100 index in London was down by more than 40 percent from its peak (*The Economist*, 2002a). The Dow Jones index had lost four years of bull-market gains by the third week of July 2002.

The European economies were not as quick as the US in starting to recover from the 2001 recession, and thus European stock markets suffered more than those in the US. By mid-2002, European stock market indexes had lost eight years of bull-market gains. The Japanese economy was still in the doldrums. Other important bourses around the globe, particularly those in Asia, were volatile and sunk in gloom. Three large emerging market economies of the Western hemisphere, namely Argentina, Brazil, and Uruguay, were facing serious economic disruption by the middle of 2002. The problems facing the three countries were different, and required different approaches for resolution; the only thing they had in common was that outside help was needed to resolve them. Therefore, there was no likelihood of acceleration in financial flows to emerging market economies in the short term.[23]

According to the *Global Financial Stability Report*, December 2002,[24] investor sentiment continued to deteriorate sharply during the third quarter of 2002, and the external financing environment for the emerging market economies remained singularly unsupportive (IMF, 2002b). Investor apprehension over the problem economies of the Western hemisphere worsened. Notwithstanding an increase in volatility, there were no signs of a broad-based contagion. In the primary markets, unsecured access was effectively closed to non-investment grade issuers from Latin America. Conversely, Asian and Eastern European issuers experienced relatively open access. In the short term, risks for emerging markets were expected to remain elevated due to the turbulent external environment and uncertainty over policy continuity. Weakness and volatility in the mature equity markets was also detrimental to emerging market financing.

The cumulative gross issuance of bonds, bank loans, and equities in the nine months to September 2002 fell well below the 2001 level. It also lagged issuance levels of the previous five years by a significant margin, and it was highly concentrated in investment grade credits. In the third quarter of 2002, gross funding of emerging markets on international capital markets declined to $28.8 billion from $31.8 billion in the second quarter and $37.1 billion in the first.[25] Bond issuance plummeted, with quarterly issuance down in the third quarter of 2002 by 40 percent from the second quarter, declining to the levels seen in the aftermath of the Asian crisis. The drop in bond issuance was partially offset by syndicated loan commitments. Likewise, equity placements remained modest – with Asian issuers accounting for the bulk of new offerings.[26]

Although there was a modest rise in syndicated lending to the emerging markets in the third quarter of 2002, the syndicated loan market witnessed a considerable decline in volume in 2002, to levels seen in 1994–1995. This downturn in primary market syndications reflected a lack of demand by corporates for credit amid the slowdown in global economic growth and uncertainty about the prospects for global recovery. On the supply side, banks further reined in and tightened lending conditions. This was the result of sizable losses suffered by them following several high-profile bankruptcies in the United States and Europe in late 2001 and 2002. The second major reason that weighed heavily on global bankers' decisions was losses on banks' Argentine exposures and uncertainty over Brazil's outlook. Consequently, the risk appetite of investors was exceedingly low (see IMF, 2002b).

The post-bubble global economy continued to be fragile. Despite weak GDP growth in 2002, the US economy outperformed the Euro zone and Japan. During the early months of 2003, stock markets around the globe plunged. In the first two months, the S&P 500 shed around 2 percent, Germany's DAX was down by 6 percent, and the FTSE 100 fell by 12 percent, to a seven-year low. This collapse was blamed on the tepid global economic recovery and prospects of war in the Middle East. European markets fell more than the US market because the Euro-zone economies were in worse shape. A major risk for the emerging market economies in 2003 is that the global economy will not gather momentum in the course of the year. A key factor in this regard is whether robust US consumer spending can persist without a revival of confidence based on a sustained increase in profits and job recovery (IIF, 2003).

In Chapter 1 (Section 5) we saw that the economic and financial environment, both domestic and global, sways capital flows to emerging market economies immensely. Capital flows during 2002 testify to this fact. The global financial market environment was characterized by slipping stock market indexes, high levels of real and implied volatility, sharply widening credit spreads, the withdrawal of large banks from risk-taking in response to loan losses, and declining equity prices. This environment disturbed several emerging market economies, and global capital flows remained weak. The feast-or-famine dynamic that had developed in 2001 continued in 2002 – that is, a market differentiation among borrowers by perceived credit quality persisted during 2002. Brazil and other sub-investment grade issuers faced high credit spreads, whereas Asian borrowers benefited from near-record low spreads. All the Asian emerging market economies, except the Philippines, were supported by regional liquidity and a solid investor base. The degree of spread compression for investment-grade issuers was partially driven by a search for yield on the part of European institutional investors. Spreads for the East European economies that signed the accession treaty to join the EU in April 2003 also declined substantially (IMF, 2003b).[27]

There was little favorable impact of the end of the destructive conflict in Iraq, in the second quarter of 2003. While the Serious Acute Respiratory Syndrome (SARS) outbreak seemed to have peaked outside China in May 2003, its economic effects continued to ripple across Asia and beyond, and it became a drag over the global economy in the early second quarter of 2003. Despite the sharp decline in oil prices to $25 a barrel, the global economy continued to look weak.[28] Two of its major weaknesses that persisted were the repercussions of the bursting of the bubble of the 1990s, and excessive reliance on the US economy for pulling the global economy out of its moribund state. Between 1995 and 2002, the US economy accounted for more than half of the growth of the global economy. Its strengths were its economic flexibility, strong productivity growth, and sound macroeconomic policy. Its projected growth for 2003 was 2.2 percent, which was hardly a surge but was much better than that projected for Europe and Japan. Economic projections by the IMF (2003a) were of below-trend growth for all the world's major economies during 2003. In the second quarter of 2003, the Japanese economy was on the brink of its fourth recession in 10 years and the Nikkei index was at its lowest point since 1985. The period when Japan's economic model was the envy of the industrial and emerging market economies seemed a long time ago. Germany, the Euro zone's largest economy, continued to be in the doldrums, and there was little prospect of a pick-up in the short-term.[29]

On the global currency front, the scenario had undergone a market change during 2002–2003. There were sharp upheavals in the foreign exchange markets, and the figures speak for themselves. By mid-2003, the euro had risen by about 25 percent against the dollar. The dollar lost more than 15 percent of its value in trade-weighted terms – that is, against a broader range of currencies. The appreciation of the yen was causing consternation in the Japanese government. By mid-2003, the pound had slumped to its lowest level against the euro for six years. The deregulation of international capital markets meant that, on the whole, only emerging market economies had to worry much about what foreign-exchange dealers were up to. However, the very large swings in the value of the main reserve currencies are having a big impact on economic policy-making in the world's biggest economies and creating uncertainties.

The risk of the future external environment remaining unsupportive is palpable. Prospects of a strong recovery in the global economy remain far from certain. Equity markets are exposed to price correction. With such uncertainty in global economic milieu, short-term expectations of a strong recovery in global capital flows to the emerging market economies are not realistic. Investor discrimination is likely to prevail, and the perception of credit quality will be a strong determinant of capital flows in the short term. Therefore, until the global economy enters a robust recovery phase, the feast-or-famine dynamic is likely to continue in the foreseeable future.

9 Summary and conclusions

Private capital flows to emerging market economies are determined by the economic fundamentals of the recipient economy as well as the external economic environment, which includes both regional and global environments. Financial markets reward sound financial and macroeconomic policies and commitment to reforms by the emerging market policy mandarins. Incongruous and unpragmatic macroeconomic and financial policies destabilize economies, and financial markets are sensitive to policy inconsistencies and their outcome. Market disapproval is forthwith reflected in the direction of financial flows.

The global economic policy milieu during the first half of the 1990s worked strongly toward stimulating private capital flows to the emerging market economies. Some of the principal strands of the new policy environment included wide-ranging liberalization and structural adjustments in this group of economies, adoption of market-friendly strategies, acceptance of the Washington consensus, and increasing institutionalization of savings in the industrial economies. Improved fundamentals in the emerging market economies, the strengthening of the trend toward globalization, and a stable global economic environment also provided strong stimulants to capital inflows in these economies. Private capital flows into the emerging market economies went on increasing in a monotonic manner, and peaked in 1996. The global economic environment was transformed by the crisis in Thailand in July 1997, and financial flows to emerging market economies declined until net flows were reduced to a trickle in 2001. Although crises in Turkey and Argentina did not have a contagious effect, the global economic milieu was questionable in 2001 and 2002. Due to recurrent crises, there was a serious loss of investor confidence in the emerging market economies, and consequently net portfolio investment turned negative.

The presence of institutional investors in the global financial markets exposed the emerging market economies to some vulnerabilities. They could potentially take substantial short positions in a weak currency. When financial sector weaknesses become apparent, institutional investors and currency speculators are attracted, making a currency crisis imminent, and the well-known "herding" behavior of investors immediately makes this situation worse. The currency markets over-react because it is the agents who manage investment, and not the principals. Economies with inflexible exchange rate regimes are considered more vulnerable by speculators. History has demonstrated that speculative currency runs have occurred in periods of high capital mobility and fixed exchange rates.

However, the blame heaped on speculators for a currency crisis is perhaps excessive. Evidence is available to show that speculators only determine the timing of the eruption of a crisis; it would have occurred without their endeavors anyway. Hedge funds have also drawn a lot of ire. Although they are market players, a level-headed analysis shows that they cannot precipitate a currency crisis on their own, when there are no price bubbles. Normally, central banks resort to adopting sterilized intervention as the first defensive strategy against a speculative run. Raising short-term interest rates to dissuade speculators from taking short positions in the domestic currencies is another method, although this defensive strategy cannot be sustained for a long time. To reduce the volatility-creating activities of hedge funds, policy-makers can consider raising margin and collateral requirements for all financial market participants. Such measures would discourage hedge funds more than other investors, because they are heavy users of credit. Central banks should not adopt inflexible exchange rate pegs; not adhering to unsustainable pegs can work as a helpful defensive strategy. The strongest defense against a speculative run is to have a macroeconomic environment that is sound, functional, and pragmatic, a currency peg that is realistic and flexible, and a financial sector with a well-laid out framework of prudential norms. In addition, the excessively rapid liberalization of capital accounts does more harm than good to the financial sector of an economy; the liberalization of capital accounts should be cautious and sequential. That is, the liberalization of short-term flows should gradually follow that for long-term flows.

The debacle of Enron and Andersen in Wall Street was followed by the WorldCom disaster. Revelations of one accounting scandal after another drove Wall Street – and with it other important stock markets around the globe – to the edge of a precipice. The global financial and economic environment was putatively depressed by these events. Estimates for 2003 were, therefore, of the continuance poor financial flows to emerging market economies.

3 Financial liberalization in the emerging market economies

Growth, volatility, or both?

1 Introduction

When the post-World War II era began, the strategy of financial repression was endemic, leading to inefficient capital allocation and languishing financial intermediation. A group of developing economies adopted gradual financial liberalization seriously, and succeeded in becoming what became known as the emerging market economies – a rapidly globalizing group of economies. The final outcome was more rapid real growth than in the past and also compared to the non-globalizing group of economies. The flip side of this coin is that in the recent past liberalization has been squarely blamed for strong bouts of volatility in the emerging market economies.

The basic objectives of this chapter are to study in depth the financial liberalization process in the various segments of the emerging market economies, and to observe whether the resulting assertion of rapid real GDP growth holds. The financial and macroeconomic turbulence in the emerging market economies during the 1990s and early 2000s, which gave a new perspective to the financial liberalization process, is elaborated in a detailed manner. It was believed that capital account liberalization led to volatility, which in turn led to support for the strategy of restrictive global capital flows. The unrestricted trans-border capital flows were blamed for disorderly, if on occasions totally erratic, capital market behavior, both domestically and globally. Whether the recent spate of emerging market crises has a relationship with financial liberalization is the other focus of this chapter.

The structure of this chapter is as follows. After taking a long-term perspective on financial repression and financial liberalization in Section 2, the focus is on the liberalization–growth nexus in Section 3. Capital account liberalization and whether it leads to growth and/or volatility, or both, are the issues on which Sections 4 and 5 dwell. The relatively recent phenomenon of liberalization in equity markets, its pace and intensity, are delved into in Section 6. How it has contributed to the recent rise in volatility in the emerging markets is also discussed in Section 7. The last section briefly summarizes the principal conclusions of the chapter.

2   Financial repression and liberalization

Financial distortions commonly affect the functioning of financial systems in most developing economies. Until the early 1970s, domestic financial repression was widespread. Even some of the industrial economies suffered from some features of financial distortion and repression. Controls on interest rates, size of bank loans, prohibitions on foreign currency denominated deposits and loans, and dual currency markets, were endemic. The common and garden variety of repressive policies included controls over interest rates on both deposits and loans, as well as over exchange rates, capital markets, and capital flows. Government policies of directing credit were an important part of financial repression. Therefore, often government-favored sectors and industries obtained credit at negative real interest rates, while others had to depend upon the expensive and unstable informal credit market. In many cases even the government-favored firms were nurtured with negative real interest rate finances, creating opportunities for rent-seeking.

In the post-World War II era, during the 1950s and 1960s, policies related to directing credit segmented domestic financial markets. In addition, in many developing economies the banking sector had either partial or complete public ownership. It typically led to negative real interest rates for the depositors, eventually discouraging saving. Equity markets in the developing economies were small, underdeveloped, and restricted – i.e. non-residents were not allowed to participate in the domestic equity markets. Due to ceilings on interest rates, capital accumulation was severely restricted in the developing economies. It should be noted that these economies were, by definition, capital-scarce. The cumulative impact of financial repression was decimated domestic saving rates, inefficient capital allocation, and an inefficient and languishing financial intermediation process. Economic growth endeavors suffered. During this period, policy mandarins incorrectly considered financial repression to be an accepted policy stance for economic growth and academics were yet to raise their dissent strongly against this stance.

Many developing economies took note of the adverse macroeconomic impact of financial repression, albeit belatedly. The ones that were subsequently classified as the emerging market economies began to liberalize their financial sector and markets in the mid-1970s. This liberalization was characterized by several means: first, by reforming the banking sector, along with the deregulation of domestic interest rates; second, by opening the capital account to varying degrees; and third, restrictive measures on domestic equity markets, as well as those on foreign ownership of financial assets, began to be dismantled. The elimination of interest rate controls not only changed the nature and composition of the market on bank loans and deposits, but at a later stage also attracted international capital flows. Elimination of credit rationing and controls contributed to the expansion of hitherto infant stock markets. When the liberalization process is occurring, liberalization across the individual segments of the financial market is important. Identifying and prioritizing the liberalization of the segment that catalyzes the entire domestic financial market and the domestic economy has a salutary effect on the liberalizing economy.

The financial liberalization measures enumerated above included lifting numerous small and large financial controls, eliminating restrictive policies like credit rationing to favored sectors and industries, dismantling foreign currency-related regulations, and relaxing official barriers to consolidation. The process of financial market liberalization has been an important catalyst for the integration of global financial markets. As liberalization progressed, global market investors were allowed to own domestic securities. The removal of prohibitions on repatriation of dividends and interest generally followed. These reform measures brought about a radical change in the operation of financial systems and macroeconomic management. With multiple exchange rates gone and capital controls dismantled, domestic firms began to borrow abroad. Liberalization of the equity markets provided global investors with opportunities to invest in the emerging market economies' securities. The domestic investors in these economies were able to transact in global securities. It was believed that financial liberalization reduced the costs of financing (in this case external financing) for the firms, and therefore promoted growth (Rajan and Zingales, 1998). In other words, firms that needed external finance in economies that were liberalizing their financial sector during this period grew disproportionately faster than those in economies that were not liberalizing their financial sector.

Over the preceding two decades, many emerging market governments have significantly relaxed official barriers and gradually deregulated, as noted in the preceding paragraph. Deregulation has influenced the restructuring process through changes in entry conditions and market competition. In the new deregulated environment, legal and regulatory frameworks have been reconsidered and given a much needed focus. In the past their focus was consumer protection and the prevention of institutional failures. However, the contemporary focus of the legal and regulatory framework is no longer strict regulatory control but is rather creating a financial system that is based on enhancing market and institutional efficiency through competition. The three principal elements of the new system are: (1) the adoption of market culture and market discipline; (2) regulation and supervision; and (3) risk-based capital deployment guidelines. This system is obviously less concerned with the prevention of institutional failure. Instead of being protective of financial services providers, the new environment encourages banks to fend for themselves in the marketplace – as non-financial businesses have always done. Thus, there was a radical change in the objectives and philosophy of financial markets.

Kaminsky and Schmukler (2001a) studied the progress of financial liberalization over the 1972–1999 period in both the Group of 7 (G-7) industrial economies and various regional sub-groups in the developing world.[1] They prepared a composite index of liberalization of various segments of financial markets, including the capital accounts, domestic financial systems, and stock markets. They found that during the period under review, removal of financially repressive measures was slow albeit continuous globally. They also concluded that the G-7 industrial economies were the first and the quickest to liberalize their financial sectors. It is possible that disenchantment with the restrictive policies of the interwar years had something to do with their eagerness to liberalize financially at the first possible opportunity. By mid-1970s, the financial sector in the G-7 economies was considerably liberalized and not many restrictive practices were left untouched. Financial liberalization measures were adopted early in the West European economies and followed through in a rapid manner.

Several emerging market economies of Asia, particularly those of East Asia, steadily liberalized their financial sector after 1972. They were followed by the emerging market economies of Southeast Asia. After 1995, progress in further liberalization slowed down in these economies; it seems that their liberalization endeavors reached a plateau after this time point.

In the emerging market economies of Latin America, financial repression was removed in an uneven manner. In the early 1970s, this country group liberalized its financial sector rapidly. During this period, it was spearheaded by the southern cone economies. They advanced toward adopting *laissez faire* financial policies that encouraged private sector participation as much as possible. Governments in the southern cone economies tried to adopt a hands-off stand during this period; however, much to their chagrin, the outcome of rapid and extensive liberalization was a large number of bankruptcies and generalized financial crisis in Latin American economies. After the debt crisis of 1982, financial liberalization was neglected in this country group. During the 1989–1992 period maximum progress took place in this direction (Kaminsky and Schmukler, 2001a). In the latter half of the 1990s, the emerging market economies of Latin America not only returned to liberalization in earnest, but also implemented wide-ranging regulatory and supervisory program mechanisms so that future crises could be avoided.

3 Financial liberalization and growth nexus

The effects of controls on financial markets, capital flows, and economic growth have been a prolific area for empirical research in international economics. Researchers in economic growth have also addressed the issue of the financial liberalization and development of the financial sector. Whether it has contributed to rapid growth in the emerging market economies is an important, albeit difficult, question to answer. Although researchers in several disciplines have studied the financial liberalization–

economic growth nexus, both theoretically and empirically, there is no categorical conclusion regarding the contribution of financial liberalization to economic growth in the emerging market economies. Neither theory provides a clear answer regarding how liberalization impacts growth, and nor do empirical studies. Many of these studies have remained inconclusive.[2] Most researchers have tended to focus on the effects of deregulation over domestic financial markets, like the stock markets and banking sector. Besides, subsumed into financial liberalization is the issue of capital account liberalization *per se*. It has remained a controversial policy measure, and its effect has been little understood, although long debated. While several attempts have been made, measuring its impact remains a problem-ridden task.[3]

There are four important causes behind this disappointing state of affairs. The first hurdle was the lack of homogeneous measures of financial liberalization policies across countries and across time.[4] Second, while several empirical studies were attempted, in general their scope was limited. They focused on one kind of reform measures, or the elimination of controls on one particular financial market. Some concentrated on the elimination of controls on the banking sector, others on stock markets, and yet others focused narrowly on capital account liberalization. However, as noted above, financial repression can take many forms. Restrictive measures on one market not only affect it directly but also affect the other financial markets indirectly. As expected, narrowly focused studies produce inadequate and incomplete evaluation of the effects of financial liberalization.

The third hurdle, the problem of omitted variables, is to be found in almost all empirical studies. Financial liberalization is seldom adopted as a solitary or exclusive policy measure, but is generally part of a comprehensive liberalization policy package including measures like trade liberalization, improved investment policies, privatization, and strengthening of private property rights. Sachs and Warner (1995) emphasized that policy choices in these areas are important determinants of long-term growth. Therefore, to calculate the impact of financial liberalization on economic growth it is vitally important to control for all the other reform measures that were adopted as a part of the larger policy package. Lastly, in addition to these shortcomings, Eichengreen (2002) pointed out that each emerging market economies is *sui generis*. Each one has different macroeconomic, financial, and political traits. Additionally, each economy has its idiosyncratic institutional strengths and weaknesses. While quantifying the growth impact of financial liberalization, these differences must be taken into account. A lack of this perspective further adds to the difficulties of the empirical studies, as well as putting a question mark over the acceptability of their conclusions.

Models based on perfect market assumptions tend to conclude that liberalization has welfare-inducing implications for market participants, both lenders and borrowers. Well-known theories posited by McKinnon (1973) and Shaw (1973), among others, have pointed out that welfare-enhancing effects of financial liberalization can be related to the interest rate mechanism. In a liberalized regime, the interest rates rise (or fall) to their competitive market equilibrium level, which leads to the efficient allocation of productive resources. The second channel of welfare gains could be through capital account liberalization. Third, in a developing economy setting, it is not inappropriate to assume that financial markets are imperfect and capital constraints are endemic (Hubbard, 1998). Given these circumstances, external finance will be typically more expensive than domestic finance, which in turn will make the rate of domestic investment sensitive to external capital flows. In such developing economies, if equity markets are liberalized then one of the direct effects should be the easing of capital constraint because more global capital can flow in. A possible indirect effect may be an improvement in the quality of corporate governance, which is sure to lead to improvement in risk sharing. Together, these two effects should force the cost of capital down.

Among the financial economists, Goldsmith (1969) was the first to address the issue of the growth impact of financial liberalization, followed by seminal contributions by McKinnon (1973) and Shaw (1973). Their proposition regarding this relationship was simple and positive. They concurred that liberalization favorably affects economic growth by: first, strengthening the size and improving the efficiency of the domestic financial system; second, allowing domestic firms to access the global financial markets; and third, improving the level of corporate governance in the domestic financial system and thereby reducing the agency problems. The focus of McKinnon (1973) and of Shaw (1973) was also the advantages of reducing financial repression prevalent during their period. They pointed out that the advantages of reducing financial restrictions included higher savings rates, improved allocation of resources, and a lack of compulsion to adopt dualistic growth policies.

The inclusion of static and dynamic factors subsequently refined this scenario. Financial liberalization promotes foreign competition in the domestic banking and non-banking financial sectors, reducing the cost of capital. It allows the financial institutions in the emerging market economies to adopt the newest financial know-how, instruments, products, and technologies. Financial deregulation and reforms fuel institutional reforms. Additionally, when domestic firms begin accessing the global capital market, their cost of capital declines and raises the level of domestic investment. There can be little doubt that there are static and dynamic impacts of these developments as well, which in turn buttress GDP growth rate.[5] As firms begin to tap global capital and securities markets, a large font of capital and stockholder base becomes available to them. Domestic financial constraints are eased by the availability of a greater quantum of capital (Gilchrist and Himmelberg, 1998).

In addition, there is an important indirect effect. Capital allocation by markets putatively improves the efficiency of allocation, and financial resources head for sectors with a comparative advantage that were constrained during the period of financial repression (Sarkissian and Schill, 2003). A good deal of evidence of these static and dynamic effects has been provided by several emerging market economies. The liberalized emerging markets came to have an opportunity to grow and develop like their counterparts in the advanced industrial economies.

Recent studies have supported what McKinnon and Shaw posited three decades ago; that is, that corporate governance in the emerging market economies was favorably affected by financial liberalization. Competition from foreign banking and non-banking firms did exert pressure on their domestic counterparts to adopt *à la mode* financial and banking practices as well as internationally accepted accounting standards, regulatory practices, and supervision norms. Financial liberalization also promotes transparency and accountability, reducing adverse selection and moral hazard problems. These improvements in corporate government tend to reduce the cost of borrowing in the banking sector and securities markets.[6] Other than promoting competition, liberalization enhances the opportunities for smoothing out the effects of real shocks. In this respect, liberalization, including capital account liberalization, plays a stabilizing role.

However, this line of logic has been challenged. Skeptics have argued that it is not necessarily true that access to the global capital market will increase the availability of capital. When firms are allowed to list on bourses abroad, this can potentially inhibit the development of domestic financial markets and reduce domestic liquidity. In the process, the depth of the domestic financial markets suffers. The inverse correlation between the amounts of aggregate capital raised by firms in emerging market economies in Latin America in the American Depository Receipt (ADR) market and the number of initial public offerings (IPOs) in the domestic markets corroborates this argument (Moel, 2001).

Skeptics also argue that efficiency in capital allocation cannot come about by mere removal of distortions caused by financial repression. As alluded to earlier, removal of one set of distortions cannot be welfare enhancing when many other distortions remain in tact. For instance, there were cases of capital account was liberalization when tariff barriers were kept high for import competing industries. In such a cases, capital went to industries that did not have comparative advantage, which was not welfare enhancing. If anything, it was welfare diminishing.

Furthermore, Stiglitz (2000a) has contended that in an environment of information asymmetries in the financial markets, there is little possibility of financial liberalization leading to welfare improvement as a rule. So far we have ignored moral hazards, which should be added to asymmetric information in the developing economies.[7] Stiglitz's contention applies *a foretiori* to an environment where corporate governance is weak and property rights are not strongly held. Merely liberalizing financial markets would never ensure the flow of capital to uses where its marginal product exceeds its opportunity cost. Therefore, Stiglitz supported certain forms of financial repression and credit rationing. He argued that if credit is channeled toward the export sector or toward those with high technological spillover, the final result would no doubt be acceleration of the growth rate (Stiglitz, 1994). However, his argument is not without its downside. This kind of financial repression is a throwback to the past. It increases the power of bureaucracy and promotes rent-seeking behavior. In capital allocation decisions, the competence of bureaucrats was generally found to be less than that in imperfect markets.

Information asymmetry, alluded to in the preceding paragraph, is perhaps the most often cited asymmetry in capital markets. Asymmetries exist in the goods markets as well, but they are far more in number as well as more pronounced in asset markets. Due to information barriers, geographical distances, and cultural differences, the problem of information asymmetry is exacerbated in the international capital markets. In addition, market imperfections of this genre are further magnified in the international capital markets owing to difficulties in entering into and enforcing contracts across borders. Information asymmetries do lead (and have led) to over-reactions by global investors on both sides, investing freely and withdrawing massively (Zeira, 1999). The growing globalization of capital markets and declining transaction costs can (and did) make global investors rationally "exuberant." In such an environment, information asymmetry increases the probability of herding behavior, which manifests itself in "excesses," or booms and busts, in the international capital markets (Calvo and Mendoza, 2000). Information asymmetry also generates market behavioral patterns such as momentum trading, noise, trading, bandwagon effects, and short-termism (see Chapter 1, Section 5 for definitions).

Numerous empirical studies of the impact of financial liberalization on growth are available in the literature, and several of them are cited below. They have essentially taken two routes for selecting variables to deploy and for quantifying their results; some of them selected one proxy variable or the other for financial liberalization, while others focused on specific liberalization strategies for quantifying how liberalization affected growth. Earlier empirical studies were narrow and considered the real interest rates to be adequate measure for financial repression. These studies considered positivity or otherwise of interest rates to be an important indicator, and assumed that economies with negative real interest rates were financially repressed while those with positive real interest rates were not. These studies concluded that the growth rate in economies with negative real interest rates suffered, and its opposite was equally true. This indicator of financial repression was subsequently rejected as being inadequate, and some studies adopted the ratio of credit to the private sector to GDP as a measure of financial liberalization (De Gregorio and Guidotti, 1993). Other indicators of financial development were also taken as proxies of liberalization.

After several cross-country studies with large numbers of sample countries, a gradual consensus emerged on financial development and liberalization affecting growth rate in a significantly positive manner. Deregulation creates an environment that greatly facilitates economic growth.[8] As discussed below, the evidence of the benefits of financial liberalization and deregulation on real per capita GDP growth was found to be strong. Reinhart and Tokatlidid (2002) not only supported this result but also added that financial liberalization delivers a higher level of foreign direct investment (FDI) and gross capital flows. However, the catch is that this occurred only in the higher-income emerging markets. Financial liberalization appears to deliver financial deepening, but again in the higher-income emerging markets. Economies that shunned financial repression – or more realistically dropped it at an early stage of development – and liberalized their financial sector stood a better chance of becoming emerging market economies.

Although the general acceptability and robustness of these results was high, they need to be considered with a degree of skepticism. While they related financial liberalization to growth, they ignored other structural and macroeconomic developments that were progressing with the implementation of financial liberalization measures. Simultaneity of reform measures was a capital issue that made it difficult to isolate the effects of financial components of the reform package. While it was possible that financial liberalization played a leading role, it was certainly not the most crucial one, and never the only strategy affecting the growth rate in the economies being studied. Under certain circumstances, financial liberalization can have no impact at all on financial development. Emerging economies in Latin American have provided evidence of this. Using 30-year data from the World Development Indicators, Galindo *et al.* (2002) demonstrated that all regions experienced a significant impact on their financial systems as they liberalized. Latin American economies were an exception to this generalization, recording a decline in the size of their financial system during the financial liberalization period in Latin America.

Empirical research focusing on specific liberalization strategies for quantifying how liberalization affects growth has not made a great deal of headway. Not many researchers have tried this route, essentially because of the constraints related to liberalization data. Bekaert *et al.* (2002) did one of the few comprehensive cross-country studies of this kind. They took a dynamic panel of industrial and developing economies and conducted a number of empirical exercises that instill confidence in their results. The results survived several econometric robustness experiments, including controlling for the global business cycle. In addition, they were found to be robust to alternative measurements of the liberalization variable. Although the liberalization variable was a 0/1 indicator, these authors also used a number of variables that measured the intensity and comprehensiveness of the equity market liberalization. They concluded that stock market liberalization affected growth permanently. When they augmented the standard set of variables used in economic growth research with an indicator variable for equity market liberalization, they found that liberalization of equity markets led to a 1 percent increase in annual real per capita GDP growth over a five-year period. This increase was found to be statistically significant. They also showed that financial liberalization increased the investment/GDP ratio and factor productivity. The 1 percent increase in real GDP is surprisingly large, even counterintuitive. However, it can partly be explained by the fact that equity market liberalization measures are intertwined with both macroeconomic reforms and other financial sector developments.

Indirect transmission channels between financial liberalization and growth rate have also been studied. Important among these studies is one by Laeven (2000), which took 20-year data for 13 emerging market economies to conclude that liberalization process eased financial constraints, particularly those faced by large domestic firms. The results of Galindo *et al.* (2001) are important in that they infer that financial liberalization enhances the allocative efficiency of investment. Although some of these studies have controlled for parallel ongoing reforms, the simultaneity of reforms argument applies to this set of studies also because it is unclear how large the controls were. It is difficult to determine whether these controls were large enough to isolate the effects of financial liberalization.

Galindo *et al.* (2002) addressed this issue from a cross-industry–country panel data perspective. They improved upon Rajan and Zingales' (1998) methodology; their approach allowed isolation of the impact of financial liberalization on growth. Using a time series of cross-industry–country data for 28 economies, they estimated the same empirical model as Rajan and Zingales (1998). Their inference was that financial liberalization is an instrument that under certain conditions can promote financial sector development, which in turn "can stimulate the relative growth rate of sectors that rely on external funding." However, they found that a caveat is essential; that is, for rapid growth other structural reforms that ensure the proper behavior of financial markets are also essential. Financial liberalization is necessary, albeit not sufficient, for rapid growth. In a fully liberalized economy, "the impact of liberalization on the domestic credit market growth can be null" if regulatory and institutional support are lacking.

Integration with the global markets and institutions tends to speed up the reform process to achieve a resilient financial system. Summing up these arguments, it can be concluded that the emerging market economies have benefited from financial liberalization in two ways. The first was by having an increased access to the global pool of capital, which helped to raise the level of investment and output. The second channel of benefit was improvement in the efficiency of capital allocation. Both of these are known to underpin economic growth. Despite the polemicists, the current drift of opinion among the international economists is toward financial liberalization and deregulation. They endorse the removal of capital controls because they consider capital markets to be efficient. In a control-free financial environment, capital is likely to flow toward the most lucrative destination. The opposing view, which supports controls or gradual liberalization, argues that financial liberalization amounts to lurching into excesses of trans-border financial movements. This logic in the international economics literature as well as in the capital market literature is based on the view that market failures and distortions pervade capital markets around the world.

If, as stated above, a consensus has emerged on financial development and liberalization affecting growth rate in a significantly positive manner, why do so many economies still have an under-developed financial sector? A common (if simplistic) answer is that it is due to a lack of demand. Demand for financial development is determined by economic growth and industrialization. It has been observed that economies at the same level of general development differ widely in their level of financial development. Several alternative explanations for this have been provided, including the lack of social capital necessary for financial development, and weak legal, cultural, and political systems. Countries with a common law and strong minority investor protection have better-developed financial (particularly securities) markets. Structuralists have also tried to provide an explanation for the differences in the level of financial development. According to them, in some economies there can be real structural impediments to the development of the financial sector. Once these impediments are overcome, the supply of finance should rise to meet the demand.

The experiences of the last two decades demonstrate that financial liberalization is not risk-free. It has been observed that it leads to over-borrowing, and McKinnon and Pill (1999) have presented a formal framework demonstrating how and when financial liberalization may lead to this. This propensity was found to be magnified when domestic financial liberalization was undertaken along with, or a little before, capital account liberalization. As the rising levels of debts are in foreign currency, the economy soon becomes vulnerable to exchange rate fluctuations. Thus, financial liberalization becomes the cause of volatility. This issue is discussed in Chapter 5.

4   Capital account liberalization and growth

Although capital account liberalization is subsumed in financial liberalization, it has been an important issue for the emerging market economies, and deserves to be analyzed as a distinct policy move. During the last quarter-century, several emerging market economies that were capital-poor permitted non-residents to participate in their domestic stock markets. In the wake of the recent economic and financial crises in several emerging market economies, capital account liberalization has taken on additional importance. Some of the blame for the recent crises has attached to premature or poorly sequenced liberalization of the capital account, and this is dealt with below.

Over the years, two broad views have emerged regarding how capital account liberalization affects an economy – particularly the financial sector. The allocative efficiency view is the older and better debated of the two. To state it briefly, when capital account barriers on the flow of capital are removed, trans-border capital movements begin. Capital tends to move from capital-abundant economies, where the marginal rate of return is lower, to capital-scarce economies, where the marginal rate of return is rationally expected to be higher. In the latter country group the cost of capital declines, which in turn favorably impacts investment and output (Fischer, 1998; Stulz, 1999b; Mishkin, 2001a).

The newer view was put forward by Rodrik (1998) and Stiglitz (2000a, 2000b). It was called the "animal spirit," an expression used first by John Maynard Keynes for the psychology of business people. This treated the older view of the impact of capital account liberalization as simplistic, if not downright fanciful. The proponents of this view believe that capital account liberalization does not result in the efficient allocation of financial resources because international capital movements have little connection with real economic activity in the host economies. They posited that capital account liberalization has no impact on domestic investment, output or any real variable with non-trivial welfare implications.

Opening the stock markets for non-residents comprises a discrete change in the degree of capital account openness. As several emerging market economies liberalized their capital accounts and allowed non-residents to purchase shares in their stock markets, statistical data to examine the two above-mentioned hypotheses regarding the impact of capital account liberalization empirically are readily available. Allocative efficiency hypothesis can be tested in two ways, with the help of time series data, for the prices and quantities of capital during the liberalization period (Chari and Henry, 2002a). The first method is to examine whether the cost of capital has been driven down and Tobin's q the asset market value of installed capital goods relative to their replacement cost driven up by the inflows of global capital after the liberalization of the capital account. The second testing method is that profit-maximizing firms may respond to the rising level of Tobin's q by increasing the investment in physical capital. This increase in the level of investment would continue until the asset market value of capital goods and their replacement costs have equalized. If the allocative efficiency hypothesis is correct, data should reveal a temporary increase in Tobin's q as well as in investment after the capital account is liberalized. However, if the "animal spirit" view is correct, there should be no discernible increase in the prices and quantity of capital inflows during the liberalization episode.

Chari and Henry (2002a) made time series and cross-sectional estimates using data for 1980–1994 for 369 firms in India, Jordan, Korea, Malaysia, and Thailand, and found that time series results were more consistent with the allocative efficiency hypothesis than with the animal spirit or psychology-of-the-business-people hypothesis. They concluded that a typical firm experiences an increase in both Tobin's q and investment during the liberalization episode. For their sample firms they found that during the year the capital market was liberalized, the growth rate of capital stocks exceeded their pre-liberalization mean by 4.1 percent. During the next three years the average growth rate of capital stock for the 369 firms in the sample exceeded its pre-liberalization mean by 6.1 percent. As opposed to this, cross-sectional estimates were found to be more consistent with the animal spirit hypothesis. Same or similar results have been arrived at by other recent studies. For instance, Bekaert and Harvey (2001) and Henry (2000a, 2000b) have provided evidence of capital market and stock market liberalization leading to higher stock prices and more investment in the economy. Conversely, Rodrik (1998) has provided evidence from aggregate cross-sectional data of no significant relationship between the investment/GDP ratios in the sample economies and openness of capital account, supporting the animal spirit hypothesis.

These results need to be interpreted carefully. The two sets of results suggest that neither of the two hypotheses provides a completely accurate view of the impact of liberalization of the capital account. Although liberalization of the capital account may encourage the movement of capital from capital-abundant to capital-scarce economies, this policy measure alone is certainly not enough to ensure the efficient allocation of productive capital between firms and sectors.

5   Capital account liberalization and volatility

The capital account is liberalized by removing statutory restrictions on cross-border global capital flows, which in turn is an important facet of general financial liberalization. It entails the relaxation or removal of controls on transactions in the capital and financial accounts of the balance-of-payments. One of the most important removals of restriction is on the convertibility of foreign exchange. Macroeconomic and financial volatility are a well-known downside of financial liberalization, and capital account liberalization is frequently blamed for causing volatility. As alluded to earlier, in the early 1970s the emerging market economies of the Western hemisphere liberalized to end their much-criticized financial repression. Soon these economies found themselves in the midst of macroeconomic crises and hoards of bankruptcies. After the emerging market financial crises of the 1990s and early 2000s – which claimed a good number of emerging market economies as their victims – this characteristic of financial market liberalization acquired a new significance.

Kaminsky and Reinhart (1999a) have established a link between financial liberalization and economic, financial, and balance-of-payments crises. All of these crises are traumatic and have high economic and social costs. The individual emerging market economies suffer as much as the global economy. The emerging market economies of East and Southeast Asia had successfully established their reputation as high performers, but in 1997 several of them succumbed to their worst recessions in decades. The global banking and financial system was also adversely affected on several occasions during this period. Global capital market flows to emerging market economies, which were booming in the early and mid-1990s, had declined to a trickle by 1997 and 1998. By 2002, capital markets flows to emerging market economies in the form of bank lending, bond lending, equity flows and other flows had not recovered, although foreign direct investment (FDI) had held firm.

An important casualty of these crises was the rising trend toward financial liberalization, both at domestic and global tiers. Opinion leaders such as Paul Krugman (1998) and Joe Stiglitz (1999) began opposing financial liberalization and supporting restrictive global capital flows.[9] They began to blame unrestricted trans-border capital flows for disorderly, if on occasions totally erratic, capital market behavior, both domestically and globally. Their logic was that restrictions on global capital flows would help in moderating the "excessive boom–bust" pattern in financial markets so prevalent in the 1990s and early 2000s. Krugman (1998) even suggested controls on capital outflows, which sounded like an archaic notion.[10] In the early 1970s, this and similar propositions were opposed as being inefficient and counter-productive. The indiscriminate advocacy of greater financial liberalization and development virtually stopped. The saving grace behind the proposals for restriction over capital flows was that they were more of less intended to be short term, for the purpose of handling a crisis situation and for obstructing the disorderly retreat of global investors in a crisis-ridden economy. As a permanent policy measure, these proposals did not win many supporters.

Distortionary macroeconomic policies and volatility have been found to be closely related. Inapt macroeconomic policies such as excessive government spending, high inflation, and an over-valued exchange rate render an economy prone to crisis. Demirguc-Kunt and Detriagiache (1998) blamed macroeconomic and financial instability on the lack of institutional development in an economy. The likelihood of financial crisis in the wake of financial liberalization declines with a rising level of institutional development. Creating and strengthening institutions is the task of the governments, and thus government intervention in the system in the form of (1) institutional development, (2) prudential regulation and (3) supervision has a convincing justification. At least in the early stages, governments in the emerging market economies need to ensure proper functioning of the financial system and therefore to intervene more than in the later stages, when these developments have made a reasonable progress. If regulation and supervision progress hand in hand with financial liberalization, the negative impact of financial liberalization on the emerging market economy can be reined in (Das, 2002).

In the early stages, liberalization can have a destabilizing effect over the financial sector because it abruptly increases the exposure to credit risk and foreign exchange risk – *a fortiori* when liberalization is undertaken in an environment of macroeconomic stability. In a newly liberalized financial environment, managers lack the experience to manage the two risks named earlier and have a tendency to push toward riskier investments. In such a financial environment, even soundly managed banks feel it to be a good strategy to build up large open foreign positions abroad to finance domestic assets, or to engage in foreign exchange lending to domestic residents. As stated previously, this situation calls for government intervention and strengthening of the regulatory and supervisory framework.

6 Degree of liberalization of global ownership of equities

Quantifying the degree of capital account liberalization is not considered to be an easy exercise. Therefore, there is a predominance of qualitative measures of liberalization. They largely build on the comprehensive, country-wise data and information annually compiled by the International Monetary Fund (IMF) and published in the *Annual Report on Exchange Arrangements and Exchange Restrictions*. This publication documents rules (and annual changes in them) regarding restrictions or liberalization of capital inflows in the IMF member economies. It does not provide any indication of the intensity of capital controls, and its frequency of data is also low. Some recent empirical studies have tried to score the intensity of capital controls (Quinn, 1997). Recent finance literature treats capital account liberalization as either a one-time event or a structural break, although both of these approaches need refinement (Edison and Warnock, 2001).

When capital account liberalization is treated as either a one-time event or a structural break, the general assumption is that all episodes of liberalization are comparable and that they have equal intensity and pace. It does not have to be so. In reality, each economy is *sui generis* in this regard, and has its own intensity and pace of liberalization. Liberalization measures take may different forms. Some are partial while others are complete, some are a one-time event and others are a gradual dénouement. For instance, in the emerging economies of the Western hemisphere, liberalization was much faster than that in those of Asia. It was also launched earlier than in Asia. Measuring the intensity of liberalization with the help of the annual measures of capital controls formed with the help of dummy variables is not helpful because it hardly provides any indication of the intensity of capital controls.

A measure is required that both takes into account the intensity of controls and has a greater frequency than annual, for the emerging market economies and other economies. Edison and Warnock (2001) have devised a monthly measure of the intensity of controls for a liberalizing economy, which is simple to construct. It also calibrates the intensity of controls at a point in time (or the static view), as well as their evolution through time (or the dynamic view). Their monthly measure is based on the International Finance Corporation (IFC) data and is the ratio of the market capitalizations underlying a county's investable and global indexes as computed by the IFC. The IFC has been calculating these two indexes for the emerging market economies for some time. The global index (IFCg) is designed to represent the market, while the investable index (IFCi) represents the portion of the market available to the global investors. Thus, the ratio of market capitalizations of an emerging market economy's IFCi and IFCg indexes is a quantitative measure of the availability of the economy's equities to global investors. One minus the ratio becomes a measure of the intensity of capital controls.

$$\text{Intensity of capital controls} = 1 - \frac{\text{IFCi}}{\text{IFCg}}$$

These IFC data have been available for a long time (since December 1988), but attracted the attention of only a few researchers. Empirical research did not use them adequately. Another version of this measure was used by Bachatta and van Wincoop (2000) to conclude that in general, liberalization in the emerging economies appeared to be gradual. This again was not followed up by other empirical studies as a viable measure of capital controls. Chari and Henry (2001) used firm-level IFC data to examine the salient features of firms in which global investors tend to invest, and the firms in which they choose not to invest. One weakness of the measure devised by Edison and Warnock (2001) is that it is narrow, because it only focuses on global ownership of domestic equities. The flip side of this coin is that it is readily available at high (monthly) frequency, starting in 1988, for all the emerging market economies. Its lends itself to empirical analysis of cross-sectional and time-series data sets. The fact that it is based on the rich IFC database makes this measure easy to compile.[11]

Intensity and pace of liberalization

Using this monthly measure, Edison and Warnock (2001) computed the intensity and pace of liberalization for 29 emerging market economies. Their results are reported briefly below. There were 10 Asian emerging market economies in their sample, which included China, India, Indonesia, Korea, Malaysia, Pakistan, the Philippines, Sri Lanka, Taiwan, and Thailand. Restrictions in India were initially quite high – much higher than those in the Western hemisphere – but in all these economies they fell during the course of the 1990s. In the mid-1990s, Malaysia had the minimum restrictions on foreign ownership of stocks and was the most open economy in Asia. At this time, the other Asian emerging markets had foreign equity ownership limits ranging from 10 percent in Taiwan to 49 percent in Thailand. However, there was retrograde motion in several Asian emerging market economies. In spite of declining restrictions in the early 1990s, India, the Philippines, and Sri Lanka were no more open in the early 2000s than they were in 1990. Because of the crisis, Malaysia briefly reinstituted restrictions and controls in 1998, and dismantled them thereafter.

As regards the dynamic scenario of capital market liberalization, each Asian economy was found to be different in the timing, extent, and evolution of its liberalization process. Korea, Indonesia, Malaysia, and Thailand were not very open economies in the 1990s, but they relaxed equity ownership restrictions over the decade. The relaxation process was greatly accelerated in 1997 and 1998. For India and Sri Lanka, liberalization was more or less a one-time event. Progress was slow and occurred very little after 1990–1991. There was a gradual relaxation in China after 1993, although the pace accelerated after 1998. Only a few Chinese H-shares were listed in Hong Kong SAR before 1993, and this listing increased markedly after 1998. In 2000, the Chinese market was still about 60 percent closed to global investors.

The emerging market economies of the Western hemisphere included in the sample were Argentina, Brazil, Chile, Colombia, Mexico, Peru, and Venezuela. The evolution process of liberalization in the Western hemisphere was markedly different from that in Asia. These economies had much lower restrictions on equity ownership by global investors in 1990 than did the emerging market economies of Asia. After 1990, liberalization in these economies was far more extensive than in Asia. Equity ownership restrictions were almost negligible in Argentina in 1990, and its equity market was almost completely open to foreign investment. The other emerging markets were not far behind. Mexico had liberalized its equity markets by 1990, followed by Brazil and Peru. Brazil made a retrograde move in 1993 and increased the restrictions on global investors to stem the tide of capital inflows.

Chile showed a mixed picture in the 1990s, liberalizing in the early part of the decade and instituting capital controls in the mid-1990s. The latter were targeted at short-term capital inflows, as Chile favored medium- and long-term capital inflows but was skeptical of the short-term ones. In Venezuela, liberalization was slower to start than in the neighboring emerging market economies. Also, Venezuela underwent a policy reversal by nationalizing the banking sector in 1996. Banks were privatized again, and foreign investors were allowed to buy in.

In Eastern Europe, Hungary was the earliest to start liberalization in 1993, although at present Poland has the most open economy. Regarding Greece, Portugal, and Turkey, restrictions were lower than those in the emerging markets of Asia but higher than those in the Western hemisphere. Turkey launched its liberalization process early. Gradual relaxation took place in Jordan, Morocco, South Africa, and Zimbabwe. Of these economies, Zimbabwe partially reversed its liberalization process in 1998, and Jordan and Zimbabwe both instituted stringent restrictions. As opposed to this, South Africa has remained open to foreign investment (Edison and Warnock, 2001).

7   Liberalization of equity markets, and volatility

During the recent episodes of crisis in the emerging market economies, stock markets displayed an excessive boom–bust behavior. Many asked the question, "Did liberalization of the equity market cause it?" To answer this question, Kaminsky and Schmukler (2002) examined the possible varying time-patterns in the financial cycles before and after financial liberalization in 28 emerging market and industrial economies since 1973. They focused on the duration of the upturns and downturns in the financial markets and on the magnitude of cycles, taking into account the fact that the characteristics of stock market cycles have changed over time. They compared the characteristics of these cycles during episodes of repression and financial liberalization.

Kaminsky and Schmukler (2002) answered the question posed above in a negative manner. They took into account the financial crises in the emerging and industrial economies, including the crises of the 1990s, before concluding that financial cycles in the equity markets were not intensified by financial liberalization. If anything, the opposite appeared to be the truth: equity market cycles become smoother after liberalization. Interestingly, they found inter-temporal differences in the impact of financial liberalization on the equity market. Liberalization tended to trigger more explosive financial cycles in the immediate aftermath of financial liberalization but in the four years after liberalization equity market volatility became markedly less pronounced. This observation applied to both the emerging market economies and the matured industrial economies.

In this scheme of things, the integration of domestic equity markets in emerging market economies with the global financial markets contributes to a decline in volatility. The expectations of non-resident investors influence this development. Better skills and information enable non-resident investors to monitor the management of the firms in which they are purchasing stocks. Before liberalization, domestic investors were unable to do this because they did not have the capability. Equity market liberalization also allows domestic firms, at least the large ones, to access matured capital markets for capital. When firms list on the large global bourses, they find themselves within the jurisdiction of a superior legal system to that they had at home, and they need to become more transparent and respond to the higher information disclosure standards of their new hosts. During the 1990s and 2000s a good number of firms from the emerging market economies, particularly Asia and Latin America, began to list on foreign stock markets. These developments and new institutional norms tend to attenuate "excessive" financial cycles. In addition, as this kind of two-way expansion and diversification progresses, equity markets in the emerging market economies become less sensitive to actions of single large investors, which also dampens the tendency toward market volatility.

8 Summary and conclusions

Evidence suggests that financial repression and resulting distortions affected functioning of financial systems in most developing economies. Until the early 1970s, domestic financial repression was widespread and even some of the industrial economies suffered from symptoms of financial distortion and repression. These caused very low domestic saving rates, inefficient capital allocation, and languishing financial intermediation. Economic growth suffered. Several emerging market economies of today earnestly took to liberalizing their financial sector.

Although the financial liberalization and growth nexus has been extensively studied by economists of differing views, there have been several difficulties in establishing a direct link. Early studies of scholars such as Goldsmith, McKinnon, and Shaw considered this link to be a direct, simple and positive one. It worked by strengthening the size and improving the efficiency of the domestic financial system, by allowing domestic firms to access the global financial markets, and by improving the level of corporate governance in the domestic financial system and thereby reducing the agency problems.

This scenario has been studied and refined by including static and dynamic factors. A good deal of evidence was provided by several emerging market economies regarding foreign competition promoting efficiency in the domestic banking and non-banking financial sectors, leading to a reduction in the cost of capital. Also, when domestic firms begin to access the global capital market, the cost of capital declines and the level of domestic investment rises. There can be little doubt that there are static and dynamic impacts of these developments. The efficiency of capital allocation by markets improves, and financial resources head for sectors with a comparative advantage that were constrained during the period of financial repression. Recent studies have also supported what McKinnon and Shaw posited three decades ago; that is, that corporate governance in the emerging market economies is favorably affected by financial liberalization. Financial deregulation and reforms fuel institutional reforms, and integration with the global markets and institutions tends to speed up the reform process to achieve a resilient financial system. Thus, liberalized emerging markets come to have an opportunity to grow and develop like their counterparts in the advanced industrial economies.

However, this line of logic has been challenged. Skeptics argue that it is not necessarily true that access to global capital market will increase the availability of capital. They also argue that efficiency in capital allocation cannot come about merely by the removal of distortions caused by financial repression. In an environment of information asymmetries in the financial market, there is little possibility of financial liberalization leading to welfare improvement. Moral hazard should be added to the asymmetric information in the developing economies.

A gradual consensus has now emerged on financial development and liberalization affecting growth rate in a significantly positive manner. Deregulation creates an environment that greatly facilitates economic growth. Evidence regarding the benefits of financial liberalization and deregulation on real per capita GDP growth is strong, but while it is possible that financial liberalization plays a leading role, it is certainly not the most crucial one and it is never the only strategy affecting growth rate.

Two clear and opposing views have emerged regarding how capital account liberalization affects an economy, particularly the financial sector. The allocative efficiency view holds that when capital account barriers on the flow of capital are removed, trans-border capital movements begin. Capital tends to move from capital-abundant economies, where the marginal rate of return is lower, to capital-scarce economies, where the marginal rate of return is expected to be higher. The newer view has been christened the "animal spirit" (or the psychology of business people), and considers the older view of the impact of capital account liberalization to be simplistic, if not downright fanciful. The proponents of this view believe that capital account liberalization does not result in the efficient allocation of financial resources because international capital movements have little connection with real economic activity. However, most empirical studies concur with the allocative efficiency hypothesis.

It was believed that capital account liberalization leads to volatility, which led to support for restrictive global capital flows. The unrestricted trans-border capital flows were blamed for disorderly, if on occasions totally erratic, capital market behavior, both domestically and globally. The logic was that restrictions on global capital flows would help in moderating the excessive boom–bust pattern in financial markets that was so prevalent in the 1990s and early 2000s. An important result of this view was that financial market liberalization and reforms slowed down. However, as a permanent policy measure, these proposals not to liberalize the capital account did not win many supporters.

During the recent episodes of crisis in the emerging market economies, stock markets have displayed an excessive boom–bust behavior. Some believed that it was the liberalization of equity markets that was to blame for their volatility. Empirical studies showed that the equity markets' volatility was not intensified by financial liberalization; if anything, the opposite is true, and equity market cycles become smoother after liberalization. Interestingly, inter-temporal differences in the impact of financial liberalization over the equity market have been found. Liberalization has tended to trigger more explosive financial cycles in the immediate aftermath of financial liberalization, but in the four years after liberalization the equity market volatility becomes markedly less pronounced. In this scheme of things, the integration of domestic equity markets in the emerging market economies with the global financial markets contributes to a decline in volatility.

4 Evolving financial market structure in the emerging market economies

1 Evolving financial services industry

The scope of the financial services industry is broad, and includes commercial banking, investment banking, insurance, and asset management. It also includes other types of financial activity, such as securities exchanges and specialty finance. The several segments of the industry are closely intertwined. The coverage in this chapter, however, does include all the strands of the financial services industry and is necessarily limited to its principal substantive segments.

Although the global financial markets remained in a state of flux throughout the twentieth century, transformations since the early 1970s have been nothing short of dramatic. Global forces for change included advances in information communication technology (ICT), making remote access to trading systems ubiquitous. Also, innovations in ICT and the development of new instruments in the financial market became self-reinforcing. Furthermore, financial deregulation and liberalization at the national level, opening up to international competition, and globalization of financial and real markets, were significant change agents. Additionally, changes in corporate behavior, such as growing disintermediation and increased shareholder pressure for financial performance, were the prime movers behind the transformation in the financial services sector in the emerging market economies.

Advancing globalization during the 1980s and the 1990s increased trans-border capital flows and tightened the links between financial markets in the emerging markets and global financial centers. Growth of global financial markets was further accelerated by improvements in the fundamentals, particularly by more rapid economic growth in the emerging market and matured industrial economies. It was also assisted by economic and structural reforms (such as the privatization of state-owned banks in the Central and Eastern European economies) in the emerging market and transition economies. Lastly, the recent spate of banking and financial crises have accentuated the pressures for transformation.

Notwithstanding the recent decline in capital flows, the evidence of the preceding quarter-century suggests that financial markets in the emerging market economies have become increasingly deep and resilient.

2 Consolidation in banking services

Consolidation is a powerful force that causes change and is generally responsible for significant value added. Financial consolidation and financial globalization are phenomena that cut across national boundaries in many dimensions, affecting not only the economy in which these measures are taken, but also the global financial activity. In the so-called Group of Ten (G-10) economies there has been a high level of merger and acquisitions (M&A) activity over the last three decades, particularly during the 1990s.[1]

The declining significance and relevance of the traditional banking industry is one of the important impacts of recent transformations in the financial services industry. This observation applies to matured industrial economies and emerging market economies alike. Due to the increased ease of entry and the commodity-like nature of many wholesale financial products, competition in domestic and global banking industry has markedly intensified. Consequently margins have narrowed, promoting M&As in both domestic and global banking. M&As are methods of consolidation where a change in control takes place through a transfer of ownership. These two methods are generally not distinguished from each other. They strongly bind the participating firms and can have a substantial effect on economic structure.

In many cases M&As were necessary for the survival of the constituent partners. They took place not only between banks, but also between banks and non-bank financial firms. They were not limited to banks and non-bank financial institutions in domestic markets, but extended to include these institutions abroad. M&As became a frequent option for banks seeking to build a global retail system. The state of constant evolution and continuous consolidation had its own travails and raised numerous positive and normative issues in the emerging market economies and in the financial markets in matured industrial economies (IMF, 2000; G-10, 2001; IMF, 2001). This chapter dwells on the evolution of the financial market structure in the emerging market economies, as well as on the consolidation of their banking system.[2]

Events and developments that drove the process of evolution and consolidation in the emerging markets were by and large the same as those in the matured industrial economies. However, there were several idiosyncratic features specific to the emerging market economies. For instance, while international M&As were highly uncommon and infrequent in the industrial economies, they took place in large numbers in the emerging market economies. An overwhelming proportion of the consolidation activities in these markets was accounted for by the cross-border M&As.

Second, consolidations in the industrial economies were essentially a way of eliminating excess capacity. It was assumed that bankruptcy was a less efficient and high-cost exit option. In the emerging market economies, consolidation took place to deal with the economic and financial crisis-related problems. Third, market forces led to and dominated the consolidation process in the industrial economies, whereas the financial authorities in the emerging market economies frequently guided the consolidation process.[3]

One of the commonest motivations behind M&As was cost savings and revenue enhancements. Most M&As involved firms competing in the same segment of the financial services industry and the same country, with domestic mergers involving firms in different segments being the second most common type of transaction. The number of joint ventures and strategic alliances increased over the 1990s, while the number of banking firms decreased in all the G-10 countries. The concentration of the banking industry, as measured by the percentage of a country's deposits controlled by the largest banks, tended to increase (G-10, 2001). In these respects, the emerging market economies followed the G-10 economies with a considerable time lag. In the area of consolidation of banking services, more or less similar trends were observed in them.

Bank consolidation in the matured industrial economies has been thoroughly studied, while that in the emerging markets has been neglected by both scholars and multilateral financial institutions. Gelos and Roldos (2002) attempted to make up for this gap by quantifying changes in the market structure in the banking sector in the emerging market economies. Employing the methodology developed by Panzar and Rosse (1987), they delved into the principal forces shaping bank consolidation in the emerging market economies. They also described the patterns of consolidation and concentration using traditional indicators of market structure. The methodology developed by Panzar and Rosse (1987) was essentially based on the relationship between revenue and marginal costs. In the past it was used on cross-sectional data from the matured industrial economies.[4]

Gelos and Roldos' (2002) conclusions are noteworthy, and are as follows. Between 1994 and 2000, the total number of banks declined in all the emerging market economies. In some cases, but not all, this decline reflected a systematic increase in consolidation and market concentration. The emerging market economies of Central Europe provide a good example of where a decline in the number of banks took place with lower market concentration and consolidation. The measures of market concentration used were: (1) the shares of deposits of the largest banks in total bank deposits; and (2) the Herfindahl–Hirshman (HH) indexes.[5] In this set of economies the banking system had a tradition of higher concentration than in the other emerging market economies. The 1990s, particularly the latter half, saw a sharp decline in market concentration. The reason was that the former state-owned banks were losing market shares to the more dynamic medium-sized banks, reducing the market concentration of the former. These economies had followed the policy of liberal entry policies, facilitating market entry of the new banks, and the new entrants found it easy to slice away the market share of the large, old-fashioned, inefficient, state-owned banks. Another reason why the state-owned banks lost their market share was their clean-up operations, which were essential before they could be made into attractive propositions for privatization. Investors in the global market would not have been attracted toward large banks with tardy balance sheets.

Market consolidation strategies in the emerging market economies of Central Europe took hold as late as in 2000. Although these economies were under-banked in terms of banking assets and deposits, the number of banks in each one of them was quite high. Shareholders encouraged M&As of many weak banks with the strong domestic ones. Consolidation was intended to promote stability. A large number of foreign banks were also being established in these emerging markets, which again took over several smaller and weaker domestic banks. Some of the foreign banks that had a large presence in this region merged, which consolidated their respective subsidiaries. A great deal of these activities took place in 2000.

The experiences of the emerging market economies of Asia are similar. The number of banks declined in the five Asian crisis (1997–1998) economies, while the market concentration of banks fell.[6] This was unlike the trend in the G-10 economies, where the concentration of the banking industry had tended to increase. The declining market concentration in the Asian emerging market economies was reflected in the falling market share of deposits of not only the largest three banks but also the largest ten banks in each one of these economies, as well as in declining HH indexes. The crisis resolution in Korea and Malaysia entailed a great deal of consolidation. Monetary authorities took a great deal of interest and played a proactive role, continuing reforms and consolidation even after the first-stage measures of crisis resolution. In the Philippines and Thailand, monetary authorities did not intervene in the consolidation process and left it to market forces.

The experiences in the emerging market economies of Latin America were different from those of the above two regions. The reason was that the financial crises struck this region earlier than in the other two regions, and consequently, the process of consolidation started earlier. The number of banks declined in all the emerging market economies of Latin America, in particular in Argentina and Brazil. However, this decline went hand in hand with the rising market concentration of banks as measured by the share in total deposits and by the HH indexes. In this group of countries the market concentration of banks followed the same trend as that in the G-10 economies.

Although the consolidation of the banking industry has progressed in the emerging market economies, there is still a lot to be done. Many emerging economies, particularly those in Asia, still have a large number of deposit-taking institutions such as savings and various types of mutual and co-operative banks, and similar intermediaries like building societies, thrift, savings and loan associations, credit unions, post office banks, and finance companies. These institutions badly need streamlining and consolidation.

Regarding the role of the monetary authorities in guiding the consolidation process, they were active in the earlier stages but subsequently played second fiddle to the market forces. This is reflected in the promotion and guidance process in Argentina and Brazil. Initially authorities carried through the process in earnest and succeeded in reducing the number of banks sharply. Strong and weak banking institutions were separated from each other, and the former were provided with subsidized loans to merge with the latter (Peek and Rosengren, 2000). The domestic banks also took the initiative for M&A operations to remain competitive. In Mexico, the consolidation process has made greater progress than in the other Latin American economies. As in the other emerging economies of the region, both indicators of concentration indicate that market concentration in the banking industry in Mexico has increased significantly.

A good deal of progress has been achieved in the consolidation of financial services in general, and the banking industry in particular, in the emerging market economies. Wondering whether it has progressed so far as to start affecting competition in an adverse manner is quite valid. Although consolidation has gone on for a while now, Gelos and Roldos (2002) have concluded that "Consolidation in the emerging market banking system has, to a large extent, not yet translated into a decline in competitive pressure." In Argentina and Mexico, the two emerging market economies where it has advanced furthest, its adverse effects on competition are far from significant.

3   Development of bond markets

Although since the mid-1990s bond markets have recorded considerable growth in the emerging market economies, they still are small both in absolute terms and relative to their counterpart in the matured industrial economies. On average their volume is equivalent to about one-third of the GDP, whereas in most matured industrial economies the outstanding amounts in the bond markets are as large as, or frequently larger than, the GDP.[7] As regards the typology of bond issuance, there are two principal kinds: domestic bond issuance, and international bond issuance. Domestic bonds are further divided into two types, namely public sector bonds and private sector bonds. Similarly, during the 1990s emerging market economies were able to raise private capital from issues of medium- and long-term bonds in the global financial markets. Both the corporates and the governments in the emerging market economies issued them. The following two sub-sections deal with the qualitative and quantitative aspects of bond market developments and issuance in the emerging market economies.

Qualitative aspects

In the past, both endogenous and exogenous macro- and micro-economic factors influenced the creation and growth of bond markets in the matured industrial economies.[8] Although we need to take account of the change in time periods, a similar set of forces has been found to be at work in providing impetus to the development of bond markets in the emerging market economies in the contemporary period. Brisk development of financial markets and gradual growth of the institutional structure supporting bond markets were the principal endogenous factors. Two of the most important policy events that provided direct impetus to the growth of bond markets in the emerging market economies were liberalization of the financial sector – both domestic and external – and deregulation. These intensified competition among bond issuers and portfolio adjustment among investors.

However, it is widely believed in the profession that some of the exogenous factors provided a greater fillip to the development of bond markets than did the endogenous ones. The factors at play were fiscal adjustments, adoption of macroeconomic stabilization measures, and large flows of global capital into the emerging market economies. In addition, the emerging market financial crises, particularly the Asian crisis, provided a definite support to the development of bond markets by underpinning corporate, financial and banking reform, and restructuring endeavors.

In the past, a pressing need to finance the public sector budget deficit forced many governments to develop bond markets. This was essentially because they wanted to eschew monetary financing of budget deficits. The same macroeconomic logic applies today to the emerging markets that have been trying to create and strengthen bond markets. As central banks increasingly became more independent, governments in the emerging market economies found it difficult to monetize their budget deficits during the 1990s. This made reliance on bond-market financing greater for the emerging market governments during the 1990s. It has been observed that the emerging market economies that ran large fiscal deficits (as a percentage of GDP) also issued more public sector bonds in the domestic and international markets. Some emerging markets issued large public sector bonds with the express objective of developing and strengthening their bond markets. Chile, Hong Kong SAR, and Malaysia come in this category. Consequently, all three reported substantial public sector surpluses by 2000.

Emerging market crises, particularly those of the latter half of the 1990s, and the large corporate and financial sector restructuring endeavors that followed, engendered the need for massive financial resources. The post-crisis restructuring costs were estimated to be high – between 15 percent and 30 percent of the GDP. Resources needed for restructuring could not be raised easily in a crisis-affected economy, and raising them served as another motive for the development and expansion of bond markets. Many governments financed their restructuring by issuing long-term government bonds in their domestic markets. For instance, in Indonesia, which had very small bond markets, bond market activity suddenly took off after the 1998 crisis. The Indonesian government issued $60 billion in rupiah bonds for the purpose of bank and corporate restructuring.

During the last two decades, privatization and financial globalization have coalesced to usher a considerable amount of external capital into the emerging market economies, and this inflow has had to be sterilized by the monetary authorities. Initially, central banks issued short-term bills to sterilize them. This policy move was considered sufficient to attain the sterilization objective. As time went by and global capital inflows strengthened, most emerging market governments began issuing long-term government bonds for this purpose. Consequently, by 2000 a clear positive cross-country relationship had evolved between global private capital inflows and the size of the public sector bond market in the emerging market economies.

A good lesson from the history of bond-market development in the industrial economies is that as the corporate sector develops and demands more capital for productive investment, so do the bond markets. In their growth process, many firms approach the bond market to finance their assets. During the 1990s, the largest and most successful brand-named firms found that the bond markets were the most efficient instrument for financing their assets. This implies that there should be a positive cross-country relationship between real economic growth and the size of the domestic bond market, and the emerging market economies were not an exception to this paradigm. Mihaljek *et al.* (2002) found that this relationship existed for the emerging market economies when private and public sector bond issuance in the domestic market is considered. As these economies expanded, they increasingly began to rely on domestic public and private sector issuance to finance growth. However, when only the corporate bond market is considered, this relationship weakens considerably. Korea and Malaysia turned out to be the only two high-growth emerging market economies that had also successfully developed large corporate bond markets. As opposed to them, China, India, Mexico, and Poland were able to finance their growth without developing large corporate bond markets, and the reliance of this group on bond markets was exceedingly light.

The bond market issuance activity in the global market was adversely affected in 2002 (see next section). One of the reasons for this weakness was the new set of rules that the IMF was creating for dealing with emerging markets that cannot repay their debts. In April 2002, the IMF published its new plan for orderly restructuring of unsustainable sovereign debts.[9] The objective of this plan was to "facilitate orderly, predictable, and rapid restructuring of unsustainable debt" as well as to "help preserve asset values and protect creditors' rights, while paving the way toward an agreement that helps the debtor return to viability and growth." This plan, christened the sovereign debt restructuring mechanism (SDRM), was not finalized until the first quarter of 2003. However, debate between the global creditors' community, emerging market governments, the IMF, and the academic community had not ended. If appropriately designed and implemented, SDRM could help to reduce the costs of restructuring for sovereign debtors and their creditors, and contribute to the general efficiency of global capital markets. There was a pressing need for such an arrangement in the wake of the emerging market crises of the late 1990s and early 2000s.

When restructuring of a sovereign bond is necessary, present practice requires unanimity among the bondholders. However, the SDRM proposes an alternative. The fundamental idea behind it was sound and sensible. It borrows or mimics some features of the corporate bankruptcy laws in the US, and the so-called "cram-down" provision of US bankruptcy law has been taken over for an international application. Accordingly, the majority of the creditors can arrive at a restructuring plan, and this provision forces the terms of a restructuring arrangement arrived at by them on all the creditors. Thus, the SDRM allows a majority of creditors to force the minority to accept a plan. As in cases of filing for Chapter 11, the SDRM could sanction a standstill on debt repayments and allow defaulting emerging market economies to issue a new senior debt. However, both lenders and borrowers have expressed their disenchantment with the SDRM. Most global investors, bankers, and financiers have already voted against it because their principal concern is that SDRM would "erode their rights as creditors, make defaults easier and more frequent and as a result dry up the market for emerging market bonds" (*The Economist*, 2003d). The emerging market governments are critical of the plan because they fear that the addition of renegotiation-friendly provisions to loan contracts will raise borrowing costs, making it more difficult for them to access the global capital markets. This worry especially disturbed the Latin American emerging markets, and they vociferously expressed it, because they needed foreign capital to deepen their domestic financial markets.

The system allows lenders in the international bond markets weak creditors' rights because they cannot acquire the assets of sovereign defaulters. As they are poorly protected, their concern is not entirely irrational. If the emerging markets have been characterized by high interest rates, they have also displayed a penchant for over-borrowing, and frequent instances of defaults. Lenders believed that the new IMF plan did not promise a definite systemic improvement for them.

Although SDRM mimics the US bankruptcy law, it does so in a skewed manner. It mimics those aspects of the law that are kind to the debtors more, although the domestic debt restructurings in the US are to be done in an ambiance of protecting "the best interest of the creditors." In addition, Shleifer (2003) believed that a procedure that allows a defaulting sovereign debtor to issue new bonds would remove the most powerful deterrent to default, namely the lack of access to global capital markets. In his view, therefore, SDRM cannot bring any systemic improvement, and the worries of the creditors are based on a valid reason. Looked at objectively, creditors' rights are not necessarily weakened, because under the SDRM it is the creditors that have the overall control of the procedure. If SDRM succeeds in producing rapid and efficient default work-outs, it would help the bonds of defaulting emerging market economies to keep more of their value. Thus, SDRM is not worthy of outright rejection from all quarters.

Quantitative aspects

Bond market-related statistical data are available for 21 emerging market economies.[10] At the end of 1994, these 21 economies had $0.97 trillion outstanding in domestic and international bonds. By the end of 2000, the outstanding amount had increased to $1.9 trillion, which implies 100 percent growth in six years (Mihaljek *et al*, 2002).

According to the BIS statistics, domestic bonds accounted for 79 percent of the bonds outstanding at the end of 2000 in these 21 emerging market economies, while public sector bonds accounted for 64 percent.[11] Thus, public sector bonds issued in the domestic market account formed the largest market share, and private sector domestic bond issues followed them. The smallest market segment was held by public and private sector international bonds. This scenario did not change appreciably between 1994 and 2000, although minor changes were observed. For instance, the share of international bonds increased somewhat in Central Europe and Latin America, although little change was observed in Asia in this respect.

Notwithstanding their rapid growth over the 1994–2000 period, bond markets have remained puny in most emerging market economies. Measured as a percentage of the GDP, the outstanding amounts were the tiniest in Peru (8 percent) in 2000, and in the Russian Federation and Thailand (both 10 percent). Only two emerging market economies could boast reasonable-sized bond markets, namely Malaysia (102 percent) and Korea (70 percent). In 2000, the bond markets in Malaysia had the unique distinction of having outstanding amounts that were greater than the GDP. These were the only two emerging markets comparable in size to matured industrial economies such as Germany and the United Kingdom (UK). In addition, in Chile, Hungary, Brazil, and Singapore, bond market growth was substantial. In these four emerging market economies, the outstanding amounts were more than 50 percent of the GDP.

The private sector bond markets constitute another market segment that has remained highly underdeveloped in the emerging market economies, and has continued to be tiny compared to those in the industrial economies. In 2000, in Colombia, Indonesia, and the Russian Federation, the outstanding amounts in private sector bond market accounted for only 1 percent of the GDP of these countries. On average, in 2000 the total amount outstanding in the private sector bond markets in the 21 emerging market economies under consideration was 18 percent of the GDP. In the industrial economies these markets are much larger in size. For instance, in the United States (US), where the corporate bond market is the most developed, the outstanding amount in the private sector bond markets was 79 percent of the GDP, in Japan it was 34 percent, in Germany 76 percent, and in the UK 82 percent. Malaysia and Korea once again have the best developed private sector bond market segments. With 67 percent of the DGP and 50 percent of the GDP outstanding in this market segment, they are comparable in size to the industrial economies.

Annual bond issuance activity in the emerging market economies provides several important insights into the development of these markets and the growth in their volume. Over the 1994–2000 period total bond issuance amounted to $2.2 trillion (an annual rate of issuance of $300 billion). Two noteworthy features emerged from the issuance activity: first, of the total bond market issuance, Latin American emerging market economies accounted for almost half; and second, in private sector issuance Asian emerging market economies led the way and accounted for the bulk of private sector issuance. Central Europe lagged considerably behind Asia and Latin America in terms of issuance in general, and in terms of private sector bond issuance in particular. During the 1994–2000 period, Brazil was the largest bond issuer ($132 billion), followed by Malaysia ($81 billion), Hungary ($70 billion), Hong Kong SAR ($69 billion), and Korea ($65 billion). The volume of total annual bond issuance activity remained at the same level (at approximately $280 billion) in 1995 and in 2000, and total issuance activity peaked in 1995 at $370 billion. It fell in 1996, after the Mexican crisis. Following the Asian and Russian crises it declined to its lowest level, and in 1999 it was a mere $250 billion. As regards the private sector issuance activity, it declined dramatically after the Asian crisis. The fall was due to the thorough corporate and financial sector restructuring adopted by the Asian emerging market economies.[12]

The market for emerging market bonds was reduced to a shadow of its former self in 2002. According to the Institute of International Finance (IIF) statistics, emerging market economies raised a mere $12 billion in 2002 and the IIF predicted that 2003 would not be much better. Uncertainty regarding the global economy obviously played a leading part in forcing these bond market flows to shrink to such a low level (see Chapter 2). The second reason was that, having suffered losses in crises from Asia to Russia to Argentina, global investors are no longer starry-eyed about emerging market bonds. Third, investors and bankers are also disaffected about the IMF's attempt to create a new set of rules for dealing with countries that cannot repay their debts.

In 2002, the return on emerging market bonds, as reflected by the JP Morgan Emerging Market Bond Index Plus (EMBI+), was 14.2 percent, while US Treasury yields declined to 8 percent – which was a near-historic low rate of returns. The strong returns masked both regional differences and differences in credit segments. As a rule, bonds at the low end of the credit rating spectrum performed considerably less well than their high-grade counterparts. Bonds for the emerging market economies outside the Western hemisphere benefited from narrowing of spreads, and posted a 26 percent return for 2002, while those for Latin American economies posted 7 percent returns. The spreads widened considerably for the latter group of emerging economies (IMF, 2003b). Asian issuers dominated 2002, while the large Western hemisphere issuers remained passive and Venezuela was shunned by global investors. They continued to add to an already overweighted position on Russia. The reason was market credit upgrade; it was being anticipated that Russian bonds would soon be upgraded further.

Brady bond: demise of the market?

As set out in Chapter 1 (Section 6), the institution of the Brady Plan in 1989 helped those emerging market economies that were struggling with the debt-servicing problems of the early 1980s. This group essentially comprised the emerging market economies of the Western hemisphere, although it was not limited to them. Brady bonds were not considered to be part of the normal bond issuance activity. The first Brady bonds were issued with the restructuring of Mexico's defaulted sovereign loans in 1990, and soon the market in Brady bonds became a large and liquid debt market. Commercial and investment banks were among the first to invest in Brady bonds, but the investor base subsequently widened to include mutual funds, insurance companies, and other institutional investors. The different classes of Brady bonds include fixed-rate, floating-rate, collateralized and uncollateralized. Also, there were numerous different issuers of Brady bonds. By the mid-1990s, the availability of derivative facilities made it possible to develop a rich and varied set of sovereign and interest-rate investment strategies.

The peak period for the Brady bonds was 1997, when Peru concluded its sovereign debt restructuring. At this point, the stock of dollar-denominated outstanding Brady bonds peaked at $156 billion. A steady decline in the stock of Brady bonds set in after this peak. Market conditions improved after 1994, which encouraged several important Brady bond-issuing emerging markets to retire their outstanding bonds, and this process continued with other smaller issuers following suit. There were a series of buybacks as well as exchanges of Brady bonds for uncollateralized global and Eurobonds. These exchanges were made at significantly lower spreads.

In April 1996, Mexico used the proceeds of a 20-year global bond to retire $1.2 billion of discount Brady bonds in September. Following Mexico's example, the Philippines exchanged one-third of its par bonds for $60 million of 20-year uncollateralized Eurobonds. This swap freed up $183 million of collateral in US treasury bonds for the Philippines. There was the demonstration effect, and the same strategy was soon adopted by Ecuador, Panama, and Poland. They bought back their Brady bonds, bringing their stock to a low level. By the late 1990s market participants felt that the market in Brady bonds had outlived its usefulness, although the Cote d'Ivoire and Vietnam went counter to the grain and entered the market during this period with their Brady bonds. However, in terms of size these were not significant entrants, and their additions to the stock were not enough to offset the amounts retired by Brazil, Ecuador, Panama, and Poland over the same period. Brazil was the largest Brady bond country, with close to $50 billion outstanding. Owing to this large volume of retirement the stock of Brady bonds has gone on dwindling, which has raised concern regarding the size of the Brady bond market and the liquidity of emerging debt markets.

Of indexed bonds and original sin

Broad consensus exists on the utility of inflation-indexed or inflation-linked bonds. For one, they make the sharing of risk between issuers of bonds and investors possible. Also, they go to complete the bond markets in the emerging market economies and deepen them. When an emerging market government issues inflation-indexed bonds, this is seen as reducing the cost of educating the global investors regarding the benefits of these instruments. It also reduces the co-ordination problems in the adoption of alternative units of account mentioned in the following paragraph (IMF, 2003b). The flip side of the coin is that the indexation suggested above is generally difficult to reverse. Indexing to foreign currencies, or dollarization of debt, which is another kind of indexation, could potentially create financial instability in the domestic financial markets, which in turn can have a high cost for the emerging market in terms of loss of access to the global capital markets.

Chile developed and made exemplary use of the long-term inflation-linked bonds in its corporate bond market. These bonds are indexed to *Unidat de Fomebto* (or UF), which is a unit of account linked to the Chilean consumer price index (CPI). First, developing a government and corporate bond market using this link, and second, making use of UF a legal requirement, have been the two important pillars of the Chilean bond market development strategy (Walker, 2002). Institutional investors in Chile needed to invest for the long term, and therefore, corporates issued long-term inflation-indexed bonds with maturity of up to 30 years. Although indexed bond markets had existed for over two decades in Chile, they suddenly picked up momentum after 2000 and tripled in volume in the three years between 2000 and 2002. The reason was that the global financial environment had become unsupportive and therefore it became imperative for the Chilean corporates to turn to the domestic bond market. The maturities of corporate bonds went on extending, and at least 10 years were added to average maturities between 1990 and 2000.

While indexation has its benefits, it can have some serious negative repercussions. It can complicate monetary policy objectives and have a harmful impact on the local fixed income and derivatives markets. For one, knowing that there is a hedge against inflation may change the object-ives and attitude of policy-makers toward price stability in the domestic economy, and they may begin to feel blasé about rising prices. Also, after being established in the financial markets, indexing may expand in the economy to labor markets. A well-known drawback of indexation is that global investors may be dissuaded by it because they may find it confusing to calculate the performance of their investment in an unfamiliar unit of account. Institutional investors and asset managers generally prefer the so-called "plain vanilla bonds," which have clean exposures (IMF, 2003b). Indexing to foreign currencies, or dollarization of debt, as noted above, is the second variety of indexing. The emerging markets of the Western hemisphere have used this method of issuing bonds extensively. They developed their domestic bond markets by issuing dollar-denominated bonds.

Emerging markets have not been able to issue a great deal of non-indexed bonds denominated in their domestic currency simply because governments have control over their monetary policy and they can poten-tially "inflate away their debt." The moral hazard issue also comes into play here. If corporates expect to be bailed out by their governments – as was the case in the Asian economies during the 1997–1998 crisis – they would prefer to issue all their debts in the dollar (Burnside *et al.*, 2001). Inadequate development of the domestic financial markets and weak national policies and institutions are some of the other cogent reasons behind the issuance of dollar-denominated bonds in several emerging markets.

Available IMF statistical data show that major industrial economies, like Japan, Switzerland, the UK, and the US, which issued over a third of global debt during the 1990s, also issued more than two-thirds of the global debt in their domestic currencies. The developing economies were at the other extreme, issuing only 10 percent of the global debt, 1 percent of which was denominated in their own currencies. The European economies that belong to the Euro zone displayed a more balanced approach, particularly after the introduction of the euro in January 1999.[13] The proportion of dollar-denominated debt is small in the European emerging markets, while it is the highest in the emerging markets of the Western hemisphere. As the exposition above reveals, a large majority of the emerging market economies cannot issue bonds denominated in their own currencies.

The inability of emerging markets to issue international bonds denominated in their domestic currencies was referred to as the "original sin" by Eichengreen *et al.* (2002), and they proposed a way out. According to them, poor domestic policies, reflected in high inflation rates, do not explain the high proportion of dollar-denominated bonds issued by the emerging market economies. The only robust determinant of the proportion of dollar-denominated bonds is the size of the country or the economy. To resolve this problem, mere strengthening of domestic policies and institutions would not be enough. There are several problems created by the structure and operations of international financial markets, and international initiatives need to be taken to resolve these problems.[14]

A multi-stage plan has been sketched out by Eichengreen *et al.* (2002) for the emerging market economies to issue their international bonds denominated in their domestic currencies. This plan can be executed with the help of international financial institutions (IFIs) like the World Bank, and the regional multilateral financial institutions. The sub-regional financial institutions like the Caribbean Development Bank can also be involved in it. That the IFIs issued almost half of their internationally placed bonds in exotic currencies during the 1990s was the starting point for their plan. In most cases these loans were swapped and the repayment obligations finally fell in the dollar, which in turn provided support to currency swap markets.

The first stage of the mechanism devised by Eichengreen *et al.* (2002) is to choose a well-diversified basket of emerging market currencies and evolve a currency basket index. This basket serves to overcome the relatively small size of some of the issuers. The methodology of computing this index entails calculating the end-of-period exchange rate of the emerging market economy chosen, divided by the CPI in the same month. The weights in the index are the emerging markets' relative GDP adjusted at purchasing power parity. The index computed by Eichengreen *et al.* (2002) demonstrated that its volatility was in line with that of major global currencies. This index also demonstrated a negative correlation with the real private consumption growth in the G-7 economies.

The second stage is for the IFIs to issue debt denominated in this index, and eventually the Group of 10 (G-10) economies will follow suit. The IFIs can also convert the dollar loans made to the emerging markets in the index into local currency CPI-indexed loans. This dispels the currency mismatch generated by the issuance of the proposed bonds. Likewise, the

G-10 economies can undertake currency swaps with each individual emerging market economy in the index, which has twin benefits: first, the emerging market will succeed in eliminating the currency mismatch, and second, the G-10 economy will have a useful hedge against its original sin.

The third stage in this mechanism is that once a liquid market in this kind of indexed debt develops successfully, global investors might want to add credit risk to the index. They can buy the local currency debt of the emerging market economies in the index, which in turn will promote the development of these domestic currency bonds. To be sure, this plan is innovative. However, analysts at the IMF believe that its implementation and acceptance in the global capital markets may pose problems (see IMF, 2003b). That said, those plans also serve that are drawn up and go unimplemented (with apologies to John Milton!).

4   Banks *vis-à-vis* bond markets

Although, the significance of the banking sector has been on the decline for some time (as stated in Section 1), the financial system in the emerging market economies is still essentially based on commercial banks. In a majority of them the banks dominate the financial services industry, and in some they do so in an overwhelming manner. The slow growth of the bond markets is having a decisive impact over the banking system in these economies. With their expansion, some of financing business of the banks has begun to be taken over by the bond markets. Whether this will undercut and undermine the banking sector or not is the concern of those in this sector. Conversely, if a growing bond market implies a reduction in the vulnerability of the corporate sector to the infirmities of banks, the objective of the central bank to support steady economic growth is served well.

It is not necessary that the growth of the bond markets should be completely at the cost of the banking sector, and vice versa. The two can play complementary as well as mutually supporting roles. On their part, banks play a role in the development of both private and public sector bond markets. According to Hawkins (2002), banks are among the "most important issuers, holders, dealers, advisers, underwriters, guarantors, trustees, custodians, and registrars in this market." He further remarks that: "banks are deriving more of their profits from such activities and less from lending. For this reason, it is important to have healthy banks to have a sound bond market. And a bond market may improve the health of the banks, by improving market discipline." Thus, the two cannot only co-exist but can also have a profitable and symbiotic relationship. In this unique relationship, banks and bond markets can not only compete with but also strengthen each other.

A cross-country study of 21 emerging market economies found that both banking and bond markets were larger, when measured as a proportion of the DGP, in the economies with higher GDP. This was a general trend, although some countries with a large GDP did have small bond markets. China is an exception of this kind; the reason is that the banking sector dominates the financial system under a socialist market system, although China is moving away from the socialist economic structure. The corporate bond market is of recent vintage in China, and therefore will take time to develop. As noted above, as the financial services industry grows toward maturity, the banking sector develops earlier than the bond markets. The reasons for this trend to emerge are: (1) in a low household-income economy, family units prefer keeping their savings as liquid short-term bank deposits; (2) institutional investors either do not exist or are small; and (3) the information and legal infrastructure is either weak or is not in place (Shirai, 2001; Hawkins, 2002). In addition, only highly rated corporations issue corporate bonds; the ones with a low rating do not issue bonds, or only very seldom. At an early stage of development, economies characteristically have low GDP and do not have many corporations that are rated highly by the financial markets, and therefore, corporate bond issuance activity remains subdued until the growth process has gained momentum.

When the financial services industry is in its infancy, private or corporate bond markets can in no way supplant the banking system of an economy. The lesson from history in this regard is that in the process of growth of the financial services industry, the banking system is the first to be developed, as well as being developed much earlier than the bond markets.[15] Bond markets – particularly corporate bond issuance – develop at a rather later stage in the development of the financial services industry, and begin taking over bank lending business only when they are large and well developed. In the US, where the corporate bond markets are most developed, they took over a significant amount of lending business from domestic banks long ago. In the Western European economies, growth of the corporate bond market has been much slower than that in the US. In the emerging market economies, only Korea has recorded considerable growth in its corporate bond market sector in terms of amounts outstanding. In other emerging market economies, corporate bonds markets have continued to remain small. At their present stage of development they have merely begun supplementing bank lending as a source of finance for the private sector.

Alan Greenspan referred to the supplementary role of the bond markets as a "spare tire" for the banks (Greenspan, 2000) – that is, when banks have balance sheet related problems in making advances to the corporate sector, the slack can be picked up by the bond markets. Throughout the 1990s in the US and during the latter half of the 1990s in Hong Kong SAR, banks adopted a conservative stance in lending to the corporate sector. This was the time and opportunity for the bond markets to play their "spare tire" role in the financial system. The reverse is also feasible – for instance, when the bond markets dry up due to macroeconomic instability of some nature, the banking sector may substitute itself as the principal source of finance. This situation was recently observed in Thailand in 1997, and during the sovereign default of 1998 in the Russian Federation.

The "spare tire" doctrine has been challenged, and some consider it too simplistic. The logic followed by the challengers is that bank lending to the corporate sector only slows down in periods of general loss of confidence in the economy, and during such periods it is also difficult to issue bonds. During periods of macroeconomic instability bond markets are likely to dry up even before banks become reluctant lenders. In support of this line of logic, Jiang *et al.* (2001) conducted an empirical exercise to conclude that bank lending and bond issuance are positively and strongly correlated both in the OECD economies and in the emerging market economies. However, bond markets have been observed to provide some offsets to bank lending.

5   Effect of globalization on the banking structure

Financial globalization progressed *pari passu* with advances in ICT, and financial deregulation and liberalization in the emerging market economies. While the latter facilitated the entry of global banks and financial institutions into the emerging market economies, the former made global reach feasible by lowering the costs of telecommunication and computing. The onward march of financial globalization has in myriad ways been influencing the evolution of financial structure and management practices in the emerging market economies.

The transnational corporations (TNCs) and the expanding global networks of their subsidiaries are relevant and significant change agents. They have been long-time clients of large banks based in the matured industrial economies, which in turn are global financial services providers. As they expect their banks to have the necessary financial expertise and product mix wherever they operate, they provided a strong motivation – or pull factor – for large banks to spread to different parts of the globe in tandem with the TNCs' operations.[16] Given the rapidly growing and global nature of their operations, the TNCs expect their financial services providers to meet their investment and risk management needs in any part of the globe where their operations expand. Many studies support the claim that banks tend to follow their clients – or, to be more precise, the foreign direct investment (FDI) of their clients – abroad (Miller and Parkhe, 1998; Buch, 2000). This has supported the geographical spread of large global banks into the emerging market economies, which has in turn had a definite impact on the banking structure of the financial markets in these economies.

It is, however, not clear whether FDI in the non-financial sector exerts an influence on banks to move globally, or whether it is limited to FDI in the financial sector. More targeted research on the activities of foreign banks in the emerging market economies is needed. However, there are some indications that large global banks operating in the emerging markets face less intense competition in the domestic markets of the emerging market economies. The host economy, therefore, may offer substantial profit opportunities (Clarke *et al.*, 2001).

The strategic objective of several large banks in the matured industrial economies was to build a global retail system. To this end, international M&As became a frequent option for these large banks. By acquiring an existing institution in the target market, the acquiring bank gains a more rapid foothold than would be possible with an organic growth strategy. The latter strategy is also expensive in terms of time and resources. A small number of large European banks and other global services providers adopted this strategy in dynamic regions like East and Southeast Asia – ING Baring and HSBC are good examples.

Trans-border consolidation of banking

Owing to the spread of financial globalization and deregulation, bank assets controlled by large global or foreign banks in the emerging markets have increased considerably. Many countries had restrictions on the entry of foreign banks until 1980, but after this many of them eliminated the restrictions, and this activity also accelerated during the 1990s. The entry of foreign banks into emerging market economies takes place through setting up branch operations, and establishing a local subsidiary bank or even a local headquarters. An interesting example of trans-border consolidation between an industrial economy bank on the one side and financial institutions in the emerging market economies on the other is the acquisition of large shareholdings in the Latin American financial sector by big Spanish financial institutions. Initially the Latin American economies eagerly joined hands with the large Spanish banks to be able to emulate the Spanish model of retail banking practices. This provided an opportunity for a quantum leap in retail banking practices for the Latin American economies. However, recently Spanish institutions have also acquired private pension funds in this region. The emerging markets that have participated in this exercise are Argentina, Brazil, Chile, Colombia, Mexico, Peru, and Venezuela. Thus viewed, financial globalization has been progressing with the help of M&As.

In the emerging market economies of Central Europe, in 2000 the share of foreign banks in total assets and capital was around two-thirds of the total (Hawkins and Mihaljek, 2001). A decade earlier, their average share was close to 7 percent. Such rapid expansion in the presence of foreign banks made the banking systems in these economies among the most open in the world. In the emerging markets of Latin America, the market share of foreign banks increased from 7 percent in 1990 to 40 percent in 2000.

In Asia, foreign banks increased their presence during the 1990–2000 period in the Philippines (from 9 percent to 15 percent) and Thailand (from 5 percent to 12 percent). However, due to the expansion of domestic banks the presence of foreign banks declined in Hong Kong SAR (from 89 percent to 72 percent) and Singapore (from 89 percent to 76 percent) over the same period. Similarly, in Malaysia their presence declined (from 24 percent to 18 percent) due to thorough banking sector restructuring endeavors in the latter half of the 1990s.[17] Overall, Asia has become more open to foreign banks, and Indonesia, Korea, and Thailand have raised allowable foreign equity levels in local banks to approximately 100 percent. The Philippines now allows 50 percent foreign bank ownership. On the contrary, Malaysia has kept a tight rein on foreign ownership of domestic banks and enforced a 30 percent ceiling.

According to Tschoegl (2000), the present degree of integration across the banking sectors around the globe is comparable to that on the eve of World War I. After the War ended, myriad restrictions on the entry of foreign banks were enforced by countries. The policy environment during the 1990s was radically different, and several emerging market economies were eager to allow foreign banks to operate. During the latter half of the 1990s, Venezuela, Argentina, the Czech Republic, Poland, Chile, and Hungary globalized their domestic banking sector more with the help of the foreign banks than did the other emerging market economies.

Financial globalization immediately impacts upon the institutions providing wholesale financial services. They have an instant opportunity to expand the scale of their operations and alter the competitive dynamics of several market segments in the emerging market economy (Calomiris and Karceski, 1998). Many financial products whose utilization was previously limited to the matured industrial economies are now available globally through competing firms. Although some traditional retail banking products and services are still available locally or regionally, a small number of global services providers have begun to make inroads in these areas into emerging market economies. Consequently, national or regional financial institutions feel obliged to respond to the threat posed by global services providers. They have to offer either parallel products or better pricing to stay in the game. To be able to do so they need to pay a good deal of attention to their operations and management style and improve the efficiency of their operations.

Factors promoting globalization of banking

There are several factors that draw large global banks to emerging market economies. One of the many reasons why they are attracted toward expansion in the emerging market and other developing economies is, as alluded to above, the opportunity for profitable operations in a less competitive environment. As the local banks are weak and smaller than them, foreign banks can exploit local profit opportunities easily. During the latter half of the 1990s, Hungary was quick to open its banking sector to foreign banks, which lost no time in becoming involved in domestic retail banking, both in consumer lending and in deposit taking. This example provides evidence of a profit motive driving the expansion of foreign banks in the emerging market economies. Chile, Poland, and the Czech Republic also had the same experience, albeit to a lesser extent than Hungary.

Claessens *et al.* (2001a) modeled the presence of foreign banks across 80 developing economies, including all the emerging markets, and found that large money-centered banks and other global banks were attracted to economies that have low taxes and high per capital incomes. In a more comprehensive study, using a richer data set, Focarelli and Pozzolo (2000) modeled the location choices of 143 banks across 28 countries. They included variables such as GDP growth prospects and competitiveness of the banking sector in their study. Their conclusion was that foreign banks entered countries where expected GDP growth rate in the short- and medium-term was higher and where the banking sector was less efficient.

They found that the host country's initial GDP per capita and inflation rate were negatively correlated with the presence of foreign banks, while the stock market capitalization was positively correlated. The signs on these three relationships were found to be the same by Levine (1999). Therefore, these results are interpreted to mean that foreign banks have a decisive preference for entering economies with high GDP growth prospects. In addition, areas where the banking sector uses capital inefficiently were found to be attractive locations by the foreign banks. The inefficient capital use was reflected by a higher average cost of operations, lower net interest margins minus charge-offs, and higher cash flows. The entering foreign banks justify being attracted by such an inefficient market by following the strategy of taking over and restructuring the banking institutions with the help of their higher quality human and financial resources. These two studies also found that foreign banks' presence was higher in countries where average bank size was smaller. The entering foreign banks found that smaller banks are easier to acquire and restructure, which helps them in establishing their market presence in a new country in a short span of time.

When countries have stringent restrictions on the entry of foreign banks, the immediate outcome is that the domestic banking sector faces only limited competition and inefficient banks continue to function. Barth *et al.* (2001) have provided cross-country evidence that more stringent entry restrictions are associated with higher net interest margins and overhead costs. Although foreign banks prefer the inefficient banks and financial markets, they tend to shun those having stringent entry restrictions (Clarke *et al.*, 2001).

Impact of trans-border consolidation of banking

Following the liberal mode of current policy thinking, the World Trade Organization (WTO) has laid down adoption of a liberal approach in allowing the entry of foreign banks into the domestic markets as a condition of membership. The Organization for Economic Co-operation and Development (OECD) and the European Union (EU) also promote a liberal approach to the entry of foreign banks. Global, regional, and foreign banks wish to enter an emerging market to expand their reach into profitable markets. On their part, financial and central banking authorities in the emerging market economies are generally eager to expand their presence to improve the stability of their financial systems and to reduce the cost of recapitalization of weak domestic banks. Demirguc-Kunt *et al.* (1998) posit that the entry of large global financial institutions tends to strengthen emerging markets' financial systems, and lower the probability that a macroeconomic and financial crisis will occur. A cross-country econometric study by Mathieson and Roldos (2001) concluded that a banking crisis in the previous three-year period tends to raise foreign banks' participation in the domestic banking system by 10 percentage points.

When large banks and financial institutions from matured industrial economies and global financial services providers enter an emerging market economy, the financial and monetary authorities in the home economy make a concerted endeavor to modernize their financial and banking sector and bring it in line with the prevailing practices in the matured industrial economies. Competitive pressures created by the entry of large global financial institutions in the emerging market economies lead to a reduction in per unit operating costs and higher general systemic efficiency. Claessens *et al.* (2001a) found that it also led to smaller margins between deposit and lending rates. Offering better-customized services is another option open to the national and regional institutions. Several individual case studies of emerging markets are available that demonstrate that with financial globalization and the entry of foreign banks, the efficiency level in the domestic financial sector rises.[18]

The domestic banking and financial sector in the emerging market economy benefits from the entry of the large foreign banks in several direct and indirect ways. The strong solvency position of the acquiring foreign banks strengthens the financial base of the banks that are being acquired in the emerging markets. Also, after making an acquisition, foreign banks lose little time in implementing strategies that increase shareholder value. The benefit to the acquiring banks is that the new enterprises that are created after M&As earn higher intermediation margins, which are not possible in the industrial economies because of intense competition. As the emerging market economies and their financial sectors are known for high risk, instability, and volatility, the new joint ventures and M&As face higher risks. It is believed that the acquiring foreign banks introduce better management processes and risk management practices in the new ventures, which results in higher quality corporate management. The ultimate effect is a reduction in institutional volatility as well as enhancement of profitability of the newly created institution.

The end result of the entry of large global and foreign banks into the emerging markets is a strengthened domestic banking and financial sector. These banks have far more diversified portfolios, as they have access to sources of funds from around the globe. This not only reduces their risk exposure but also ensures that they are insulated from the negative shocks and other pernicious developments in the emerging market they are entering. Second, the entry of large global and foreign banks, as alluded to earlier, also leads to the adoption of best practices in the domestic banking and financial sector in the emerging markets, particularly in areas like risk management (see Chapter 5, Section 7). The ultimate result is a more efficient banking and financial sector. Third, due to the presence of the foreign banks, governments are less likely to bail out banks when they have solvency problems. This game is well understood. When the likelihood of a government bailout is low, banks in the emerging markets behave in a more prudent and disciplined manner, which in turn causes moral hazard to be reduced (Mishkin, 2001a).

Globalization has impacted the financial structure in the emerging market economies by underpinning a shift from a bank-centered system to a market-based one. Over the years, capital markets have expanded, and become more liquid and efficient. With this development, it has been observed that the preferences of the highest rated investment grade creditors have changed. They increasingly prefer commercial paper and bond markets to traditional banks and insurance products. Margins on loans for this quality of borrowers have been driven down to the extent that only the most efficient financial institutions are able to provide them with credit. On the deposit side of the banking business, a large outflow is observed to a wide range of non-bank financial institutions and to different kinds of competing financial products. For instance, mutual funds and related products effectively out-compete the bank deposit option.

In a short span of time, financial globalization has also ushered in far-reaching changes in corporate governance in the financial sector. Corporate governance implies the organizational structure and the system of checks and balances in a business or financial institution. With expanding financial globalization, the stocks of financial and non-bank financial institutions have come to be held by a wider investor clientele. This includes stockholders from the emerging market economies. The new set of stockholders is not only geographically widely spread, but is also younger and financially savvy. Pressure for change in corporate governance has largely come from stockholders outside the home country of the institution, essentially from the new set of stockholders, who have increasingly demanded a high and uniform standard of corporate governance and reporting system from the large financial institutions. Ongoing change in the global investor demography has also contributed significantly to the demands for improved and more professional corporate governance. The concept of "shareholder value" has become more entrenched and widespread than ever. The focus of indicators such as return on assets (ROA) and return on equity (ROE) has become common. While estimating performance results of the financial institutions, these measurable performance results are taken into account by the new set of stockholders. Such demands have had a discernible impact over the corporate governance in the financial and non-financial institutions that have globally-spread operations.

6   The effect of globalization on stock markets

Over the last two decades, stock markets in the emerging market economies have grown considerably. Market capitalization in the emerging market economies has risen from $488 billion in 1988 to $2,659 billion in 2000. Likewise, annual trading on their domestic stock exchanges has soared from $411 billion to $2,515 billion over the same period.[19] The reasons for this rapid growth were enumerated in Section 1. Large stock markets now operate like a well-connected global network, and ICT advances have facilitated remote access to this network from the emerging market economies. Some emerging markets, like Chile, Korea, and Taiwan, have become well integrated into this network.[20] Migration of stock exchange activity from the emerging markets to highly liquid large bourses abroad has been an important consequence of the globalization of stock markets.

The development of domestic stock markets has been found to depend on the development of a sound legal system, and particularly on creating a system of protecting minority rights. This is a necessary condition, although far from sufficient. No stock markets have been seen to develop without an adequate legal base. Second, apart from the legal infrastructure, macroeconomic stability and the size of the investor base (particularly the institutional investor base) are important determinants of stock market capitalization. Third, it is dependent on the development of other segments of the financial services industry. Fourth, trading behavior and liquidity are the other determinants of the future growth pattern of a stock exchange. Large differences have been observed in the stock markets and trading volumes in comparable emerging market economies, and these differences essentially seem to be due to institutional differences. Fifth, a cross-country study has shown that turnover in a stock market is *inter alia* dependent on the inverse of the trading costs – that is, commissions and other fees (Domowitz *et al.*, 2001). Sixth, at the firm level, new primary offerings of stocks across countries have a direct bearing on the accounting framework, the level of investor protection, and the extent of access to the domestic markets for global investors.[21]

To analyze the recent investment trends among the global investors in the emerging market economies, Griffin *et al.* (2003) conducted an extensive study with high frequency (daily) data from stock markets in India, Indonesia, Korea, the Philippines, Taiwan, and Thailand in Asia, and South Africa in Africa.[22] The sample period for the study was 1996–2001, which coincided with the data series. The advantage of deploying high frequency (daily) data is that it allows better examination of lead–lag dynamics between inflows and outflows, which with lower frequency (monthly or quarterly) data may appear to be contemporaneous relationships. These stock exchanges kept extensive data records of foreign investors' activities, including trade by both global institutional investors and individual investors. The stock exchanges in Korea and Taiwan classify data for these two categories separately, but a major part of the foreign equity flow in these two countries was due to institutional investors.

The time-series plots of the market indexes, as well as the cumulative global capital flows into equity market, showed several interesting features. First, external capital inflows into the emerging market economies showed a weak positive relationship with the movement of market indexes. They did not show massive capital flights with large equity market down moves. For instance, during the crisis in the Russian Federation there was a discernible sell-off only in Korea, and none in other emerging markets in the sample. Second, the sample period (1996–2001) was one of net foreign capital inflows in the sample economies. The Philippines and Thailand were the only exceptions where net equity flows turned strongly negative in 1999. Third, the volatility of net inflows through the equity markets varied from economy to economy, with Indonesia and Korea showing substantial movements and greater volatility.

Griffin *et al.* (2003) used a simple model of equilibrium equity flows, which predicted that equity flows toward an emerging market economy would increase with the return of that economy's stock market. When the emerging market in question was small, the model predicted that equity flows toward the country would increase with stock returns in bigger markets. This is called the external or global influence on the equity flows to the emerging market economies (see Chapter 1, Section 5). The daily flow data from the sample emerging markets supported these two hypotheses. Global investors increase their investment in the equity markets as soon as they notice that the returns are high, and their reaction time is short – often less than a day. Using a bivariate structural Vector Autoregression (VAR), the significance of regional returns was examined. Equity flows increased following strong regional equity returns. North American returns were particularly important in determining equity flows toward the emerging market economies of Asia, and had an economically and statistically significant effect on flows toward India, Indonesia, Korea, Taiwan, and Thailand. These findings were robust when exchange rate effects, cross-country flow dynamics, and the potential asymmetric effects of positive and negative returns were taken into account.

This model provided evidence of a world where foreign investors from industrial economies buy shares from emerging market economies following positive international market performance. Conversely, these investors moved out of emerging market stocks following negative international stock market performance. The past performance of a stock market in the emerging market economy was found to be positively correlated with foreign investment flows. Also, inflows into these equity markets increased rapidly when the US stock market performed well, irrespective of the local market's performance. Thus, external or global factors were found to have a significant influence over the global equity investment in the emerging market economies (Chapter 1, Section 5).

Cross-listing of stocks on global bourses

Among the large corporations in the emerging markets, a new trend of cross-listing on large global stock exchanges developed and gained momentum during the 1990s. By cross-listing, emerging market firms demonstrate that they are trying to lower the cost of the capital and are working toward maximizing shareholders' wealth by cross-listing offshore. There is a close relationship between cross-listing and the quality of corporate governance in the home country of the firm; whenever the corporate governance framework is weak in the home country, firms eagerly cross-list abroad. This is done to protect the interests of minority shareholders, and by doing so firms reveal their intent to prospective investors to take minority shareholder's rights seriously and intend to protect them.

There are apparent costs and benefits of cross-listing offshore. On the benefit side, high liquidity of the large global stock exchanges adds to the value of stocks of the emerging markets. Also, it lowers borrowing costs. However, the migration of shares affects market capitalization and value added, and may involve high domestic costs. Trading volumes have tended to decline at bourses in emerging markets, particularly those in Latin America and Central Europe, which in turn has brought about a decline in income from trading activity in these stock markets. Looking forward, as financial globalization progresses further, access to information improves even more, and markets become more standardized in terms of corporate governance, the cross-listing trend is likely to accelerate.

With financial globalization, the trend toward migration of stocks has continued to be strengthened. For some stock exchanges in the emerging markets, around half the trading and listing has migrated offshore. A large migration of trading activity may even make domestic stock exchanges unsustainable. Karolyi (2003) has emphasized that cross-listing does not contribute to development of local stock markets in the emerging market economies. On the basis of a study of twelve emerging market economies in Asia and Latin America, he concluded that antagonists have valid concerns about the deleterious impact of the integration of global equity markets through instruments like ADRs (American Depositary Receipts). The exodus of shares to large bourses offshore would curtain all the domestic equity market activities, and the flow of orders for domestic brokers and business for the investment banks, accounting firms, and other support services firms might decline so much that it would become difficult for these firms to form a critical mass of domestic business activity. This poses a serious question for the policy-makers in the emerging market economies regarding what policy to adopt regarding the development of stock markets. They need to explore whether domestic firms are cross-listing offshore because of weak market fundamentals at home. There is a likely possibility of firms intending to shun an institutionally weak financial system in favor of the one with strong market fundamentals.

However, Claessens *et al.* (2002) do not agree with this dichotomy of trading and listing at domestic stock exchanges and offshore. To them, this distinction is spurious. Their analysis concluded that the very process of developing and strengthening domestic stock exchanges also increases domestic firms' ability to access offshore exchanges. Improved fundamentals may no doubt increase domestic activity, but an increasing amount of this activity will occur offshore. They concluded that better domestic "fundamentals spur the degree of migration in capital raising, listing and trading on exchanges abroad." The policy implication of this for the emerging markets is that they need to go on improving and strengthening the domestic fundamentals so that more and more firms can participate in the domestic raising of capital, and those that can are able to access offshore bourses. The end result is additional investable resources

Although the depository receipts (DRs) were in no way a novel instrument, their use by the emerging markets has expanded considerably only recently.[23] As financial globalization has progressed, cross-listings and DRs programs have grown. Their pace of expansion has kept up with the global integration of equity markets over the last two decades. One of the stylized facts of the equity market is home bias, yet the popularity of DRs is on the rise in the US and other large stock exchanges (Karolyi and Stulz, 2003). DRs benefit investors in the local and global markets alike, with liquidity, transparency, and ease in trading being their well-recognized advantages. They facilitate trading in shares of corporates in emerging market and industrial economies. DRs are marketed by depository banks, and are perceived as being one of the most cost-effective instruments of global investment and diversification programs.

By 2000, approximately $600 billion in equity had been raised through DRs at the New York Stock Exchange (NYSE) alone. In 2000, more than 125 DR offerings were made in the American and European stock markets by the emerging market economies. Stock trading also migrated from the bourses in emerging markets to large global stock markets. In 2000, trading in American Depositary Receipts (ADRs) amounted to $1,185 billion, which was 17 percent of the total trading in the domestic stock exchanges in the emerging markets (Claessens *et al.*, 2002).[24] According to the statistics compiled by the Bank of New York, there were 1,500 ADR programs in 2001 for companies in 85 countries globally. This included more than 600 ADR programs trading on major US stock exchanges.[25] Cross-listed firms from the emerging market economies appear to be well integrated into the US portfolios. The weights in US portfolios of cross-listed stocks were found to be in line with the weights predicted by a float-adjusted international version of the classical capital asset pricing model (ICAPM). The sheer size of the cross-listing effect on US portfolios is striking. In the sample of Edison and Warnock (2003), US investors held, on average, 7 percent of the market capitalization of firms that were not cross-listed, but 27 percent of the market capitalization of those firms that were cross-listed. The US investors also demonstrated a preference for large stocks, and for stocks for emerging economies with fewer ownership restrictions.

Emerging market firms can cross-list their stocks on the NYSE or NASDAQ as ordinary listings, global registered shares, and New York registered shares. A highly popular vehicle for listing in the US is ADRs, which are negotiable certificates that confer ownership of shares in the emerging market economy on the investor in New York. They are quoted, traded, and pay dividends in US dollars. When the emerging market stocks are listed in the City in London, naturally stocks are traded in pounds sterling. Trading occurs in accordance with the clearing and settlement regulations of the market in which they are traded. The ADR program is sponsored by a bank, which functions as a depositary bank and provides custodian and safekeeping services for a nominal charge (Karolyi, 2003).

Global equity markets: shifting correlations

The correlation structure of global equity markets has been thoroughly studied. Theoretical, empirical, and statistical studies on international correlations are legion. Similarly, extensive literature exists on the benefits of international diversification. The concept of mutual funds holding equal proportion of international securities was born in eighteenth-century Holland, and quantitative analyses of international diversification date back to the early nineteenth century.[26] Goetzmann *et al.* (2003) documented the correlation structure of global equity markets from the middle of the nineteenth century to the current period. To be sure, there were data limitations; this is to be expected in such long time-series data. Their tests suggested that the structure of global equity correlations has shifted continuously and considerably through time, reaching several peaks, in the late nineteenth century, early twentieth century, the so-called Great

Depression of the 1930s, and the late twentieth century. It is currently near a historical high – approaching levels of correlation that last existed during the Great Depression. Interestingly, unlike the 1930s, the late 1990s were a period of prosperity in the global equity markets. Thus, the diversification benefits of global equity investment have not been constant.

The late twentieth century was similar to the late nineteenth century in terms of the free flow of capital across national orders, although this freedom was greater then than now. Periods of free capital movement are generally associated with high correlations among global equity markets. Owing to the growth of the emerging market economies over the last two decades, the opportunity set for the global equity investors has expanded dramatically. At the same time, correlations of the major equity markets have increased. Consequently, the benefits of international diversification have also increased in the recent period.

The time series of average correlations in the equity markets show a pattern consistent with the letter "W," with the first and third peaks of the "W" coinciding with a high degree of financial globalization in the world economy. These two peaks lay at the two ends of the twentieth century. Goetzmann *et al.* (2003) broke down the pattern of correlation through time, and found that close to half of the benefits of diversification available at present to the global equity investors are due to the increasing number of emerging market economies available to them, while the balance is due to lower average correlations in the industrial economies. This indicates to the globally significant role of the equity markets in emerging market economies.

7   Summary and conclusions

The financial services industry has a wide scope, and comprises several closely related segments. As a consequence of recent transformations, the significance of the banking sector has been on the decline globally. The emerging market economies are no exception to this generalization. The recent evolution of the financial sector and its consolidation has been driven more or less by the same set of events and developments as those in the matured economies.

Consolidation of the financial sector and international M&As in the emerging market economies has frequently been guided by financial authorities instead of by market forces. The consolidation endeavors have not only influenced the emerging market economies in which they were undertaken in a favorable manner, but also the global economy. Cost savings and revenue enhancements generally motivated consolidation moves. As a consequence of consolidation, the total number of banks declined in all the emerging market economies, and market concentration – as measured by the share in total deposits and by the HH indexes – has fallen. The emerging market economies of Latin America are an exception in this respect; although the number of banks declined in Latin America as well, this was accompanied by a rising market concentration of banks.

Although since the mid-1990s, bond markets have recorded a remarkable growth in the emerging market economies, they still are small in absolute as well as in relative terms. As in the matured industrial economies, both endogenous and exogenous macro- and micro-economic factors have influenced the creation and growth of bond markets in the emerging market economies. It is widely believed that exogenous factors played a greater role in the development of bond markets in the emerging market economies. The factors at play were fiscal adjustments, the adoption of macroeconomic stabilization measures, and large flows of global capital into the emerging market economies. In addition, the emerging market financial crises, particularly the Asian crisis, provided a definite support to the development of bond markets by underpinning corporate, financial and banking reform and restructuring endeavors. Domestic bonds dominated the issuance activity. Also, public sector bonds accounted for 64 percent of the total amount outstanding. Among the emerging market economies, Korea and Malaysia had the largest bond markets when measured as a proportion of GDP. Total issuance activity peaked in 1995 at $370 billion. It fell in 1996, after the Mexican crisis, and following the Asian and Russian crises in 1998 it declined to its lowest level. In 1999, it was mere $250 billion. As regards private sector issuance activity, it declined dramatically after the Asian crisis.

The slow growth of the bond markets is having a decisive impact on the banking system in the emerging market economies. With their expansion, some of the financing business of the banks has begun to be taken over by the bond markets. It is not necessary that the growth of the bond markets should be completely at the cost of the banking sector, and vice versa. The two can not only co-exist, but also have a profitable and symbiotic relationship.

The onward march of financial globalization has in a myriad of ways influenced the evolution of financial structure and management practices in the emerging market economies. Transformations brought about by the TNCs and the large banks in the matured industrial economies that were busy building a global retail system are significant in this regard. Many industrial economy banks have made acquisitions of large shareholdings in the emerging market banks. Financial globalization has impacted upon the institutions providing wholesale financial services. The domestic banking and financial sector in the emerging market economy has benefited from the entry of the large foreign banks in several direct and indirect ways. In a short span of time, financial globalization has also ushered in far-reaching changes in corporate governance in the financial sector.

Stock markets in the emerging economies have grown considerably over the last two decades. Financial globalization has stimulated the tendency of cross-listing in these economies at the offshore stock exchanges. Carried to the extreme, this trend can have definitive pernicious effects on the domestic bourses. However, a dichotomous approach in this regard is not helpful. The very process of developing and strengthening domestic stock exchanges also increases the domestic firms' ability to access offshore exchanges. Improved fundamentals may no doubt increase the domestic activity, but an increasing amount of this activity will occur offshore. The end result is additional investable resources.

5 Financial and macroeconomic instability in the emerging market economies

1 Financial and macroeconomic instability

The enormous increase in liquid assets that has taken place with financial globalization is beneficial to global financial market participants. When capital flows take place easily and smoothly into and out of emerging market economies, these economies benefit from more investment as well as an increased ability to diversify risk. The flip side of this coin is that the enormous increase in liquid assets and global inflows and outflows of capital can be worrisome for several reasons: it erodes central banks' ability to exercise monetary control; it tends to appreciate currency and triggers inflationary pressures; it may facilitate the opening of speculative positions; and it may cause the quality of credit in the system to decline. This could create serious instability in financial markets as well as in real markets.

Empirical research has demonstrated that on the one hand these inflows into emerging markets can reduce the cost of capital in the domestic markets, which in turn favorably affects investment.[1] Rapid and sustained growth in the recipient economy is the eventual result. On the other hand, empirical research has also demonstrated the opposite. Rapid capital inflows in a financially globalized world can create boom–bust cycles in the host economy. Volatility can be caused by both domestic and external factors, which in turn can aggravate the fragilities of the domestic banking and financial systems. Capital flows have been known to spawn panics and manias in the recent past, and this issue has intrigued a good number of economists.

Many studies have found a tenuous link between the variables on the two sides of this equation. Rapid transborder capital flows have frequently caused macroeconomic instability or even a crash.[2] Currency, macroeconomic, and financial crises of the recent past indicate the inordinate tendency of financial markets to experience sharp boom–bust cycles. During the boom phase of the cycle, both lenders and borrowers generally underestimate the risks involved in high levels of lending and indebtedness. Over-lending and over-borrowing do not become obvious until the downswing of the financial market cycle begins. This reflects information asymmetry as well as a radical change in expectations with the arrival of new information. These changes in expectations and the resulting decisions not only tend to affect the financial markets seriously, but also exacerbate the uncertainty inherent to the inter-temporal decisions that underlie financial transactions.

If global capital inflows can finance high investment rates and current account deficits, raising sustainable growth rates and living standards, they can also inflate real exchange rates. An inflated exchange rate has a large potential for destabilizing an emerging market economy (see Chapter 1, Section 4). Its immediate effect is weakened export competitiveness. Many recent financial crises, particularly those in Asia, were preceded by exchange rate appreciations. These encourage excessive resource allocation to the non-traded goods sectors. When global investors find that the real exchange rates are high, it undermines their confidence in the emerging market and they are ready to exit to safe havens. Their sudden exit, followed by herding behavior, contributes to a crisis situation.[3]

At the beginning of the twenty-first century, financial instability and volatility became one of the most significant challenges faced by the emerging market economies. Compared to the 1990s and the early 2000s, episodes of financial instability and crises were infrequent in the 1980s. Once they made most people's eyes glaze over and "were subjects of intense interest to only a limited clientele, many of whom wore green eyeshades" (Blinder, 2003). This generalization does not hold good any longer, and financial instability has unfortunately acquired a mass audience since the early 1990s and the European ERM crisis of 1992–1993.[4]

Since this time point, crises have also attracted a great deal of scholarly attention and consequently a large volume of so-called crisis literature has emerged. Severe financial instability, crises, sovereign defaults, and stunning currency collapses in Latin America after mid-1982, Venezuela in 1994, Mexico in 1994–1995, East and Southeast Asia in 1997–1998), the Russian Federation in 1998, Brazil and Ecuador in 1999, Turkey in 2001, Argentina in 2000–2002, and Venezuela in 2002–2003, have pushed the subject to the front page of the financial daily press.[5] Three of these crises, namely the ERM crisis, the Latin American crisis (which began in Mexico in 1994), and the Asian crisis, turned out to be region-wide financial and currency crises. Many of them caused a global ripple effect. Overwhelmed by their frequency, Paul Volcker (1999) remarked that these crises – domestic, regional and global – were "built into the human genome."

Financial sector instability leads to serious macroeconomic instability. Numerous instances of financial sector instability leading to macroeconomic instability are available for the preceding quarter-century, both in the emerging markets and in the matured industrial economies. Instances of instability and crises in the emerging market economies outnumbered those in the matured industrial economies. Does this imply that the financial systems in the emerging markets are more fragile to capital mobility? Wyplosz (2001) found that external financial liberalization and capital mobility is more destabilizing in the emerging markets than in the industrial economies. The probability of the creation of a boom–bust cycle in an emerging market is higher than that in an industrial economy.

As financial globalization progresses and domestic liberalization and integration with the global economy increases, the tendency toward a boom–bust cycle declines. Diversification of asset portfolios and healthier development of the financial sector combine to impart stability to the economy. However, there is little comfort in the fact that a liberalized and open globally-integrated economy is more stable and less volatile over the long haul. The very process of liberalization and globalization increases volatility and the risk of crisis. Therefore, the World Bank (2002b) emphasizes the distinction between being open on the one hand and becoming open on the other. While the former is associated with greater stability, the latter, under certain circumstances, can lead to financial and exchange rate crises, with high costs to the economy.

China: an exception to instability?

China, the largest emerging market economy, remained unaffected by the Asian crisis of 1997–1998. It appeared that the crisis passed China by. The economy was helped by the currency reforms of 1994–1995 and by the fact that it was not convertible. When the Asian crisis broke out China had large foreign currency reserves, which helped it in keeping the contagion at bay.[6] It graciously offered to help the crisis-affected Asian economies. However, in early 2003, due to several financial sector weaknesses, it was being compared to the Asian economies of 1997. According to the official statistics, 25.4 percent of the bank loans (or around $600 billion) in China were classified as non-performing. Goldman Sachs estimated that a minimum of 44 percent of China's GDP would be needed to clean up China's banking mess.[7] The poor record of bank lending is more a fault of the government than of the bankers, as the cost of China's transition from a planned to a market economy was placed in the banks' loan books rather than issuing government debt.

At the end of 2002, the government announced that Goldman Sachs and Morgan Stanley would be allowed to form joint ventures with one of the four asset management companies that were set up in 1999. A large number of cases of corporate malfeasance and accounting malpractices have come to surface. In 2003, the highest court of the country allowed class action law suits against these companies. The decade-old stock market is dominated by state-owned enterprises (SOEs) that were listed for political rather than economic reasons. Around two-thirds of the market capitalization is not traded, and there is no corporate bond market. Many China analysts have questioned whether China is ready for a serious bout of financial instability (*The Economist*, 2003b). Although China's banking sector in 2003 is in as poor a shape as that of Indonesia and Thailand in 1997, it does not have companies with large foreign currency debts. Another helpful factor is that the renminbi yuan is still not a convertible currency.

2   High costs of crashes

The immediate macroeconomic costs of the financial sector problems have been large in terms of foregone growth, inefficient financial intermediation, and impaired public confidence in the financial system. All these infirmities have medium- and long-term implications for the affected economies. A financial crisis leads to capital flight and a drop in investment levels far below the financial autarky levels. Furthermore, crisis resolution endeavors have their own cost. Fiscal and quasi-fiscal outlays for restructuring the financial and banking sector can be as high as 15 percent to 30 percent of the GDP of the crisis-affected economy. This cost, in most cases, is borne by the public exchequer.

In an endeavor to quantify the cost of macroeconomic stability, Easterly and Kraay (1999) found that an increase in the standard deviation of GDP growth reduces the annual average rate of per capita growth by one-fifth of 1 percent per annum. An earlier study by the Inter-American Development Bank (IDB, 1995) controlled for the other determinants of secular rate of growth that are standard in the empirical literature, and found that the growth rate is negatively correlated to volatility of terms of trade, of real exchange rate, of monetary policy, and of fiscal policy. Of these, terms of trade volatility and exchange rate volatility were associated with the largest negative effect over GDP growth (Easterly and Kraay, 1999; Guillaumont *et al.*, 1999). The negative association of volatility with growth reflects adverse impacts on both productivity and investment. So far we have focused on the impact of volatility on GDP growth and excluded a major source of volatility, namely the financial and economic crises. They are incompatible with GDP growth and force an economy to *ad hoc* and stop–go policies. Crises are known to disrupt the domestic financial system, cause distress in the corporate sector, and force a decline in private and public investment.

Financial sector problems and volatility not only have macroeconomic and financial costs, but also entail painful social costs. They adversely impact social indicators like income distribution, poverty levels, and educational attainments. The poor, unskilled, and uneducated suffer disproportionately from volatility because they are unable to hedge their incomes. Hedging offsets an existing risk exposure and entails taking an opposite position in the same or similar risk, for example by buying derivatives contracts.

Financial sector instability entails serious spillover or contagion risks, which can have a direct devastating effect on the global financial community. Crises have been known to spread regionally as well as managing adversely to affect the global financial markets (see Section 6). The debt crisis of 1982, which started in Mexico and spread to the other Latin American emerging market economies, brought the global banking and financial industry perilously close to collapse. The Mexican crisis of 1994 affected the emerging market economies in the Western hemisphere, as did the financial crisis in Thailand, which started in July 1997 and spread to several Asian economies that had been known for their stellar economic performance over the preceding two decades. The contagion effect can potentially have an economically financially devastating effect,[8] and therefore crisis-affected economies are frequently assisted by large stable economies (such as the United States) or by supranational institutions (such as the International Monetary Fund).

Financial conflagrations became too frequent, too devastating, and too contagious to be ignored by investors, bankers, financial and monetary policy-makers, the financial firefighters in multilateral institutions, the economics profession in general, and the students of emerging market economies in particular. Many academicians believed that multilateral institutions neither understood the rationale of instability and crises completely, nor succeeded in predicting the severity of the shrinkage of output in the crisis-affected emerging market economies. They also frequently failed to predict the timing, pace, and strength of the recoveries (IMF, 1998b; Lane *et al.*, 1999). Overall, they succeeded in creating an impression that they were not up to the job.

The IMF was roundly criticized for its poor understanding of the causal factors behind the crises and contagions, as well as for its inability to devise an optimal rescue package for the affected economies. Its observations and policy errors were particularly conspicuous during the Asian crisis (Das, 2000a). It was easy to be vituperative about the IMF because its programs for several crisis-affected economies were short-sighted, even incorrect. They were criticized as "knee-jerk reactions" and "one size fits all" rescue packages. Mid-course corrections were needed after several IMF rescue programs were prescribed and launched.[9] The economics profession was critical (albeit divided) of the manner in which the IMF handled various episodes of economic instability in the emerging market economies. There was little agreement in the economics profession regarding what would have been the optimal manner of handling each emerging market financial and macroeconomic crisis. Stiglitz (2000a, 2000b) was one of the constant and vitriolic critics of the flaws in the IMF rescue programs prepared for the affected economies, although not everything done by the IMF was incorrect and some of the criticism was unfair. For instance, the analytical prowess of the IMF professionals was far from those of "third rank students from first-rate universities."[10] The quality and quantity of research published by the IMF testifies to this fact.

An additional (if unsavory) intrinsic role that the IMF has played is that of the scapegoat. Governments in dire financial straits have to impose unpopular policies, and they blame the IMF for those policies. Moreover, borrowers looking for a way out and donor countries unhappy with policy failure all have blamed the IMF in the past. It does not deserve all the criticism heaped on it. In mid-January 2003, when the IMF rolled over loans for Argentina, it was widely criticized for taking another mis-step. On its part, the IMF could not allow its bigger borrowers to be "left twisting in the wind," not only because this could have serious adverse consequences for these clients but also because of the serious consequences it could have for the emerging markets in general. When, after a year of negotiations with the Argentine government, the IMF agreed to roll over a $6.6 billion loan, after acknowledging "exceptional risks to the Fund," it was branded a "weak" institution (*The Economist*, 2003c). However, the ongoing crisis in Argentina, while it did not cause a contagion in the region or affect the group of emerging market economies, did bring neighboring Uruguay to its knees and make the global financial markets concerned about the economic situation in Brazil. As the stakes were high, the IMF had to relent because of these strategic considerations. In the process, it earned the accusation of being a weak institution. IMF's recent handing of Brazil, Indonesia, and Turkey has inspired a similar reaction from its stakeholders.

3 Emerging market financial crises during 2000–2002

As stated above, the financial crises of the 1990s afflicted major middle-income emerging market economies and spilled over into the 2000–2002 period. The contagious effect of the crisis of the 1990s spread both regionally and in some cases globally. Few generalizations can be made regarding the causes of each one of these crises and of the economic instability in countries that were the sources of crises. They differed in several important respects. Common elements in all instances were shortcomings in external financial management, and defects in corporate and financial sector governance. Turkey and Argentina both had serious problems in these areas, as did economies affected by the earlier crises of the 1990s.

The Argentinian crisis was born out of the build-up of vulnerabilities after the highly successful exchange rate-based stabilization program of the early 1990s. Argentina had adopted a dollar-based currency board in 1991, which had served the economy well by curing it of a serious and long-standing inflation problem. The Turkish crisis was rooted in its high public sector deficit, which reached 12 percent of the GNP in 2000. This was compounded by high levels of public sector debt, reaching 90 percent of the GNP, and difficulties in rolling over short-term debts. These debts were as large as the foreign exchange reserves of Turkey. Adoption of a crawling peg regime did not work for Turkey. The objective was to reduce the high inflation rate, but it encouraged large capital inflows, resulting in a substantial build-up of foreign exchange liabilities for the banking system. In February 2001, it had to be abandoned.

A conspicuous difference between these two crises and the ones in the 1990s regards the contagion effect to other emerging market economies and other debt markets. While the crises of the 1990s had a quick and decisive effect, in the cases of Turkey and Argentina this effect was close to none. Evidence of investors retreating from other emerging markets due to crisis in these two economies was infinitesimal. Even Brazil was not seriously affected by crisis in its neighbor to the south, although Argentina and Brazil are two economies that are closely related in any state of the global economy. The correlation between secondary market bond spreads in different emerging market economies is a measure of spread of contagion. Between Argentina and 15 other emerging market economies, correlation of spreads on bonds rose from 0.27 before the exacerbation of the crisis to 0.47 after the crisis became full-blown in October 2000. Similarly, correlations of spreads on Turkish bonds increased from 0.12 before the crisis to 0.39 after the crisis (World Bank, 2002c). It cannot be ignored that this was the period of global slowdown, when there is a general rise in spreads and also in the volatility of spreads. Therefore, measured correlations tended to rise with increases in volatility. That the Argentinian crisis did not set off a serious contagion is noteworthy, because it was a crisis of large dimensions, eventually leading to a sovereign default. It was comparable to the August 1998 default by the Russian Federation, which spawned serious dislocation across global financial markets

Further evidence of the weak impact of crises in these two economies on the other emerging markets is provided by the index of emerging market spreads, which had remained almost stationary until September 2001. Again, there is no evidence from the stock market prices showing that the Argentine or Turkish crises affected other emerging market economies, except for a small impact on the Brazilian stock market. One reason for the weak contagion effect was the missing element of surprise; investors were aware of the problems and the possible outcome. Besides, most investors were less leveraged this time than during the earlier crises, and therefore they did not need to liquidate assets across the board to meet margin calls.[11] Overall, Brazil succeeded in resisting direct contagion from the crisis in Argentina reasonably well.

Contagions need not go through the regional or global economy like an avalanche. Experience with so many crises shows that they can be contained. Most emerging market economies that are well integrated with the global capital markets have strengthened their ability to withstand shocks by adopting flexible exchange rate regimes, disciplined domestic monetary policies, and, most importantly, limited short-term external liabilities and limited near-term refinancing needs. These measures help in stalling the spread of problems.

4 Fundamentals of financial and macroeconomic stability

Financial stability in an emerging market economy has a direct bearing on two conditions. The first relates to the macroeconomic and structural conditions in the real economy, which not only affect the financial decisions but also form the environment in which the financial system operates. The second condition relates to the financial system *per se*, that is, how robust the financial markets and institutions are, and the manner in which financial transactions are conducted.[12] Whether financial transactions are carried out in a strict regulatory environment and under supervision or are done in an arbitrary manner has a great deal of impact on the financial stability in an emerging market economy.

How the real economy operates is an important and relevant, if not critical, issue that determines the stability (or lack of it) of the financial markets. The manner in which the real economy operates provides basic signals to which the financial system responds. Instability and/or distortions in the real economy will inevitably cause financial instability, no matter how robust the system. The positive side of having a robust financial system is that, first, it reduces the risk of financial instability when the real economy malfunctions, and second, when financial instability is created, a robust financial system limits the impact of the resulting crisis. The cost of restructuring and returning to normalcy under such conditions is less than when the financial system is weak. Lastly, requisite institutions and capabilities are not sufficient for maintaining financial stability, although they are necessary. Social consensus and political commitment supporting the policies and measures needed for continued financial stability are indispensable.

The preceding paragraph refers to a robust financial system. The BIS (1997) defines it as a system that can stand the so-called "test of the market." If a financial system remains functional and works efficiently under a wide range of market circumstances, it qualifies to be called robust. The necessary characteristics of a robust financial system are flexibility, resilience, and internal stability. A robust financial market system must be able to deliver on the following fundamentals: it should (1) allocate finance efficiently under a full range of market circumstances; (2) continue performing market functions and making expeditious payments under market disturbances; and (3) not generate financial shocks of its own or magnify the external ones it receives.

The robustness of financial markets is determined by how efficiently they are able to perform three basic market functions: (1) maintain an incentive structure for the market agents and financial actors; (2) generate and make available information that has a bearing on financial decision-making; and (3) intermediate between financial markets and financial actors, thus providing the capability for institutions and individuals to respond to market incentives and utilize market information.

5   Financial and macroeconomic instability: exploring the causality

The emerging market crises of the 1980s and those of the 1990s were different from each other. The crises of the early 1980s were brought about by heavy borrowings by several Latin American governments in the international capital markets. They were encouraged by low real interest rates (or low LIBOR in real terms) and the high commodity prices they received for their exports. When real interest rates (LIBOR) soared and the recessionary conditions in the US weakened the demand for their exports, as well as prices, the indebted countries found it difficult to service their debts. The result was serious impairment of the balance sheets of the money-centered banks in the US and Europe. There was a distinct possibility of a systemic banking crisis in global economy. As opposed to this, the crises of the 1990s were primarily caused by a combination of unsustainable current account deficits, excessive short-term foreign debts, and weak domestic and financial systems. Although the experiences of each crisis country were unique, one or more of these crisis conditions were always present. In addition, both domestic and global factors were responsible for causing financial and macroeconomic instability, although it is difficult to determine which is the bigger villain. It is not possible to conclude from the available evidence whether one or another set of causal factors has been the principal destabilizing influence over the emerging market economies, and researchers in this area continue to disagree. In many episodes of recent financial crises the two sets of causal factors seemed to be feeding on each other, setting in motion a downward spiral and eventually triggering a crisis. The following two sub-sections analyze the domestic and global causal factors separately.

Domestic origins of financial and macroeconomic instability

Over the preceding quarter-century, it has been repeatedly observed that macroeconomic instability and crises in the emerging market economies have frequently been caused by problems in the domestic financial sector, particularly the domestic banking sector. The reason is that the banking sector became, and has remained, the dominant channel of financial intermediation in the emerging market economies. This sector has been responsible for more than three-fourths of financial intermediation in a majority of them. This observation applies more to the Asian and Latin American emerging market economies than to others. It made the banking sector a potential candidate responsible for the vulnerability of the financial sector. Although other financial institutions can also be a source of vulnerability, in most emerging market economies they were not well capitalized, or were even seriously undercapitalized. This reduced their sphere of activity, their significance for the real sector, and therefore their capability to destabilize the financial system.

The financial sector infirmities in the emerging market economies have been found in similar areas, namely corporate governance and market discipline (Das, 2001c). The most frequent areas lacking discipline were regulatory norms and supervisory structures. In an unstable macroeconomic environment, these vulnerabilities of the financial sector readily spawn a crisis. Distortions in the real economy and serious macroeconomic policy failure also produce the same results, adversely affecting the price signals and incentives structure of a market.

Emerging market banking crises frequently followed periods of rapid economic expansion – including rapid expansion in domestic credit – which were responsible for the creation of unsustainable macroeconomic imbalances. When a period of economic downturn begins after a period of prolonged upswing, fueled by large credit expansion, capital inflows and overvalued currency, the situation is ripe for a financial crisis. Also, when slow GDP growth and a spurt in domestic credit expansion continue, the likelihood of a financial crisis increases (Frankel and Rose, 1996; Kaminsky and Reinhart, 1999b). Only having relatively lower per capita income levels makes emerging markets more crisis prone than those economies that have higher income levels (Martin and Rey, 2002).

It was observed that asset price corrections when unsustainable macroeconomic imbalances existed, along with financial sector vulnerabilities, caused a full-blown crisis. Similarly, external shocks when unsustainable macroeconomic imbalances existed, along with financial sector vulnerabilities, led to the same final outcome. As opposed to this scenario, in those emerging market economies where financial vulnerabilities did not exist and the financial system was sound, severe macroeconomic shocks were borne in a resilient manner. An illustration of this fact is Chile, which was known to have a relatively sound financial system. It was not mauled by the 1994–1995 Latin American crisis, which began in Mexico.

A close scrutiny of recent instances of emerging market crises reveals that in a financial sector, crisis causality can work both ways – that is, instability and distortions in macroeconomic framework can affect the financial institutions and markets and, conversely, financial sector vulnerabilities can be responsible for an unstable macroeconomic performance. External shocks can be magnified by either of the two sources of vulnerability.

The obvious sources of macroeconomic instability are high and variable inflation rates, rapid movements in the domestic business cycle, and unsustainable fiscal and current account positions. These can be direct sources of vulnerability faced by the banking sector through their adverse effect on asset prices and allocation of financial resources. Financial institutions can indeed hedge their portfolios against volatility, but there is little possibility of hedging macroeconomic risks or volatility completely. For instance, during the downturn of a business cycle the banking sector cannot protect itself against deterioration in the quality of loan portfolios. Banks have passively to accept erosion of their capital base and reserve position. As opposed to this, during an upturn of the business cycle, when monetary policy is relaxed, the short-term profitability of banks improves. However, the downside is that if a boom situation creates an asset price bubble, in the medium term the banking sector will be destabilized again (Lindgren *et al.*, 1996).

During the several recent instances of crisis, it was observed that macro-economic instability contributed to asset prices volatility. Several economies, both emerging market and matured industrial ones, found their real estate and equity prices falling and in turn adversely affecting the banking sector in a serious manner.[13] Swings in the asset prices were accentuated by distortions in the real economy. For instance, in many economies the tax structure is such that it encourages borrowing from banks and investments in real estate. One example is Sweden in the late 1980s. Such a tax structure creates distortions, and changes financial prices and incentives. In many emerging market economies and matured economies, shifting relative prices, like changing terms of trade, have con-tributed to difficulties for the banking sector. Chile, Malaysia, Nigeria, and Norway provide examples (Lindgren *et al.*, 1996).

The structure of emerging market economies and their management are of capital importance. Emerging market economies are structurally less diverse, and are generally blighted by one kind of rigidity or the other. Furthermore, market imperfections are common in these economies. Therefore, they tend to suffer more from macroeconomic instability than the matured industrial economies, consequently their ability to absorb external shocks is lower than that of the industrial economies.

In addition, because of the structural reasons enumerated above, the emerging market economies have demonstrated a tendency for wider swings in real exchange rates, real interest rates, private market capital inflows, and terms of trade movements. When we say wider swings we imply relative to the size of their GDP. Likewise, poor macroeconomic management has also been a source of episodes of instability. When policy-makers make frequent changes in the macroeconomic policies, ignore the growing fiscal and current account deficits until they reach a crisis proportion, allow large inflows of short-term capital or "hot money," and defend an exchange rate that is out of line with the funda-mentals, this results in the gradual sinking of the economy into a crisis situation (BIS, 1997). Macroeconomic mismanagement is readily visible in exchange rate instability. These fluctuations not only affect the open foreign exchange positions of banks and other financial institutions, but also indirectly affect the performance of the borrowers in the global market place. This category of borrowers has been growing rapidly in the emerging market economies.

Another important source of financial and macroeconomic instability seems to stem from microeconomic and institutional failures. A large number of episodes of instability and financial crisis in the emerging market economies during the decade of the 1990s can be justly blamed on microeconomic and institutional failures. There is a wide variety in these failures. Financial institutions and corporate business houses suffered from inadequate internal control mechanisms, connected lending, and insider dealing. Moral hazard worsened this bad situation. Corporate owners had little incentive to be ethically and morally upright and to supervise managers. In many emerging market economies, financial institutions were either government-owned or under government direction. Low asset quality and directed lending universally go hand in hand. The BIS (1997) contended that in many cases this was the crucial problem at the "root of the management failure" of financial systems, because in such cases commercial and prudential considerations were abandoned while social and political objectives became the guiding star. Professional and profitable running of the financial system was no longer an objective.

Even in the private sector, financial institutions frequently suffered from poor quality management and did not feel obliged to follow sound financial practices. An inadequate or weak legal framework further compounded the complex problem of lax management and lackadaisical corporate governance. BIS (1997) pointed out that:

> "unreliable payment systems and underdeveloped financial systems increased the risks which were inherent to financial transactions. Once credit quality was compromised, regulatory shortcomings and supervisory forbearance aggravated matters by failing to identify problems and preventing them from being addressed in a timely fashion."

Government regulation and supervision of financial systems on the one hand and poor risk management by the financial sector on the other were further domestic causes contributing to crises. Government regulations did not encourage financial institutions to avoid mismatches between assets and liabilities. This included unhedged foreign exchange borrowings and short-term assets financing long-term investments (Das, 2000a; Kawai *et al.*, 2001). These were high-risk practices, and made banks vulnerable to exchange rate depreciations and rising interest rates. In many emerging markets the regulatory and supervising bodies failed to keep a good eye on whether the financial institutions were capitalized adequately and whether domestic banks made sufficient loan loss provisions. Also, transparency was lacking and mandatory public disclosure of audited financial statements was not ensured. Therefore, market discipline slipped. Many of the recent crises have demonstrated that risk management in the emerging market economies was inadequate. In many cases, for instance in the Asian crisis-affected countries, highly leveraged and vulnerable corporate sectors were a crucial determinant of the depth of the crisis. Large currency depreciations abruptly inflated the size of the external debt and debt-service obligations, and this drove many large domestic financial corporations in the crisis-affected economies into a financial morass.

Closely related factors were the failures in corporate governance and management, which in turn stem from two principal reasons: first, the lack of incentives to act prudently; and second, inadequate information, low accounting standards, little monitoring, and highly inadequate reporting requirements. Financial institutions in the crisis-affected economies paid little attention to the identification of problems and making provision for them. There were cases where managers of financial institutions maintained that their capital base was adequate until the day of the collapse of the institution. Poorly managed banks and financial institutions also ignored standard credit appraisal procedures, and neither monitored borrowers nor imposed financial discipline. Inexperience, incompetence, and downright fraudulent tendencies also played a visible role in the failure of many financial institutions. These microeconomic and institutional failures had a pernicious macroeconomic impact on the economy.

Insider lending was another serious source of financial distress in many emerging market economies that suffered from macroeconomic instability and financial crises. The reason was a poor incentive structure in the domestic financial system. Many large borrowers from the banks were also their part owners, and therefore could treat the bank as a captive source of finance.[14] Arm's length dealings between lending banks and such borrowers were conceivable, but not a part of financial reality in the emerging markets (Das, 2001c). Lending to related enterprises therefore became a potent cause of bank failure. In such cases, creditworthiness of the large borrowers was not a criterion on which the loans were made. A large number of cases of banks being exploited as captive sources of finance came to light during the Asian crisis.[15]

Financial globalization and financial and macroeconomic instability

As seen in Section 4, domestic factors can be the crucial determinants of financial and macroeconomic instability, and financial globalization can also be a harbinger of crisis.[16] Before an economy is liberalized and deregulated, that is in an autarkic situation, only the domestic market players monitor the market and react to any hints of unsound macroeconomic and financial fundamentals. However, after liberalization and deregulation the scenario expands to include an additional market player, namely the global investors. Addition of this class of investors to the old group of market player has far-reaching ramifications. They add several changes to the financial market of the emerging market economies, altering its course and character dramatically. In an open economy, both domestic and global market players monitor the markets and react to any weaknesses in the fundamentals. Together they determine the long-run steady state of an economy and help it to reach its so-called "sound fundamentals" state. As long as the sound fundamentals state continues, the economy can continue functioning without any volatility.

When economies open, they become vulnerable to the imperfections in the global financial markets. This implies that financial globalization can be a potential source of macroeconomic and financial volatility in the emerging markets. Those who support this argument believe that market imperfections are more prevalent in the global financial markets than in the domestic markets. Imperfections in the global financial markets can *inter alia* cause irrational exuberance, herding behavior, speculative attacks, and market crashes.[17] Information asymmetries exacerbate this situation by catalyzing momentum trading, noise trading, bandwagon effects, and short-termism (cf. Chapter 1, Section 5).[18] Several market bubbles have been generated over the past two decades, which caused serious destability in the financial markets. The impact of imperfections in the global financial markets can be far-reaching in destabilizing even economies that have sound fundamentals. For instance, a mere market perception of the unsustainability of the exchange rate may activate speculators against that currency (see also Chapter 1, Section 3).

Notwithstanding the robustness of market fundamentals, this action can precipitate a self-fulfilling currency crisis. Several instances of such a situation have been well analyzed in the financial crisis literature. McKinnon and Pill (1999) contended that imperfections in the global financial markets could also have a weakening effect on the market fundamentals *per se*. One commonly observed example of such weakening of market fundamentals is bouts of overborrowing after liberalization and deregulation, particularly when there are implicit government guarantees. This moral hazard has led to crisis situation in several emerging markets (see Chapter 3, Section 2).

After an emerging market has become integrated with the global economy, external factors begin to have a good deal of influence on its domestic economy – so much so that financial globalization can sway the performance of the emerging market economy even in the absence of market imperfections. This can happen in an emerging market that has sound fundamentals, as noted in the preceding paragraph. As seen in Chapter 1, being able to attract global capital is a *sine qua non* of an emerging market economy, and it has tremendous advantages.

The process of integration with the global economy makes it dependent on global capital inflows. An abrupt shift in this flow is sure to create a domestic financial crisis, if not initiate a downswing of the business cycle. The shifts in the direction of global capital flows do not necessarily reflect the domestic fundamentals of the recipient emerging market. Various external factors can and have caused such abrupt shifts in the direction of capital flows in the recent past. For instance, during the 1990s, movements in global interest rates were responsible for large capital flows to Asian and Latin American economies. Other than interest rate movements, the factors that matter most are movements in the business cycle in the industrial economies, drives toward diversification of investment in the global financial centers, and regional economic developments.

Financial crises have taken place throughout history.[19] Those who have studied the long-term history of financial and macroeconomic crises and compared the financial crises of the contemporary period with those of the earlier waves of globalization do not see the contemporary period as an excessively turbulent one. At today's level of financial and economic integration, given the earlier history of crises, we should have had more frequent crises than there have been so far. The reasons for the superior performance during the contemporary period are the existence of supranational institutions at the global level, and better supervision and accounting standards at the domestic level (Bordo *et al.*, 1999).

A more recent study focused on a long period of crises in a disaggregated manner, and compared the frequency and severity of crises occurring since 1880. For the sake of clarity, the period was divided into different sub-periods, namely the gold standard era (1880–1913), the inter-war period (1919–1939), the Bretton-Woods period (1945–1971), and the contemporary period. Each one of these sub-periods is known for its own idiosyncrasies. An inter-period comparison showed that crises are more frequent in the contemporary period than they were during the gold standard period or the Bretton-Woods period. As opposed to this, the frequency of crises during the inter-war period and the contemporary period is comparable. There was little evidence regarding the severity or duration of the contemporary crises becoming worse than those of the earlier sub-periods (Bordo *et al.*, 2001).

Managing instability and crisis

The high and painful economic and social costs of financial globalization for several emerging markets in the past have been discussed above. It is vitally important to develop policies and institutions to rein in the deleterious impact of globalization so that welfare improvement becomes the principal, if not the only, outcome of globlization.[20] Many scholars have addressed the issue of limiting volatility and managing crisis in globalizing emerging markets. While there is no consensus on several issues, they do agree on several major points. For instance, it is generally agreed that foreign direct investment (FDI) and portfolio investment augment investable capital stock and have a salutary effect on growth. However, portfolio investment has some questionable traits and can potentially create serious instability in a globalizing emerging market. When capital account is liberalized and portfolio investment inflows begin, initially they tend to relax financial growth constraints and deepen capital markets. However, frequently pre-existing policy and market distortions interact with the portfolio investment inflows and create volatility and the risk of a crisis. The degree of distortion of the domestic economic environment is of material importance. In the matured industrial economies, where generally policy and market distortions are minimal, portfolio investment inflows are known to stimulate financial depth and growth. Conversely, they have been found to have a perverse effect on the financial sector in many emerging market economies, essentially because of the presence of market and financial distortions.

With the progress in globalization, it is progressively difficult to maintain statutory restrictions on the capital account without disturbing and constraining other forms of economic activity. This makes it imperative to coordinate financial liberalization with the elimination of market distortions. Absence of such coordination is sure to heighten volatility and crisis risk. To this end, if the following policy measures are adopted, they will go a long way toward dampening volatility and minimizing the risk of crisis (Das, 2003b).

One of the most significant and oft-repeated lessons from the emerging market crisis of the 1980s and 1990s is that capital account must not be prematurely liberalized. Economic and financial distortions should be addressed and eliminated and the financial sector should be strengthened before liberalizing the capital account. This lesson extends to reveal that policy reforms like the removal of implicit guarantees, the imposition of budget constraints on financial institutions, the rationalization of prudential supervision on financial institutions, and adequate capitalization of financial institutions, reduces the probability of a crisis.[21] Capital account liberalization should follow, not precede, recapitalization of the domestic banking sector.

Another important lesson from the recent crises regards the accumulation of foreign exchange reserves. They tend to provide a cushion against volatility. Some economies were able to ward off crisis by accumulation of substantial reserves.[22] Academics and policy mandarins alike have supported the strategy of having such a cushion, because it works as insurance against disruptive domestic financial effects as well as abrupt capital outflows.[23] One suggestion was that emerging markets should hold reserves equal to the total short-term liability that is going to fall due for repayment over the next 12 months (Greenspan, 1999). Another recommendation was to hold even larger reserves, as much as twice what Greenspan suggested (Bussiere and Mulder, 1999). For economies that run chronic current account deficits, even this level was considered inadequate.

There is a strong case for liberalizing the capital account in stages. It should be liberalized for foreign direct investment (FDI) long before it is liberalized for portfolio and short-term capital inflows. Although it seems intuitive, many emerging market governments did not do this, and some were even slow to adopt these priorities after a crisis. Although there are skeptics, FDI tends to be more stable than other kinds of private capital inflow. The logic is that an investor cannot unbolt and lift all the tangible components of his factors to join the herd of panicking creditors. Closely associated with liberalization at an early stage for FDI is the process of opening to external financial institutions. Entry of foreign banks and investment banking institutions is a low-cost means of upgrading the risk management capabilities of the domestic banking sector through techno-logy, skill and knowledge spill-over from the foreign to domestic banks. The foreign banks are better supervised and better capitalized, and are generally averse to risk.

Excessive capital inflows tend to be a distinctive possibility, and to ward off this problem market-friendly instruments need to be used. The much-debated Chilean approach won many admirers. Chile required a non-interest bearing deposit for one year from the investors and businesses seeking to borrow in the global capital markets. As short-term inflows pose a greater risk of volatility and crisis, the Chilean scheme of a holding period can be justified as a form of prudential supervision. It was considered to be transparent, without any administrative discretion. Besides, it was not inef-ficient and conducive to rent-seeking behavior (Ulan, 2000). Stock and bond market development also plays a supportive and meaningful role in controlling volatility. Diversifying the sources of corporate debt by develop-ing bond markets on the one hand and developing stock markets to diver-sify the sources of capital on the other, are healthy developments for the balance sheets of domestic banks and corporations. Well-developed stock and bond markets, by allowing opportunities to diversify the sources of capital, contribute to reducing the volatility of the financial system. However, foreign access to domestic stocks and bond markets should be liberalized before freeing the domestic banks to fund themselves offshore.

For the purpose of ensuring liquidity at short notice, commercial credit lines can be negotiated. These can be tapped in periods of plummeting investor sentiment, when withdrawal of capital begins. When international banks and investors refuse to roll over their loans, the financial authorities can use their credit lines as the lender-of-last-resort. Again, for a fee, these lines of credit can be rolled over and made into a standby arrangement, which contributes to the stability of the financial system. These credit facil-ities do not have the "no adverse material change" clause, which allows banks to back out at the time of a veritable crisis.

Although all these arrangements can be helpful in managing a crisis situation, there is no substitute for building credible policy-making institu-tions. This is necessary, although not sufficient, to limit volatility in a financially globalizing world. Risk of a crisis is inversely proportional to the credibility of fiscal and monetary institutions in an emerging market economy. If, over the years, these institutions have accumulated sufficient credibility and goodwill of the market, this will decisively contribute to the stability. This condition applies to both fiscal and monetary institutions (Das, 2003b).

Expenditure reduction versus expenditure switching

In the aftermath of a crisis or an adverse real shock, the affected economy is faced with a difficult decision regarding how much of the impact on the trade balance should be financed by borrowing from the global market. The alternative to it is offsetting the gap by the adjustment of macroeconomic policies. Economic theory provides guidance in this regard. Accordingly, if the crisis is judged to be largely transitory, borrowing from the global capital markets should tide it over. Failing that, official and bilateral sources of finance should be tapped. If a gap in financing persists, the IMF should supply the remaining capital. Undoubtedly the IMF would only lend conditionally, on ensuring that the borrowing emerging market follows sound economic policies and rectifies structural imbalances.

This was the neat theoretical scenario. However, the reality is different. During the crises of the 1980s and 1990s, it was observed that private capital flows from the global market had a penchant to exacerbate the real adverse shocks rather than offsetting them. While theory indicates that global capital inflows should be counter-cyclical, in practice they are pro-cyclical. For instance, during the crises of the early 1980s, contraction in the demand for commodities and the fall in their international prices (which was one of the causes of crisis for the Latin American economies) was followed by a sharp reduction in capital flows to the affected economies, not an increase. In some cases, it appeared that the withdrawal of capital was so large that it seemed to be the principal cause of the crisis.

The initial real adverse shock during the Asian crisis of 1997–1998 was a precipitous fall in global semiconductor prices as well as those of other manufactured goods in 1996. In this case also, the loss in capital inflows seriously weakened the balance of payments in the affected emerging markets. This situation was more than what became known as the "sudden stop" of capital. In Thailand, for instance, a record capital reversal took place. Capital inflows were measured at 18 percent of GDP in 1996, but decreased to a capital outflow of 8 percent of GDP in 1997. Frankel (2003) called it a record reversal of capital flows.

Given these experiences and the pro-cyclical nature of global market capital inflows, policy-makers have shifted from financing to the adjustment of macroeconomic policies. In fact, the initial real adverse shock should imply the possibility of stoppage of capital inflows, as seen above, before planning remedial measures. If this is the real scenario, should the IMF be responsible for the entire external financing needs? This is an important query, because its answer entails key issues of moral hazard, greater involvement of the lending banks in the preparation of the IMF "rescue package," and political willingness of the G-7 economies. On occasions, the larger members of the G-7 have provided financial resources of unprecedented proportions to the crisis-affected emerging economies.

Frankel (2003) has discussed two sets of policy instruments: expenditure-reducing policies and expenditure-switching policies. The former are represented by monetary contraction, and the latter by currency depreciation. The two policies target perfectly the internal balance and external balance respectively. Both currency depreciation and an interest rate rise improve trade balance, making domestic assets more attractive to global investors. A rise in the interest rate reduces expenditure (or the domestic demand for goods) and currency depreciation increases the net foreign demand for domestic goods. The greater the interest rate rise, the less currency depreciation is needed.

Critics of the IMF rescue packages contend that the monetary contractions resulting from the prescriptions of the IMF create recessionary conditions in the crisis-affected emerging markets. The well-publicized counter-opinion is that a policy mix of a lower interest rate with currency depreciation would result in achieving the target of internal balance in the crisis economy, without creating recessionary conditions. In their view, high interest rates are irrelevant because they cannot succeed in attracting global investors when there is a high probability of default in a crisis-affected economy. This may partly be correct. However, Frankel (2003) believed that this is not the most far-reaching correction in the IMF's traditional approach. Even if the high interest rates do not have a large salutary impact over the capital account, the final effect is undoubtedly favorable. In the ultimate analysis, no economy can conceive of attracting global capital by lowering interest rates.

Strong evidence is available to show that currency depreciations are contractionary in the short term, and the contractionary effect may last for two years. Textbooks provide many, sometimes up to ten, contractionary effects of currency depreciations.[24] Post-depreciation difficulties of servicing hard currency debt were found to be most difficult during the crises of the 1990s. They also caused a strong contraction in the crisis-affected economy. Notwithstanding these negative effects, the long-term impact of currency depreciation was positive. In general it stimulated net exports, and therefore, from the second year onwards when exports begin to accelerate, the overall effect on GDP growth was positive.

However, in some of the recent crisis economies, exports did not accelerate as expected. This reason was because the supply-side machinery was in disarray, which in turn was caused by corporate financial distress. Trade credit became unavailable, imports became more expensive in terms of domestic currency, and production targets – even for much needed exports – could not be met. This apparently came under the rubric of expenditure reduction, not expenditure switching. No matter how a rescue package is designed, there is little possibility of escape from a short-term recession. Should this be taken to mean that the financing-versus-adjustment framework is no longer relevant? The framework is still relevant, but only for a short period after the real adverse shock has struck the economy and before a financial or currency crisis is precipitated.

6 Summary and conclusions

In a financially globalized world, when financial flows take place easily and smoothly into and out of the emerging market economies, two outcomes are plausible; first, that these economies benefit from more investment and reduce their current account deficit, and second, that these economies face boom–bust cycles. Global capital inflows also tend to inflate real exchange rates, which have several domestic and external problematic influences. At the beginning of the twenty-first century, financial instability and volatility became one of the most significant challenges faced by emerging market economies.

The immediate macroeconomic costs of the financial sector problems have been large in terms of foregone growth, inefficient financial intermediation, and impaired public confidence in the financial system. Financial conflagrations became too frequent, too devastating, and too contagious to be ignored by investors, bankers, financial and monetary policy-makers, and the financial firefighters in multilateral institutions. Financial sector problems not only have macroeconomic costs but also entail high financial and social costs. The IMF was roundly criticized for its poor understanding of the causal factors behind the crises and contagions, as well as for its inability to devise optimal rescue packages for the affected economies

Financial stability in an emerging market economy has a direct bearing on two conditions; first, the macroeconomic and structural conditions in the real economy, and second, the financial system *per se* – that is, how robust the financial markets and institutions are. How the real economy operates is an important and relevant, if not a critical, issue that determines the stability or lack of it in the financial markets. The BIS has defined a robust financial system as one that can stand the so-called "test of the market."

Although both domestic and global factors can cause financial and macroeconomic instability, it is difficult to determine which one of them is the bigger villain. Several financial globalization related factors and those of domestic origin have been identified in this chapter. A serious downside of financial globalization is the contagion effect. There can be myriad channels – economic, non-economic, financial – for the crisis to spill over to the neighboring countries. Contagions are real and frequent, although it does not mean that all the emerging market crises have to have a contagion effect. The crises of 2000–2002 did not have any contagion effects.

For the purposes of reducing instability and controlling volatility, emerging market economies have been trying to strengthen and harmonize their financial regulatory infrastructure in a concerted manner. The process of creation and diffusion of financial regulations has undergone discernible transformation over the last half century; in particular a lot of new developments have taken place in this area over the last two decades. The same observation applies to the process of forging legal and regulatory instruments. Non-governmental bodies were born to create codes, standards, and rules of acceptable behavior, and took over what had been considered the domain of the governments in the past. Two of the modes of convergence of regulatory harmonization that came into vogue over the past two decades were the principle of minimum harmonization, and the reputationally induced disciplines. They have been the most important pillars of the current episode of financial globalization.

During the post-Bretton-Woods era, emerging market economies have not been able to benefit optimally from financial globalization because the process of financial globalization created many exchange rate related problems. Many of these problems were based on the fact that financial markets, both domestic and international, are far from perfect. Although emerging markets tried adopting a range of exchange rate arrangements, in many cases they had only limited success, and these economies continued to be bruised by crises. The flexible exchange rate arrangement has become popular among these economies, but monetary authorities in the emerging markets tended to apply it in an overly cautious manner in practice and therefore were not able to benefit from the autonomy of monetary policy. The concept of the "blessed trinity" promises improvements in their exchange rate arrangements. It entails having (1) a strong international currency, (2) a flexible exchange rate, and (3) sound institutions. If the "blessed trinity" is achieved, the emerging markets can integrate well with the global capital markets and take advantage of all the potential benefits, without falling prey to the triple crises. Of the three characteristics of the blessed trinity, the first is the most onerous and time-consuming to achieve.

6 Financial globalization and the contagion effect

1 Introduction

To be sure, a serious downside of financial globalization is the so-called "contagion effect." The communicable nature of recent financial and currency crises has been the center of economic discussions among academics as well as in policy circles. The contagion effect implies that a crisis generated in one emerging market economy is transmitted to another seemingly unrelated emerging market, if the economy is open and integrated with the global economy. In fact, the crisis may be transmitted to the whole region, even spread globally. For instance, the crisis and sovereign default in the Russian Federation in August 1998 triggered a pervasive widening of credit spreads and generalized risk aversion in the financial markets.[1] It also triggered fragilities in German banks and helped to provoke Long-Term Capital Market's (LTCM's) near-bankruptcy in September 1998, before spreading its impact around the globe.[2] By the end of 1998, as noted above, the impact of the Russian and LTCM crises combined to increase substantially the volatility in the global securities markets. A reassessment of credit and sovereign risks during this period led to large jumps in credit and liquidity spreads as well as in risk premia in both emerging market and industrial economies. This episode of financial distress has special significance because of its global ramifications (BIS, 1999).[3] Following the Russian crisis and default, many currency markets became inordinately volatile and global security markets seized-up (Loisel and Martin, 2001).

Furthermore, a crisis situation may also be initially generated in one region and affect economies of different sizes and structures in other regions, even around the globe. As seen in Chapter 2, with the progress in financial globalization there was a rapid expansion of international liquidity and an enormous increase in liquid assets available to participants in the global financial markets. There was an explosion of global capital flows in the early 1990s in the emerging market economies. However, this turned into a stampede of investors out of these very high-performing emerging market economies in 1997 (see Table 2.1). So many emerging market economies have been affected by crises and their spillover effects that some noted economists, who are respected as opinion leaders, have begun to advocate turning back the clock to the period when controls existed on transborder capital flows. Stigliz (1999), for instance, believes that the euphoria among the global investors has become excessive and needs to be cooled off by appropriate policy constraints.

2 Contagion

To describe such propagation of crisis, metaphors such as "sneeze of an economy causing pneumonia in another" were used. In professional writings this phenomenon has been given several disease-related names – like 'flu and a virus – by economists. The 1997 Asian crisis was called the Asian 'flu, the 1998 Russian sovereign default was referred to as the Russian cold, the 1999 Brazilian crisis earned the name of Brazilian fever, and the NASDAQ crash of 2000 was referred to as the NASDAQ rash. Interdependence, spillover, cross-market links, and co-movement were the other unpejorative expressions used for such propagation of emerging market crises.

Many analysts described this pattern of spread of economic and financial shocks as a contagion. The dictionary meaning of the term "contagion" is "a disease transmitted by direct or indirect contact," or "a communicable disease," or "a harmful corrupting influence." The use of the term contagion, albeit recent, has come to stand for the transmission of economic malaise across economies, regions, and globally. Before 1997, the term contagion was used only in the medical profession. A Lexis-Nexis search for scholarly articles on contagion brought forward only medical papers, not papers in economics relating to the turmoil in domestic and global financial markets. Why and how a country-specific or region-specific crisis has such widespread effect has been extensively studied by international economists. What the various macroeconomic, microeconomic, trade-related, financial, and even non-economic channels of transmission are, and how they operate, has become one of the new areas of intellectual curiosity among the economists of various genres, like macro, international and financial economists.[4]

Although comparison of the propagation of recent emerging market crises to the spread of a communicable disease seems an exaggeration, there is indeed some logic to it. For instance, contagion is an economic and financial disease which causes contraction in income levels and a fall in the standard of living in emerging market economies, and is responsible for extremely high social costs. Contagions have resulted in massive losses to individual emerging market economies, regional economies, and, on occasions, the global economy. They have caused serious economic dislocations in many cases, and are as devastating as the spread of major diseases in the past. In addition, the term contagion implies the transmission of a disease.

As the Thai crisis spread to the other neighboring Asian economies and then beyond, it became imperative to examine both what initiated the crisis in Thailand and how the crisis spread to other emerging market economies, which were seemingly performing well until that point in time. This indeed spawned an appearance of an economic crisis propagating through "direct or indirect contact" among economies. Questions arose, such as: could a currency crisis spread through direct links, like bilateral trade flows? Could it spread through an indirect link, like variations in investor sentiments? Soon these became debatable issues in the economic profession (Claessens and Forbes, 2001). In many recent cases of contagions, emerging market economies with strong fiscal current account balances have been adversely affected and driven to a crisis, or to the brink of one. It has been argued that a crisis initiated in another economy should not have affected them because of their strong fundamentals, and they blamed their subsequent difficulties on the "harmful corrupting influence" of investors in the crisis economy. Such a tendency is normally associated with a contagion (Claessens and Forbes, 2001), and thus the use of the term for the phenomenon of the spread of recent emerging market crises is rational and valid.

In the wake of the ERM (Exchange Rate Mechanism of the European Economic Community) crisis of 1992–1993, when several European economies had to depart from the ERM, issues related to the spread of crisis drew some scholarly attention. Following the peso crisis in Mexico in 1994, these issues were again considered. It was not until the Thai crisis in July 1997 that these issues drew focused attention from the policy-makers and general public who were the victims of contagions. The Thai crisis set in motion a serious contagion effect, which spread to several hitherto high-performing Asian economies in a short time span. Soon there were other crises with a menacing contagion effect, inflicting massive economic and social costs. Korea, a relatively recent member of the Organization for Economic Co-operation and Development (OECD), with relatively strong fundamentals, was impacted by the events in Thailand. The October 1997 stock market crisis in Hong Kong SAR spread to the Philippines and Singapore among the emerging markets, and France, Italy, and the United Kingdom (UK) among the industrial economies.[5] The December 1997 depreciation of the Korean won adversely affected currencies and stock markets in many countries around the globe, and several of them had few direct trade or financial links with the Korean economy. High degrees of co-movements have been observed in the emerging market economies in the past, particularly those in the Western hemisphere. These co-movements in the Latin American emerging markets were documented by Forbes and Rigobon (2000). The sovereign default in Russia and collapse of the ruble in December 1998 led to a sharp (over 50 percent) decline in the Brazilian stock market in mid-January 1999 (see Chapter 1, Section 5). The Argentinian stock market also fell, but less than that of Brazil. The

Brazilian crisis adversely affected far-flung and unrelated Bulgaria. These are some of the prominent recent examples of transmission of crises, or the contagion effect.

There have been a long debate regarding whether the contagion effect really exists. Experiences of the preceding quarter-century show that contagions are real and frequent. They were a defining feature of the emerging market economies in the 1990s. However, an amber signal is essential here. While contagions exist, it should not be taken to imply that all the country-specific or region-specific crises normally result in a contagion effect. The 1999 Ecuadorian crisis and sovereign default did not cause any contagion, and the same applies to the two recent crises in Turkey and Argentina (see Chapter 5, Section 3). While some crises do cause contagion, others do not. Notwithstanding the fact that the interest in contagion is of recent origin, extensive empirical and theoretical literature exists on testing whether contagion exists, and how one infected emerging market economy can transmit its currency, economic, and financial malaise to another. This extensive literature has been summarized by several recent studies, including those by Baig and Goldfajn (1999); Corsetti *et al.* (2000b, 2001a); Claessens *et al.* (2001b); Forbes and Rigobon (2001); Pericoli and Sbracia (2001).[6]

3   Of definitions

Fundamental linkages between economies are generally deemed to be responsible for the creation of a contagion effect. There can be myriad channels for the crisis to spill over to the neighboring countries or beyond.[7] Uniformity in the understanding or definition of a contagion has so far eluded the researchers in this area, and contagion has been taken to mean different things in different studies. What constitutes a contagion, and which situation, although contagion-like in appearance, is not a contagion, has not always been easy to pin down. For instance, emerging market crises could be synchronous across a country group or a region because of a common adverse shock, like a spurt in oil prices or in LIBOR rates.[8] Hernandez and Valdes (2001) called contagions "simultaneous bad luck," while Masson (1999) called them "monsoonal shock," or global shocks affecting a large number of (or all) economies simultaneously. Large common shocks would naturally raise the magnitude of cross-country co-movements in asset prices; however, rising cross-country correlations during a period of financial and economic turmoil is not necessarily an evidence of contagion.

Distinction has been made between fundamental-based contagions and a "real" or "true" contagion. The former arises when the infected emerging market economy is linked to the other emerging markets through trade and finance channels, whereas a real or true contagion arises when common external shocks and various channels of potential interconnection either are not present, or have been kept under control. According to Kaminski and Reinhart (2003a), a real contagion is associated with rational or irrational herding behavior on the part of global investors. Herd behavior leads to unwarranted contagion and spreads a crisis to an economy that otherwise would not have experienced a crisis or speculative attack. The consequences of momentum trading, noise trading, bandwagon effects, and short-termism[9] are similar.

"Knowing that there is a crisis elsewhere increases the probability of a crisis at home" is a simple definition of contagion adopted by Kaminsky and Reinhart (2003a). Sbracia and Zaghini (2001a, 2001b) agree with this definition. In their definition, a broad range of country-idiosyncratic fundamentals (like real exchange rate and reserves) and common fundamentals (like LIBOR rates) are controlled. According to this definition, contagion occurs through trade or financial links that give rise to "fundamental-based" spillovers. Using a similar definition, Eichengreen *et al.* (1997) studied contagion in 20 OECD economies and concluded that contagion could be explained more by trade links among economies than by any other channel of transmission. A similar and simple, if not simplistic, definition was posited by Hernandez and Valdes (2001), who defined a contagion as "country A gets into trouble because country B gets into trouble." "Trouble" in their definition implies a currency depreciation, a moratorium or other traumatic regime changes, or milder economic and financial problems, which lead an economy into a state in which global capital inflows become scarce. The scarcity of inflows is reflected by both their volume and prices. Thus, several researchers in this area of inquiry concur with the definition posited by Kaminsky and Reinhart (2003a).

Another concept of contagion at variance with the one presented in the preceding paragraph defines it as "the propagation of shocks in excess of that which can be explained by fundamentals."[10] One could take a close-to-real-life example to explain what could, or could not, be called a contagion according to this definition. If country A suffers an external shock, which, say, adversely affects its currency, this could have an adverse effect on the neighboring country B, or even countries B and C. The exports of the country originally affected by the external shock will become more competitive (because of currency depreciation) in the third-country market than those of neighbors B and C, which are assumed to be A's competitors in that market. This will work toward reducing the earnings and dividends of firms in countries B and C. As this transmission of the initial shock from A to B and C can be directly and logically explained by way of fundamentals,[11] it cannot be considered a contagion effect according to the above definition. This illustration is close to reality. During the Asian crisis, after Thailand depreciated the baht, the Malaysian ringgit came under pressure because both Malaysia and Thailand exported similar products to large regional markets, namely Japan, Hong Kong SAR, and Singapore.

Similarly, in the case of the Russian sovereign default affecting Brazilian stock (noted in Section 1), this could be considered a contagion because there was no fundamental link between the two emerging market economies. They did not compete in the same product lines in the third-country market, and they were not linked in the financial markets through common lending banks. However, deeper analysis reveals that there *was* a link, which was neither direct nor readily visible. During the crisis in the Russian Federation, the International Monetary Fund (IMF) responded in a certain manner while designing a rescue package, which gave the financial market participants an inkling of how the IMF would possibly react to the Brazilian crisis. This learning process conveyed valuable information regarding the short-term future of emerging markets that depreciated their currency or defaulted on their international obligations to the market participants, which in turn shaped their response to the crisis in Brazil. The information channel acted as a fundamental – if it can be called a fundamental – in this case. This illustration leads one to a valid query: can spillover of information from one emerging market economy to another cause a contagion?

However, the fundamental-based definition has a problem: if we go by this definition, how do we measure a fundamental, particularly in the short term? An even bigger issue than this is the lack of agreement on which cross-country linkages constitute fundamentals. To be sure, these are significant problematic issues. To circumvent them, alternative and easily testable definitions of contagion have been adopted. An early such definition classifies contagion as a shift or change in how external shocks are propagated during relatively normal or tranquil periods, and during periods of crisis. Another old definition of contagion includes only the transmission of crisis through specific channels, like herding or, *à la* Friedman (1999a), "electronic herding," or irrational investor behavior. Another simple and direct definition is a "significant increase in cross-market linkages after a shock to an individual country (or country group)." That cross-market linkages can be measured is one definitive advantage of this definition. Correlation in asset returns and probability of a speculative attack can easily be measured statistically, and therefore this definition had high utility for researchers and was widely accepted by analysts until the crises of the latter half of the 1990s broke loose. Other definitions of contagion have continued to pour in. For a short time the World Bank had a website dedicated to its definitions, although consensus in this regard is yet to be reached (Forbes and Rigobon, 2000).

Dungey *et al.* (2002) adopted the following definition: a contagion reflects "the spillover effect of unanticipated contemporaneous shock across countries." Favero and Giavazzi (2002) proposed an identical definition, while Sachs *et al.* (1996) viewed contagion as unanticipated, or residual, shock. These definitions are in complete contrast to those who think of contagion as the spillover effect of anticipated shocks across economies. Definitions proposed by Forbes and Rigobon (2000) and

Eichengreen *et al.* (1997) fall into this category. Masson (1999) attributed part of the residual process to multiple equilibria, or "sunspots." When self-fulfilling expectations lead to contagion, they are called sunspots. The multiple equilibria models are consistent with other channels of contagion, like the "wake-up call" theory (cf. Section 5).

4 Empirical and theoretical perspectives on contagion

Both in empirical and theoretical literature, there are disagreements and controversies regarding the concept of contagion. It has been explored in applications to various financial asset markets in different streams of literature. In Section 3, we saw the variety in definitions of contagion. The variety in views and approaches persists. Claessens *et al.* (2001b) have provided an overview of literature on this issue.

A large part of the extensive empirical and theoretical literature on the contagion effect, which has been alluded to above, does agree on certain basics. One such conclusion is that a contagion follows a crisis. The popular measure of a contagion in the empirical studies is estimating asset price co-movements across markets, or a cross-market correlation coefficient on returns. If one measures correlation coefficients on returns in two emerging markets, first in a tranquil period and then in a period of crisis, and compares the two, and if the latter is found to be higher, then the contagion has taken place. Most studies agree that periods of crisis coincide with high volatility of asset prices as well as high covariance of returns across national markets. Many studies also conclude that, on average, correlation between market returns is higher and increases during crises.[12] Put differently, the crisis transmission mechanism tends to strengthen after an emerging market is struck by a crisis.

It is not necessary that in a real life situation a contagion be propagated by only one channel. Various channels can operate simultaneously, with each crisis having some prominent and some partially active or semi-dormant channels operating during the propagation. The empirical literature on contagion has attempted to identify the different channels of transmission in various crises using alternative methodologies. Some studies attempted to identify the macroeconomic characteristics of crisis-infected economies before and after a crisis (cf. Section 5), and many emerging markets were found to report poor macroeconomic performance after a crisis struck another economy. Some of them soon fell into a crisis of their own.

By focusing on macroeconomic fundamentals, Sachs *et al.* (1996) identified which emerging market economies performed poorly after the Tequila crisis in Mexico in 1994. They concluded that initial exchange rate overvaluation and excessive amount of bank credit creation adversely affected the post-crisis cross-country performances. It could therefore be rationally inferred that contagion was driven by initial state of macroeconomic fundamentals in these emerging market economies. Following the Tequila crisis, empirical studies conducted during the mid-1990s assigned a lot of importance to the role played by macroeconomic fundamentals in the transmission of shocks, although subsequently this line of logic was abandoned in favor of other channels like trade and financial links.

Most theoretical thinkers now take a different tack. Some of the recent models have focused on competitive currency depreciations for providing an explanation for the bunching up of crisis-infected emerging market economies. These emphasize trade as the prime causal factor behind the spread of contagion in a group of emerging market economies, either bilateral trade or that with the other common trade partner economies. When one emerging market economy depreciates under the pressure of its domestic (or even external) problems, the other regional economies find it costly not to follow it if they have common trading partners and/or if they have a large volume of bilateral trade with the depreciating economy. The cost that the non-depreciating emerging economy incurs is in terms of loss of competitiveness of its exports and, therefore, loss of output and eventually deceleration in GDP growth rate. Thus viewed, according to this set of models, a high volume of trade among the economies that tend to depreciate in a synchronized manner should be an outstanding feature of the contagion-infected economies.

Another set of models emphasized not trade in goods and services, but trade in financial assets in an environment of information asymmetry. The fixed cost of compiling, processing, and analyzing market- and firm-specific information is high, and in an emerging market context there is never enough of this information available, which gives rise to frequent irrational herding behavior. This family of models suggests that the channel of transmission is essentially provided by the global diversification of financial portfolios of institutional investors (Calvo and Mendoza, 1998). This line of logic suggests that the emerging market economies with a large volume of internationally traded financial assets and more liquid markets are likely to be more vulnerable to the contagion effect. Asset returns would be the link that could bring down an emerging market economy, if they exhibit a high degree of co-movement with the asset returns in the crisis-infected emerging market.

Several models, as well as empirical literature, suggest that the evidence of contagion is of "sunspot variety," *à la* Kaminsky and Reinhart (2003a). Few studies delve into underlying causes. Some studies have attempted to discriminate among bilateral trade links, while other have intensively studied issues in a broad country context. Some of them have tried to explain contagion on the basis of pair-wise correlations in stock returns. A good number of empirical studies have given a lot of importance to trade linkages in the propagation of crisis, both regionally and globally.

A commonly used technique by modelers was an autoregressive conditional heteroscedasticity (ARCH) framework, which estimates the variance–covariance transmission mechanism across emerging markets. This technique shows how volatility is transmitted from one emerging market to another. Another set of papers used simplifying assumptions and exogenous events to simplify a model and directly measure changes in the propagation mechanism of the contagion. Studies that used this technique concluded that a crisis in one country increases the probability of a crisis occurring elsewhere in the world, particularly in the same region (Forbes and Rigobon, 2000). Other than these commonly used techniques, a variety of different econometric techniques were also used by researchers to test whether contagion occurred during a certain financial or currency crisis.

5 Transmission mechanism

As alluded to in Section 4, there are variegated transmission channels through which the contagion effect spreads. Identifying the relevant contagion channel is vitally important from a policy perspective, as devising an appropriate policy prescription necessarily depends upon the nature of transmission mechanism of a contagion. If the trade links between the emerging markets were the culprits, the defense mechanism would include diversification of trade, or fixing the exchange rate. Regional co-operation in the form of monetary union would also be helpful. If the banking and financial channel was responsible for the transmission of contagion, the defense measure would include the imposition of prudential accounting regulations, and strengthening market supervision norms.

One of the lessons from the recent financial crises is that non-economic factors like herding are frequently behind the propagation of contagions. Co-movements in real exchange rates and equity prices in many crises of the past could not be explained by mere fundamental linkages. However, it was observed that the economies that did not have fundamental linkages were also affected by contagion. How could this be explained? A rational explanation was that it was the herd behavior that caused investors to exit from economies that did not share fundamental linkages. Although herd behavior has high social costs, from an individual investor's point of view going with the herd is a logical way to control losses. Schmukler and Zoido-Lobaton (2001) pointed out that:[13]

> the issue of herding behavior is of multiple equilibria. If markets regard a country's state to be good, then large capital inflows can take place. If markets judge the country as being in a bad state, then rapid capital outflows and a crisis can take place. In a world of "multiple" equilibria, external shocks can quickly force the economy to shift from a "good" to a "bad" equilibrium.

Similarities in macroeconomic fundamentals

Emerging market economies with comparable macroeconomic weaknesses or poor fundamentals may propagate crisis from one economy to another, or may enter a multiple equilibria zone. When economies with similar macroeconomic weaknesses suffer from an adverse external shock, a crisis precipitates due to poor macroeconomic fundamentals. This may well be a case of simultaneous bad luck or common negative shock in a group of emerging markets. In the second and more interesting scenario, owing to information asymmetry global investors are likely to treat all such economies as equal. When one of them falls victim to a crisis, there is information spillover regarding the others with similar macroeconomic circumstances, which may be reflected in both broadening credit spreads and drastic reduction in capital inflows. This is known as the "wake-up call" effect. The final outcome is that global investors may pull out of all the emerging markets showing similarities in their macroeconomic fundamentals because they expect the same crisis situation to develop in them after an indefinite time lag. In the process, a self-fulfilling crisis may soon develop in the economies where a crisis situation was not necessarily a short-term probability.

A new trend among the regional economies is the tendency for co-movement among regional stock markets, and this has been on the rise since the 1990s. Brooks and Del Negro (2002) found that co-movement across national stock markets has increased sharply since the mid-1990s. This could well be due to economic integration among the regional economies and among the regional financial markets. Greater economic integration among regions may also be caused by the globalization-related institutional changes that have occurred over the last two decades. These new trends may have in turn contributed to increased co-movements in the emerging market economies, and transmission of contagion.

Banking and financial channel

Domestic banking crises in the past have caused financial distress in other emerging market economies. The reverse has also occurred – that is, a currency crisis abroad has caused a run on the domestic banks.[14] There are many channels through which banks can transmit a contagion. In a financially integrated world, bank investments tend to be widely, sometimes globally, spread. Like other financial institutions, they can easily transfer shocks through portfolio rebalancing decisions. Besides, bank loans are typically based on the collateral provided by the borrowers. If a crisis – no matter what kind – reduces the market value of stocks in a country, the firms and economies that were using those stocks as collateral to back their liabilities are forced to "mark to market," otherwise they may face cuts in their credit lines. Thus, crisis in one emerging market adversely affects the others.

Often emerging market economies in a region have strong financial links through common banks servicing the needs of a particular region. In many cases, there is a single common creditor country (or country group) for a region. For instance, Japanese banks traditionally served the emerging markets of Asia. Lending by Japanese banks to Asian economies was as profligate as that which led to the collapse of the Japanese real estate market in the late 1980s. In the past, the US banks likewise served the emerging markets of the Western hemisphere, although this relationship has weakened since the Mexican crisis of 1994. Western European banks have served the Russian Federation and Eastern European emerging market economies. If a bank (or group of banks) is confronted by rising non-performing loans (NPLs) in one country, worsening its "value at risk," it will call in its loan from this troubled economy. There is a high probability that the bank will try and balance its portfolio by reducing the overall risk to its assets by retrenching in all the emerging market economies of the region. Also, banks are required to comply with the capital adequacy ratio, which again requires them to withdraw from other emerging markets when they are faced with high levels of NPLs in one economy. The final outcome can be a credit crunch in several emerging market economies in a synchronized manner. Depending upon the level of NPLs, banks may have to embark on recapitalization. It is likely that it would stop loaning until its balance sheet begins to look healthy.

Sbracia and Zagini (2001a, 2001b) regard the presence of a common lending bank(s) as being "the most important source of vulnerability." Although only one example is presented here, a great deal of anecdotal evidence is available to show that common creditor banks do function as a channel for contagion to spread from an infected emerging market economy to a region. In mid-1997, before the Thai crisis, 54 percent of Thai liabilities were to the Japanese banks, which were also a major lending group for the region. Several large emerging markets of Asia, although not the Philippines, were heavily dependent on credit lines from the Japanese banks.[15] On their part, the Japanese banks found that their Thai exposure was large by any measure. As the Thai crisis unraveled, Japanese banks began calling in their short-term loans, not only in Thailand but also in other emerging markets in Asia. As a good proportion of the loans were of short-term maturity, withdrawal of loans from the region was easy. According to one view, capital flows from the Japanese banks and institutional investors had created an asset-price bubble in Thailand, and possibly in some other Asian emerging markets. Bursting this bubble caused enormous instability in these economies (King, 2001). In a short span of time, smooth inflows of credit to Asia became large outflows. Withdrawal of funds from the five emerging market economies, namely Indonesia, Korea, Malaysia, the Philippines, and Thailand, was large and rapid. Statistical data compiled by Kaminsky and Reinhart (2003a) show that Asian emerging markets received $50 billion from the Japanese banks in 1996. In 1997 this amount was minus $21 billion, making it a year of large retrenchment and causing a liquidity crunch in Asia. Similarly, during the 1982 debt crisis, when the Latin American economies fell like dominoes, the large money-centered American banks played the role played by the Japanese banks in Asia in 1997.

One of the basic functions of the banking system is the transformation of maturities. Banks transform instruments with short maturities (offered to depositors) into those with long maturities that other economic agents need. This maturity transformation function leaves banks vulnerable to runs, which can potentially be transmitted to the entire domestic banking system. Models of multiple equilibria reveal that contagions occur through this channel because a crisis in any emerging economy modifies the information set available to all economic agents (Sbracia and Zagini, 2001a). This happened in Thailand in 1997.

Instances of excessive or over-borrowing by some emerging market economies and excessive or over-lending by some indiscreet banks were found in the recent emerging market crises. Implicit or explicit government guarantees are the reason behind frequent cases of over-borrowing and over-lending. Confidence in the multilateral rescue packages and the belief that some borrowers are "too big to fail" also has the same effect. The over-borrowed financial resources were often channeled into risky projects, making the borrowing economy vulnerable to international shocks and sudden reversals of capital flows. When a crisis is created in this manner in one emerging market economy, it tends to spread to the other economies of the region in a short span of time through the banking channel.

Financial channel transmission also occurs through market practices. Institutional investors follow the practice of treating economies as complementary assets. Fund managers follow certain rules of thumb, according to which a negative shock in country A reduces demand for financial assets in country B. When the stock market declines in one country, fund managers may pull resources out of the other to rebalance their portfolios. This becomes a simple crisis transmission mechanism.

Cross-market hedging

We have seen the role of the common lending banks in the propagation of contagion, but the banks are not the only organizations lending to emerging market economies. Portfolio investment increased substantially and peaked in the mid-1990s. Institutional investors have become one of the most important categories of global investors and, in their endeavor to diversify their portfolios, linked several emerging economies in a significant manner. An important lesson of the Latin American crisis of 1994–1995 and the Asian crisis of 1997–1998 is that financial linkages created by the institutional investors form one of the commonest channels that transmit crises and embroil the entire region. In both these crises it was observed that countries were linked through internationally traded financial assets. When banks and institutional investors saw a crisis brewing in one emerging market, they naturally wanted to shift their portfolios. To achieve this objective, they had to sell assets from a third group of countries to hedge their positions, and this caused a downward pressure on the asset value in these countries, in turn developing a crisis-like situation in them. The final result was propagation of the crisis from one to two or three regional emerging markets in a short time span (Das, 2000). Kaminsky and Reinhart (2003a) show that financial sector links via common bank lenders form the most powerful channel of fundamental-based contagion. The high trade- and finance-linked cluster of economies comes next in terms of the contagion effect.

A precondition for this channel of propagation is that the asset markets are sufficiently liquid. For the emerging markets with underdeveloped bond and equity markets, portfolio flows are likely to be trivial because its bonds and equity are not globally traded in sufficient volume. In such emerging markets this channel is not likely to be consequential because of the small quantity of portfolio transactions.

Global bond and equity investment in the emerging market economies varies a great deal from economy to economy. Some, like Brazil, Hong Kong SAR, India, Korea, Malaysia, Mexico, Singapore, and Taiwan, are known for having higher proportions of global investment in their securities markets, while others, like Argentina, China, and the Philippines, are known for having lower levels. Also, there is considerable diversity in the return on assets and the correlation in asset returns across emerging market economies. Kaminsky and Reinhart (2003a) found the highest pair-wise correlations in stock returns among the Asian emerging markets, and relatively lower correlations in the Western hemisphere. There was evidence of high pair-wise correlations between Argentinian and Mexican stock returns. Thus, consideration of liquidity and correlation would suggest the plausibility of a high degree of cross-market hedging across Asian and some Latin American emerging markets. A caveat is essential here. Unlike bank lending, this channel of lending through bonds and equity is of recent origin. Therefore, this channel for the spread of contagion may not be operational in many emerging market economies.

Trade in goods and services

Trade in goods and services is of much longer standing in the emerging market economies than is trade in financial assets. Perhaps that is one reason why the literature on contagion gives a great deal of importance to this channel of transmission of contagion, with researchers believing it to be a strong channel. Trade flows and export shares are important channels of a country's vulnerability to a crisis that originates in a trading partner economy.[16] As set out in the Section 4, the trade channel is believed to operate through two routes, namely direct or bilateral trade among emerging market economies, and competition in third-country market(s). Competing economies may attempt to safeguard their own export competitiveness by depreciating their own currency – the age-old "beggar-thy-neighbor" strategy. Savvy global investors foresee the possibility of such decisions, and cut demand for the assets of the country that is trying to fight this strategy of another emerging market. By so doing they help in the generation of a crisis in that economy and a currency depreciation; in the process they validate their own expectations. Such crises are eventually a self-fulfilling phenomenon. The ERM crises of 1992–1993 were caused in this manner.[17]

Large one-country or two-country common export market(s) for various sub-sets of the emerging market economies are not difficult to identify. For instance, for the Asian emerging markets, Japan is a substantial export destination. Hong Kong SAR and Singapore also receive large volumes of exports from Indonesia, Korea, Malaysia, the Philippines, and Thailand. Likewise, the US is a large importer from the emerging markets of the Western hemisphere, as are Western European economies from the emerging markets of Eastern Europe and the Russian Federation. Although having a common export destination is a necessary condition for competitive currency depreciations and propagation of contagion, it can hardly be called sufficient. Similarity between exporters in their export product lines is another condition that must be fulfilled for contagion to be transmitted through this channel. If one emerging market economy exports a low-technology or agricultural product (say, textiles or bananas), it is difficult to reason how this can affect the export competitiveness of high-technology products (say, CPUs, motherboards or integrated circuits) from another emerging market in the common export destination. Thus, the export composition of the emerging markets plays a crucial role in determining whether the third-country trade link will play a strong role in the propagation of contagion.

Kaminsky and Reinhart (2003a) analyzed the 1994 Tequila crisis in Mexico and the 1997 Asian crisis for their contagion effect, and found that bilateral trade did not seem to work as a strong force behind the propagation of contagion. They found that the share of exports going to other neighboring emerging markets was not large in Asia. Therefore, this bilateral trade channel could only be a weak carrier of contagion during the Asian crisis, although the trade channel could certainly work for groups of Asian economies having competing export lines (like Malaysia and Thailand). Similarly, in the Western hemisphere, on the eve of the Tequila crisis, bilateral trade was not substantial among the neighboring economies. An exception to this was the discernibly large trade among the four-member trade bloc named MERCOSUR,[18] which also had a high degree of trade with Chile. In this context, it cannot be ignored that Argentina and Brazil are not considered to be highly open economies.

Compared to the emerging markets of Asia and Europe they are closed, with ratios of trade as a percentage of GDP far below those recorded in Asia and Europe.

The trade channel can also work through multiplier effects on output and GDP growth in other emerging market economies. Abheysinghe and Forbes (2003) developed a Vector Autoregression (VAR) model to estimate trade linkages and output multiplier effects between most of Asia and its major trading partners. They estimated direct and indirect linkages between the ASEAN-4 (Indonesia, Malaysia, the Philippines, and Thailand), the Asian Newly Industrialized Economies (ANIEs),[19] China, Japan, and the US, and the rest of the OECD group. A series of impulse response functions showed that even if bilateral trade linkages between two countries were weak, a shock to one of them could have a significant impact on the other economies through the indirect impact on other countries' output. Their estimates suggested that indirect cross-country linkages through output multiplier effects are important determinants of how crises are transmitted globally.

FDI flow is another channel that transmits shocks. A crisis or crisis resolution process entails the depreciation of currency. If a crisis-affected emerging market in Asia, Latin America or Eastern Europe depreciates, the neighboring economy immediately comes under pressure because it finds that it is no longer an attractive destination for fresh FDI. Emerging markets are known to compete with each other for attracting FDI flows to maintain their industrial edge. Consequently, when a crisis-affected economy depreciates its currency the neighbor or the linked economy will come under pressure to devalue as well. This could happen to not just one but all the linked economies in the region, setting a wave of currency depreciations in motion.

Non-economic channels or the "lemon" problem

Some buying and selling practices in the financial markets can create crises for emerging markets that have sound fundamentals and little reason for a crisis. The problem of information asymmetry in the global financial markets, compounded by herd behavior, not only creates capital market distortions but also spawns large co-movements across emerging market economies. In the wake of an emerging market crisis, fund managers are forced to download securities to finance possible redemptions by investors. Also, a leveraged investor facing margin calls needs to sell off asset holdings because of the pressing need for liquidity. Given the presence of asymmetric information, when the fund managers and/or investors sell "good" countries to raise the much needed liquidity, the market erroneously perceives that they are downloading poor quality or problem assets. Therefore, these securities are downloaded only at fire-sale value. This is the well known "lemon" problem. When "good" country assets begin to be downloaded at a low price, and the market reads them as being poor quality assets (or lemons), it sets in motion an exodus from these "good" country assets, in turn creating a crisis there.

Neighborhood effect

The neighborhood effect is an eclectic channel, which works through a combination of macroeconomic similarities, banking, financial and trade links, operational characteristics of institutional investors, and self-fulfilling expectations of the investors. Some analysts believe that proximity to the so-called ground-zero economy, the economy where the crisis was born, can be a strong causal factor behind a crisis in the neighboring economies (Glick and Rose, 1999).[20] Once the crisis has been precipitated in the ground-zero economy, the trade and financial channels (represented *inter alia* by competition for capital among emerging markets in the global centers) turn out to be robust predictors of the incidence of crisis in the neighboring emerging markets. Hernandez and Valdes (2001) presented evidence of the relative importance of the neighborhood effect during the Thai, Russian, and Brazilian crises, and their analysis demonstrated that competition for capital in the banking centers was most relevant during the Russian crisis.

De Gregorio and Valdes (2001) analyzed the process of propagation by delving into the behavior of four alternative crisis indicators in a sample of 20 countries during three well-known crises: the 1982–1984 debt crisis in Latin America, the 1994–1995 Mexican crisis, and the 1997–1998 Asian crisis. The contagion effect worked in all these crises. The researchers' objective was twofold: to revisit the transmission channels of crises, and to analyze whether capital controls, exchange rate flexibility, and debt maturity structure affect the extent of contagion. The results indicated that there was a strong neighborhood effect leading to a contagion. Trade links and similarity in pre-crisis growth rates also explain (albeit to a lesser extent) which countries catch the disease early and suffer more from a contagion.

Several analysts believe that, during the Asian crisis, the self-fulfilling expectations of investors played a decisive role.[21] These analysts argued that in June 1997, on the eve of the crisis in Thailand, the economic prospects in Asia were not egregious. The five economies were hardly crisis-bound. However, once the crisis started in Thailand, investors' panic transferred it to other Asian economies. Poorly informed investors re-evaluated their risk associated with Indonesia, Korea, Malaysia, and the Philippines when they saw problems arising in Thailand, and decided to pull out of the neighboring economies. In a world of self-fulfilling investors' expectations, there exist multiple equilibria. Here, an integrated global economy transferred investors' pessimistic expectations to the neighbors, causing contagion. Many analysts believe that the regional transmission of the Thai crisis was unwarranted. The other Asian economies were in a sustainable shape and, in the absence of the Thai crisis could have held their own.

6 Idiosyncrasies and stylized facts

One of the idiosyncrasies of the contagion effect is that it has a strong tendency to be a regional phenomenon rather than global. Several contagion-related studies have found evidence of the existence of this tendency.[22] The rationale is that the trade and banking and financial channels of transmission work in a stronger manner regionally than globally. Second, similarities in macroeconomic fundamentals are found to be more frequent regionally. Third, the neighborhood effect and self-fulfilling expectations of investors apparently have a regional impact. Fourth, while classifying emerging market economies, global investors tend to put all the regional economies in the same pigeonhole and judge them as similar creatures.

The sensitivity of the domestic economy to contagion is non-linear. The scenario of one or two emerging market economies – close and regional or distant and non-regional – suffering from a crisis does not have to mean that the domestic economy is also likely to follow suit. However, if several economies fall victim to a crisis, the probability of a domestic crisis soars significantly. If the crisis-infected economies are several large emerging markets and/or industrial economies, the probability of a domestic increases rises further (Kaminsky and Reinhart, 2003a).

Using the old typology – of the center and periphery – Kaminsky and Reinhart (2003b) proposed some stylized plausible routes for the contagion effect. Although the age-old concept of center and periphery was propounded by Sir Arthur Lewis in his famous theory of economic growth half a century ago, Kaminsky and Reinhart (2003b) assigned somewhat different meanings to the two terms. In their scheme of things, the center stands for countries that house the largest financial centers, like New York, London, Berlin, and Tokyo, while the periphery comprises the emerging market economies and the other developing economies. They posit that there are three patterns in the propagation of external shocks: (1) from a periphery economy to another; (2) from a periphery country to another, via a center economy; and (3) from a center economy to a periphery economy.

In the first case, if the two emerging market economies have direct trade and banking and financial links, the transmission of shocks can easily take place from one to the other. Some recent examples of this kind of transmission mechanism include the impact of the 1997 Asian crisis on Chilean exports, and the contractionary influence on Argentina of the 1999 Brazilian currency depreciation. Banking and financial links transmit shocks directly from one periphery economy to another. For instance, in 1994 the

Costa Rican banks used to borrow from the Mexican banks. As soon as the crisis struck Mexico, this source of finance dried up for Costa Rica, transmitting the financial shock directly and immediately.

In the second case, instead of direct transmission, shocks are transmitted via a center economy. Several examples of this transmission mechanism have been observed. In Section 3 of this chapter, we saw that Malaysian and Thai exports of identical products to their common market destinations (Japan, Hong Kong SAR, and Singapore) caused problems for Malaysia as soon as the Thai baht was depreciated. The crisis spread from Thailand to Malaysia via Japan. It also seems entirely plausible that the Russian virus may have spread to LTCM through Wall Street. Given the information asymmetry and the liquidity problems in the financial center, when Russia defaulted on its bonds the leveraged investors who were facing margin calls began selling their asset holdings at fire-sale prices. Soon a serious "lemon" problem arose, and the cost had to be borne by the likes of LTCM.

In the third case, transmission of shocks from the center to the periphery economies may occur due to changes in interest rates and regulatory requirements in the center economy. In July 1998, when Salomon Brothers closed down their bond arbitrage desk, this adversely affected the bond market liquidity for the emerging market economies. It made the bond markets less resilient.[23]

7   Summary and conclusions

The contagion effect is considered to be a serious downside of financial globalization. Contagion implies that a crisis generated in one emerging market economy is transmitted to another seemingly unrelated emerging market, if the economy is open and integrated with the global economy.

Although comparison of the propagation of recent emerging market crises to the spread of a communicable disease seems to be an exaggeration, there is indeed some logic to it. For instance, contagion is an economic and financial disease that causes a reduction in income levels and a fall in the standard of living in emerging market economies, and is responsible for extremely high social costs. Contagions have resulted in massive losses to individual emerging market economies, regional economies, and, on occasions, to the global economy. They have been as devastating as the spread of major diseases in the past. In addition, the term "contagion" implies the transmission aspect of a disease.

It has long been debated whether the contagion effect really exists. The experiences of the preceding quarter-century show that contagions are real and frequent. However, an amber signal is essential here. While contagions exist, this should not be taken to imply that all the country-specific or region-specific crises normally result in a contagion effect.

Uniformity in the understanding or definition of a contagion has so far eluded the analysts in this area. Contagion has been taken to mean different things in different studies. What constitutes a contagion and which situation, although contagion-like in appearance, is not a contagion has not always been easy to pin down.

One of the many definitions of contagion is: knowing that there is a crisis elsewhere increases the probability of a crisis at home. Distinction has been made between fundamental-based contagions and "real" or "true" contagions. Herd behavior leads to unwarranted contagion, and spreads a crisis to an economy which otherwise would not have experienced a crisis or speculative attack. The consequences of momentum trading, noise trading, bandwagon effects, and short-termism are similar.

In both empirical and theoretical literature, one finds that there are disagreements and controversies regarding the concept of contagion. This has been explored in applications to various financial asset markets in different streams of literature. There are variegated transmission channels through which the contagion effect spreads, and identifying the relevant contagion channel is vitally important from a policy perspective because devising an appropriate policy prescription necessarily depends upon the nature of the transmission mechanism. In this chapter we have discussed the following six transmission channels: similarities in macroeconomic fundamentals; banking and financial channels; cross-market hedging; trade in goods and services; non-economic channels or the "lemon" problem; and the neighborhood effect.

It has been observed in the past that contagions have a strong tendency to be regional phenomena rather than global. Several contagion-related studies have found evidence of the existence of this tendency.[24] The rationale is that the trade and banking and financial channels of transmission work in a stronger manner regionally than globally. Also, the sensitivity of the domestic economy to contagion is non-linear.

7 Global financial architecture and financial and regulatory infrastructure

1 Global financial architecture

Robert Rubin, the erstwhile Treasury Secretary of the United States, made a speech in 1998 calling for measures to "strengthen the international financial architecture." The metaphor he used was enthusiastically adopted by the academic and policy-making community, and has since survived in the academic writings on this issue as accepted jargon. However, it was an inapt – if not completely incorrect – metaphor. The global financial system is not quite an architect's blueprint; if anything, it is an excellent example of what the Japanese call *kaizen*, meaning an incrementally evolving phenomenon, improving marginally but continuously in stages with time. Pressures from market participants and those from emerging market and Group of 7 (G-7) governments have been responsible for this continual, if marginal, improvement in the global financial architecture. Lessons of the past are the second source of continual improvement in and evolution of the global financial system. Those who created the Bretton-Woods system drew on the lessons of the Great Depression.

The global financial system, as it presently exists, "is made up of a dense network of social, economic and financial institutions" (Eichengreen, 2003). While there is no widely agreed and tersely stated definition of what precisely constitutes global financial architecture, the term refers broadly to the framework and set of institutions, structures, and measures that can help to prevent crises or, when faced with one, help manage them better in the more integrated international financial environment. The term "global financial architecture" is also used to describe the institutions, structures, and policies that influence and control the global financial flows, including those to the emerging market economies. These institutions, structures, and policies are also charged with predicting, managing, and preventing macroeconomic instability and crises in the global economy, including those in the emerging market economies.

Any simple or elaborate plan of action for this purpose will necessarily have several facets or components. Such plans will not only include crisis prevention and crisis resolution, but also deal with weaknesses in the international financial system that contribute to the propensity for global instability. The various facets are closely intertwined, and putting one or some of them in place in isolation will not work, or will have limited impact. Readers of these lines should be warned at the outset that global financial architecture is too large a topic to be covered as a part of a chapter. This section only provides readers with a small picture, which is selective and relevant to the title of this book. This treatment is far from exhaustive and complete.

2   Radical transformation

Over the last half-century, since the creation of the Bretton-Woods system, the principal characteristics of the global financial system have undergone radical, albeit somewhat gradual, transformation. There has been an inevitable and desirable evolution. Crockett (2003) called it a transformation "from an administered or government-led to a decentralized or market-led system." This transformation was desirable because, for all their flaws, markets are a more efficient mechanism for resource allocation than any conceivable alternative.

When the allied nations met in 1994 at Bretton Woods, New Hampshire, to design a mechanism for restoring the shattered world economy to health, they created a new financial architecture which covered (1) the exchange rate regime, (2) trade and payments arrangements, (3) the balance of payments adjustment process, (4) international liquidity, and (5) financial market arrangements. The new financial order was based on clear rules laid down in the Treaty establishing the International Monetary Fund (IMF) and the World Bank. The operating characteristics of the monetary system were well defined.[1] The "administered" system was logical and coherent, and served its objective of facilitating the rehabilitation of war-ravaged post-war economies rather well. By the end of the 1950s and early 1960s, most industrial economies had started recording reasonably high rates of economic growth and they liberalized their current accounts. Capital account liberalization was slow to come. The administered system had to work well because there were few possibilities of damage by financial market inefficiencies. As the financial markets were not integrated, the contagion effect originating from problems in one country market to the other markets were limited. Also, as the financial institutions were essentially operating in a benign climate, they had little need to run high risks.

With the passage of time, the administered system revealed its weaknesses. Also, with new developments in the global economy and financial markets this system began to show its irrelevance in some areas. For instance, one of its much discussed problems concerned international liquidity. This was considered a major systemic limitation. That is, it did not have any mechanism to increase the primary liquidity with growth in the global economy, particularly with growth in world trade. Creation of an internationally controlled supply of liquidity in the form of Special Drawing Rights (SDRs) did not take place until the end of the 1960s. Second, as it was essentially a dollar-based system, the holding of dollar reserves had an important role for the global economies. This provoked the ire of other countries, particularly the West Europeans, who begrudged the unique position of the US in the global financial system. According to them, the US was absorbing the resources of the rest of the world and paying only in IOUs. Third, the IMF worried about the so-called "Triffin dilemma," that is, if the accumulation of dollar balances by the treasuries of other countries were to become larger than the US gold reserves, the confidence in conversion of the dollars into gold at pre-declared prices would be called into question, which in turn would undermine this system. Fourth, as world trade grew and an increasing number of countries liberalized their current and capital accounts, the number and size of current account disequilibria were increasing. Correction of these imbalances was a multilateral issue, and was not possible without exchange rate-related problems. Eventually, it was the relaxation of restrictions on capital movements on the one hand and growth and expansion of international financial markets on the other that weakened the administered system and made it look irrelevant.

Between 1971 and 1973, the old financial system collapsed bit by bit. Although the Smithsonian Arrangement was created after 1971, it did not last for long. No attempts to mend or recreate the old system were made after the 1973 oil crisis, when the price of crude oil quadrupled. With this, the global financial system passed a critical stage in its evolutionary phase, and a decentralized or market-led system evolved in place of the old system. The principal characteristics of the global financial system were different under the new system. Unlike the old one, all the key features in the new financial system progressively became subject to market forces – including the exchange rate mechanism, trade and payment arrangements, the current and capital account adjustment process, international liquidity provision, and the financial markets *per se*.[2] As the shift from government to market influence and control was more or less systemic and enveloped virtually all the aspects of global financial operations, some referred to the new system as a "non-system," which was incorrect. The market-based system was not necessarily unsystematic. Classical economic theory has taught us that a market-based system is more efficient than any of its alternatives. However, this theoretical dictum applies with an important proviso: that the conditions for markets to work efficiently are in place. Thus, for the new market-based system it was not so much the system or architecture that was of capital significance as the mechanism needed to make the system work efficiently.

For the market forces to make optimal allocation of resources, it is a necessary precondition that markets are both complete and efficient.

Markets are complete if market participants are able to trade all conceivable claims, actual or contingent, and they are efficient if market prices contain all knowledge and information and do not suffer from information asymmetry. Given these definitions, realistically a market can neither be fully complete nor completely efficient. Markets for contingent claims in all future states of the world do not exist. Also, markets routinely suffer from varying degrees of information asymmetry or the lack of vitally needed information by the market participants.

Under the new market-led system, the financial markets acted swiftly and imaginatively in creating a new and progressively wide range of instruments. This was their contribution to the completeness of the financial markets, without making them fully complete. The wide range of derivative instruments that became available made it possible for the market participants to make contingent transactions on the future outcomes of financial and economic variables. The flip side of this coin is that markets are prone to failure – both at national and at global level.

Advances in game theory have made it easy for us to comprehend why the financial markets are so prone to disequilibrium. This happens partly due to the fact that the assets traded in them provide services over a certain length of time, and also because it is difficult to assess the fundamental value of the assets absolutely correctly. The return on assets depends on the future states of the world and therefore has a strong element of uncertainty built into it. The value is difficult to assess correctly because of the endemic information asymmetries. As the asset values depend upon the collective expectations of future outcomes, a herd mentality and externalities can disturb them seriously. Crockett (2003) asserted that markets could not possibly be conceived to smoothly move to "socially optimal equilibria, even with rational private behavior and in the absence of mistakes of government policy." In a real-life situation, bad policies and the imprudent behavior of economic agents often compounds the problem of the disequilibrium tendencies of the financial markets. It is no secret that unsustainable macroeconomic policies have been behind many recent crises.

3   Prevailing status

As set out in Chapter 5, and also seen in the preceding section, market disequilibria and volatility have been and continue to be inherent to the functioning of the global financial markets. Information asymmetries frequently give rise to overshooting, sharp market corrections, and often crises. With the rapid globalization of capital flows and portfolios, the sophistication and dynamism of the financial world has increased enormously. However, an adequate and proper institutional and policy framework to regulate it is apparently not in place as yet. The existing framework is not adequate to deal with advancing financial globalization.

Those who have studied the recent emerging market crises know that the inadequacy and deficiency are not limited to one or two policy areas or institutions, but are systemic. They extend to both national and supra-national institutions. Shortcomings are conspicuous in the consistency of domestic macroeconomic policies, management of international liquidity, and financial supervision and regulation.

The global financial system is an organic whole, and global financial architecture is a global public good. Hence any reform plan requires collective action at the global level. There is a pressing need to reform, fundamentally and comprehensively, the various facets of it. The basic objective of reforming the global monetary and financial order is to harness the potential of global private financial flows in such a way that they contribute to the stability and growth in the global economy. Thoughtful, pragmatic and concerted action is required from the global community in this regard, particularly from the matured G-7 economies. The Group of 22 (G-22) is another important and relevant forum for this purpose.[3] That said, there is widespread recognition that global financial stability and growth also rests on robust national systems and therefore requires enhanced measures and reforms at the domestic level as well.

There is no shortage of proposals and novel ideas for reform. They have come thick and fast from both public and privates sources. Global financial architecture has been the focus of attention of policy mandarins and academics alike. The Finance Ministries of Canada, France, Germany, and the United Kingdom (UK) have proposed serious reform plans. The US Treasury has been actively involved in setting an agenda for reforms. After the Asian crisis, several Asian and other emerging market economies joined in the debate with their additional agenda items. They were *inter alia* concerned with the social impact of the crises, which, they believed, was being ignored by those charged with the management and resolution of financial and macroeconomic crises. The G-22 has published many intensive reports with the help of academics active in this area.

Several noted academic scholars and non-academic experts (such as George Soros, Henry Kaufman, and Jeffrey Garten) suggested the creation of new institutions or tinkering with the role of the Bretton-Woods twins, and think tanks and professional journals made their especial contribu-tions. Many of the proposed plans were contradictory and mutually incompatible – some went for further liberalization, while others plumped for the reimposition of capital controls. Some said that nirvana lies in greater exchange-rate flexibility, while others insisted that a global finan-cial system would be dysfunctional until a stable or fixed exchange-rate system is re-established (Eichengreen, 2003). Some thought that crisis reso-lution is the express duty of the global community, while others insisted that crises should be left for the market forces to resolve. Consequently, a voluminous amount of literature exists on the subject areas related to the global financial system.

In the wake of recent macroeconomic volatility and crises in the emerging market economies, particularly after the Asian crisis, the international community has attempted to devise a range of new initiatives to strengthen the global financial system and a good deal of action has been taken. For instance, Horst Kohler, the Managing Director of the IMF, has made many speeches on the subject of "international financial architecture," and the sovereign debt restructuring mechanism (SDRM) was designed by the IMF in April 2002. The World Bank has published many policy and research papers on this and related themes. Not all the novel ideas have been functional, ranging from intellectually appealing to operationally impractical. Some of the proposals even verged on quixotic, like the proposal regarding creating a new institution called the World Financial Authority.[4] In addition, there is a striking lack of consensus among those who have presented new ideas or plans for systemic reforms. Many of the new plans and strategies for reforms affect different countries in different ways, and therefore, in the multi-polar world of today, it is difficult to reach agreement among the country groups or countries on important financial and economic issues. The contemporary political and financial scenario greatly complicates the process of reaching an agreement. Besides, economic and financial decisions are made in a political environment. This is true for domestic as well as global economic and financial decision-making processes. In such a *mise en scène*, is it at all possible for domestic and global policy-makers (like the IMF) to work in a non-partisan and apolitical manner?

Notwithstanding the obstacles, given the significance and far-reaching implications of the issue the global community has not been passive. Several initiatives to reform and strengthen the global financial architecture are presently underway. Professor Barry Eichengreen of the University of California, Berkeley, identified four immediate areas for strengthening the global financial system. He posited that it would be a realistic, feasible and attainable target to reform and strengthen the global financial system. His so-called "four pillars" to provide further systemic support are: (1) international standards, (2) market-friendly (or Chilean-style) taxes on short-term capital inflow, (3) greater exchange-rate flexibility, and (4) collective-action clauses in loan contracts to create an alternative to ever bigger IMF bailouts. He contends that these reforms and improvements in the four areas could be a panacea for the crisis-prone global economy. Together they would strengthen crisis prevention, moderate the severity of crises, speed up the recovery of an emerging market economy after it has suffered a crisis, and contain moral hazard in international financial markets.

4   Areas of immediate reforms

Several areas of the global financial system are in need of immediate reforms, and call for global co-operation and collaboration. A brief discussion on these issues is provided below.

The Bretton-Woods twins: a privileged position

Almost since their inception, the Bretton-Woods twins have been active in creating a functional global financial architecture. Poverty alleviation is the principal mandate of the World Bank. Its familiarity and involvement with the developing and emerging market economies and its comparative strengths on social and structural issues has placed the World Bank in a privileged position in helping to devise and implement the global financial structure. In addition, it helps in bringing developing country experience and perspectives to the ongoing discussions and negotiations on reforming the global financial architecture. In the recent past the World Bank has also attempted to strengthen partnerships with the relevant standard setting bodies and other institutions in the areas of corporate governance, accounting and auditing, and insolvency regimes to forge a consensus and catalyze concerted actions (see following section).

The *raison d'etre* of the IMF was originally the surveillance of the monetary, fiscal and exchange-rate policies of the member countries, and its conditionality measures were essentially focused on these variables. In a financially globalized world, this role has expanded and the IMF has morphed its mission several times. In its present role it has evolved as a "global advice-and-rescue squad." According to Blinder (2003), it is:

> one part wealthy benefactor, one part stern schoolmarm and one part global firefighter. It lectures countries on economic orthodoxy, proffers financing in return for approved behavior and rides dramatically to rescue when countries fall prey to financial crises.

The IMF has come to acquire a pivotal role in the global financial system, and as such, it needs proactively to push for reforms to create viable alternatives to ever-larger bailouts of the crisis-affected emerging markets. The crises and the following contagion effect have had many pernicious implications, even for emerging economies that have sound fundamentals.

Managing international liquidity in such a manner that crises and contagions can be prevented would indeed reduce their adverse economic and social effects. Although this objective can be met by creating a lender of last resort, or by making the IMF play this role, existing institutional arrangements do not permit it. There are two reasons. First, it would require surrender of economic autonomy by member countries of the IMF, a notion that is abhorrent to them. Second, the IMF is cash-strapped. Its financial resources only make it feasible for it to arrange for or organize rescue packages for the crisis-affected emerging market economies. It cannot currently play the role of provider of required liquidity and prevent the march of contagions.

However, the IMF can play several salutary roles, both pre- and post-crisis. For one, it can utilize its existing facilities to help those emerging markets that are, while not crisis-stricken, facing macroeconomic difficulties that could at some later stage turn into crises, through facilities like the Compensatory and Contingency Financing Facility (CCFF). For instance, if an emerging market is facing an export price slump or demand-related problems that could affect the whole economy if unresolved, a facility like CCFF can come to its rescue. Financial resources relative to the economy's quotas can be provided so that a potential crisis is stopped in its tracks. Second, by assisting an emerging market in this manner the IMF can save it from falling a victim to a spreading contagion. The CCFF can be turned into a low conditionality financing facility, which can be used at an early stage if the emerging market economy meets certain *ex ante* criteria. Whether these criteria are being met or not can be determined during Article IV consultations. To dissuade economies from applying for low conditionality loans without a pressing need, the IMF should make them available only at a higher interest rate than for the normal IMF resources and for a shorter-term, which should be pre-determined.

When a crisis situation does develop in an emerging market that is following sound economic policies but is suffering from a short-term loss of investor confidence, the IMF can arrange for financial resources. As its own resources are limited, it will have to work in conjunction with the credit lines from creditor commercial banks. This is the crisis aversion and resolution role of the IMF. While it cannot relinquish this task, it needs to strengthen its role as a monitor of the economic management – or that of an economic policeman. The IMF needs to monitor closely the operations of the financial markets in the emerging market economies and ensure their conformity with the international financial norms. This will extend the role of the IMF to the private sector as well as to working with international committees of regulators. To this end, the following three initiatives in this area are underway in the IMF: (1) the preparation of the Reports on the Observance of Standards and Codes; (2) the preparation of the Financial Sector Assessment Program; and (3) the preparation of Public Debt Management Guidelines and a complementary Practitioner's Manual on the development of domestic markets for government debt. The outcome of the IMF's monitoring of the financial sector of the emerging market economy should be made public so that policy-makers in the economy and the global financial markets are aware of the progress or lack of it.

After a financial crisis strikes an emerging market economy, the IMF will need to take on the role of a proactive facilitator or co-ordinator of debt-restructuring negotiations. This role is that of an "honest broker" between the creditors and debtors. Debt restructuring has been an inordinately onerous process for both sides, which makes the honest broker's role highly significant. It would determine the success or failure of the negotiation process. If the IMF shows willingness to "lend into arrears," the two sides grow confident of coming to a reasonable agreement in a short span of time and the value of the assets of the emerging market economy do not hit rock bottom after the crisis. Being a pivotal institution, the IMF will need to be actively engaged in creating a standing committee of creditors as well as the "bailing in" of the lending banks. These endeavors seem a clear and viable alternative to the ever-larger bailouts.

Given the frequent episodes of instability on the one hand and the crucial role of the IMF in maintaining and enhancing the stability of the global financial system on the other, its resources need to be augmented. As the negotiations for quota increases are always protracted and painstaking, some rapid mechanisms need to be devised for this purpose. Three modes of operation can be considered. First, in a crisis situation the IMF should be able to access larger official resources than it can at present. Second, under the same set of circumstances it should be allowed to borrow from the financial markets. Third, under special circumstances and for special purpose it should also be allowed to create liquidity. This mechanism already exists. When more than one IMF member is suffering from a crisis, when there is a risk of a contagion, or when there is systemic risk, the IMF should be able to create SDRs. As the creation of these SDRs is purpose specific, they should be destroyed as soon as borrowings are repaid to the IMF.

International codes of conduct

In a financially globalized world, a consensus on international codes of conduct in financial areas is indispensable. These international codes and standards cover corporate governance, accounting standards, and financial supervision and regulation. The dissemination and transparency of financial information and data on the financial affairs of governments, banks, and corporates are equally important for strengthening market discipline. Adherence to internally accepted disclosure norms influences financial allocation and channels capital flows away from borrowing entities that do not take adequate measures to preserve their financial stability. Adhering to international codes of conduct in these areas works as a preventive measure and minimizes the incidence of a crisis. As the adage goes, "Prevention better than a cure." Some guidelines and regulations in these areas exist, which apparently were found to be inadequate during the spate of crises in the past. More comprehensive ones are being developed by several supranational institutions, including the IMF, the World Bank, the Bank for International Settlements (BIS), the Organization for Economic Co-operation and Development (OECD), the International Organization of Securities Commissions (IOSCO), and other relevant institutions. Although some progress has been made in this task, much remains to be done.

It is easy to discern that all the actionable areas enumerated in the preceding paragraph fall in the domestic domain of an emerging market economy. As stated earlier, global financial stability and growth rests *inter alia* on robust national systems. When financial markets are integrated, global financial stability cannot be attained without domestic financial stability. The former is a precursor of the latter. Domestic financial stability can in turn be attained through the development and strengthening of the appropriate institutional network. In those cases where this network is in place, it needs to be reformed to perform its task effectively and efficiently. If these domestic institutions and arrangements are not supervised to maintain high standards of operations, ensuring a stable domestic financial environment will be difficult.

Likewise, the role of financial regulation and supervision in risk management in financial institutions is of crucial importance. Poorly managed banks and integration with the global financial market has been called "combustible mix." Access to global financial resources inspires emerging market banks to take on excessive risk. On their part, the large foreign banks and investors feel enthused to provide capital to emerging market banks because of the government guarantee given to these banks. Only proper risk-management practices and stringent prudential supervision can reduce this risk. Prudential supervision to compensate for the shortcomings of banks' and corporates' risk-management practices are pre-supposed in a stable domestic financial system. Designing standards for financial regulation needs to go hand in hand with relevant global regulation and supervision. To this end there have been recommendations for creating a new financial institution, but this task can be managed cost effectively without creating an excessive number of expensive international bodies. The supervision of adoption of international standards at the national level can done by existing institutions like the BIS and the IOSCO. However, the creation of regional or sub-regional organizations for such supervision can be considered.

In a financially integrated world where crises frequently turn contagious and create systemic shocks, the global community has a common interest and duty in ensuring that all the financially globalized economies adopt an acceptable quality of domestic norms in these areas. A poor level of adherence by some can cause serious problems for all of the members of the financially globalized community.

Can this be taken as an intrusion by the international financial community into a country's internal affairs? Can the issue of sovereign rights be raised here? It has frequently been the case. However, Eichengreen (2003) disagrees with this line of logic and believes that the need for the stability of global financial markets justifies ensuring that the domestic arrangements in all the enumerated areas are functional and maintain the required degree of efficiency. According to him, internationally recognized auditing and accounting practices, in whose absence global creditors are unable accurately to assess the financial conditions of the banks and corporations to which they lend, should be extended to all the emerging market economies. Also, adequate creditors' rights must be established in all the emerging market economies so that creditors are able to monitor the economic and financial decisions of managers. Likewise, the international community needs to ensure that investor-protection laws have been enacted to prevent insider trading, market cornering, and other financial malpractices. Different emerging market economies can satisfy these desiderata in different ways, but in a world of capital market integration there is no avoiding the need for this.

Designing international codes and standards is as complex a process as the global financial system itself. The IMF has taken a good deal of initiative in this process, conducting several studies of its own and in collaboration with the Basel Committee, the BIS, and the World Bank. This validates the earlier observation regarding the complexity of the process of devising international codes and standards. No one institution can claim to have the expertise or "human resources necessary to design and monitor compliance with detailed international standards in all the relevant areas" enumerated in this section. Also, the reform agenda is so large that no international organization has enough resources, knowledge or administrative capabilities to provide advice to the emerging market economies. Therefore, the assistance of private-sector bodies must also be sought in devising best practices and standards in these areas. The International Accounting Standards Committee (IASC), the International Federation of Accountants (IFA), the International Organization of Supreme Audit Institutions (IOSAI), the International Corporate Governance Network (ICGN), and the International Committee of National Regulators or the Basel Committee can and should be called in to collaborate with the international organization. Emerging market economies are members of most of these self-organizing bodies.

Autonomy of capital account

Capital account liberalization that took place in the emerging market economies was either done unilaterally or under the guidance of the Bretton-Woods twins and the World Trade Organization (WTO). This was discussed at length in Chapter 3, particularly in Sections 3 and 4. Hindsight is said to be 20/20 vision, and in this case it reveals that capital account liberalization, when it is done abruptly and in a premature manner, without sufficiently reforming and strengthening the financial system, can lead an emerging market economy to a crisis. Turning to look at the experiences of the industrial economies, one observes that they maintained considerably long periods of capital control, followed by gradual capital account liberalization. It is now widely recognized that having a strong domestic financial system, including an efficient regulatory and supervision network, is a precondition for successful capital account liberalization.

As portfolio investment and short-term capital flows are characterized by instability, strong institutions and fundamentals are sometimes not enough to ward off a crisis when the maturity structure of borrowings is skewed toward the short term. Not only the magnitude but also the composition of inflows play an essential role in determining the stability or vulnerability of the capital flows. Therefore, during the period of a surge in capital inflows, central banking authorities in emerging markets should watch (1) when to begin controlling the capital inflows and (2) what maturity of inflows should be discouraged. Chile-type reserve requirements of short-term capital inflows have been greatly lauded by academics and policy mandarins alike. Such measures lengthen the maturity structure of the debt and are considered to be market-friendly measures, having least interference from the financial bureaucracy. Minimum-stay or minimum-liquidity requirements can also be imposed on large investment banks, mutual funds and hedge funds during such periods. A mechanism to ensure a reasonable maturity structure for external indebtedness, compatible with the export revenues, repatriated hard currency earnings and other macroeconomic variables, can be easily created as a complementary measure to ward off vulnerability.

Standstill provision

This is a post-crisis measure. In the past, when a crisis situation precipitated in an emerging market it helplessly faced financial chaos, including capital flight, sharp exchange-rate depreciation, and steep interest-rate hikes. Capital flight is exceedingly harmful for the crisis-affected economy because it turns an illiquidity problem into an insolvency one in a short period, exacerbating both economic and social costs of the crisis. Persistence of this situation is also harmful for global lenders, because the probability of repayment of debt declines.

As this scenario has been observed frequently in the past, it is now believed that a standstill on external obligations and capital account convertibility would bring some order to the chaos. The next step is to bring the two sides, creditors and debtor, to the negotiating table to reschedule the outstanding debt. Ideally, financial support to the crisis-affected economy should continue so that while negotiations for rescheduling are underway the economy continues to function. In this manner, both creditors and debtor stand a better chance of resolving a difficult problem. The standstill provision works for the creditors because it increases the probability of recovering a larger part of the value of their assets. To avoid the moral hazard on the part of the borrowers, the IMF should sanction the standstill exercise. It could then be combined with the IMF lending into arrears to make up the liquidity needed by the economy during the debt-restructuring period.

Bailing in the private sector

This is another post-crisis measure. In a financially globalizing world, something needs to be changed. In the case of a financial crisis, the global banks and other creditors should share in the burden of the crisis. This presently falls squarely on the shoulders of the taxpayers in the crisis-affected economy. Although it is difficult to ensure greater burden-sharing by the creditors, efforts to do so have been underway for sometime. So far no streamlined pattern has been designed for burden-sharing, but a case-by-case approach has been followed. It worked successfully in the cases of Korea, Pakistan and Ukraine in the past, but the procedures were neither clear nor transparent. Therefore, these burden-sharing exercises earned low marks on the international acceptability criteria. Consequently, the bailing-in approach is generally tried only in cases of small economies whose default is unlikely to threaten systemic instability. It is indeed a prudent approach from a systemic point of view, but hardly an equitable one. The global financial community needs more time and experience to develop minimum acceptable standards of clarity, transparency, and equity in this regard.

5 Antidote for financial and macroeconomic instability

Faced with the potentially destabilizing effects of financial globalization, the emerging market economies have been trying to strengthen as well as harmonize their financial regulatory infrastructure in a concerted manner. As briefly alluded to in Chapter 5 (Section 5), financial and monetary authorities in the emerging market economies are aware of the need to import international best practices as well as align domestic and international regulatory frameworks to avoid the destabilizing phenomenon of regulatory arbitrage. To this end, a financial regulatory convergence has been undertaken and is presently underway in the emerging market economies.

It was seen in Chapter 4 (Section 5) that the entry of foreign banks into and the provision of financial services and products by them in the emerging market economies has not only increased market competition but also has had a disciplining effect over them. Convergence in financial regulations across jurisdictions is essential for promoting integration with the global markets. The reverse is equally true: that is, convergence can also be a consequence of global financial integration. It does not matter which way the causality works. Convergence in financial regulations in the emerging market economies is necessary if financial integration with global markets is to proceed with reduced systemic instability.

With the acceleration in financial globalization over the past two decades, the relationship between financial integration and regulatory harmonization has become more intimate than ever before. This is so much so that the integration of financial products and services with financial regulatory frameworks is considered to be two different aspects of the same process, namely the ongoing globalization of finances. However, while the two aspects progress together, they do not generally have to move at the same pace. While market forces give a fillip to regulatory harmonization, this vitally important task should not be left to them alone because market forces and regulatory institutions often work at cross-purposes. "Coordination failures associated with market-led initiatives can generate negative systemic externalities, attracting capital toward regulated systems and institutions or generating forms of competition in laxity" that may eventually lead to financial and macroeconomic instability (Jordan and Majnoni, 2002).

Conventional wisdom is that the development and diffusion of codes and standards of good practice begins in the real sector and then spreads to the financial sector. That is, there is a relationship between the diffusion and adoption of codes and standards of good practices, and the level of development. This does not imply a shift of emphasis from the real to the financial sector; it is merely the result of considering the financial sector an instrument of economic integration.

The process of the creation and diffusion of financial regulations has undergone a discernible transformation over the last half-century. Both governmental and non-governmental institutions conventionally set rules for the financial sector. The latter category includes technical bodies and supervisory authorities. Initially, governmental organizations and bodies used to lay down the regulations for co-operation among economies. This applied to both bilateral and multilateral co-operation. However, since the 1970s non-governmental institutions begun to lead governmental institutions in the area of financial co-operation. Initiatives by technical and professional bodies increasingly began to pave the ground for action by the authorities. The first such initiative taken by a non-governmental technical body was the Basel Committee of Banking Supervisions (BCBS), created in 1975 in the aftermath of the Herstatt collapse in Germany. The basic objective of the BCBS was to underpin the supervision and co-ordination of banks that have widely spread international operations so that a Herstatt-like crisis did not reoccur.

The process of forging legal and regulatory instruments has also undergone a transformation. Initially, governments entered into treaties which entailed a long drawn-out negotiation and ratification process. This process was not only slow and inefficient, but was also incompatible with the needs of the world of finance, which moved at a rapid pace in developing new financial instruments. Therefore, non-governmental bodies were born to create codes, standards, and rules of acceptable behavior. These frameworks of regulation were different from the traditional treaties, and were intended to shape common behavior without changing the legal frameworks. At the global level, since the mid-1980s several non-institutional informal groups like G-3, G-5, G-7, G-10, G-20 and G-30 have been created and function productively and efficiently. The successful existence of these groups reflects the contributions made to productive international co-operation in the area of international finance. The process of the creation of a new regulatory framework as well as harmonization took a markedly different route from that of the past.[5]

There are different modes of regulatory harmonization. Forming a monetary union is one oft-utilized government-induced mode. Regulatory harmonization has also worked in those parts of the globe where one or more large and successful economies have exerted a gravitational pull for neighboring economies. In such cases, the large economy works as a catalyst and initiates the process of regulatory alignment for the other economies to follow. The experiences of regions that have followed these modes demonstrates that adopting the principle of minimum harmonization reduces the difficulties of creating a top-down harmonization system. This principle has had immense utility for global financial integration in the recent past. In addition, market mechanisms have made a large contribution by successfully developing and enforcing financial standards through reputational disciplines. These market-determined standards are set and maintained by large dominant institutions which have long-established reputations. The principle of minimum harmonization and the reputationally induced disciplines have been the most important pillars of the current episode of financial globalization. These two principles have played a greater role than the standards and codes of financial regulation (Jordan and Lubrano, 2002).

These two principles became instantly popular for the following three reasons. First, together the principles reflected both the regulatory discipline and functionality of a market. Little wonder they appealed to both market regulators and market players. Second, their generality made them attractive to economies with different economic histories and levels of economic growth. Third, the most important trait of these two principles was their conceptual simplicity. It should be noted that the two principles did not present a novel approach; they were part of a system of law that followed the practice of having norms that did not have the binding force of legislation.[6] Such conventions have been christened "soft law" due to the lack of a codified procedure for their definition and enforcement (Giovanoli, 2001). In national legal systems, soft law amounts to the adoption of codes of best practices prevalent at an international level and accepted by a group of large countries. They are non-binding and voluntary in nature, and are referred to as "codes of conduct," "guidelines," or "recommendations."[7]

In 1988, the BCBS created what became known as "the Basel 1988 Accord." It has also been called "the New Basel Capital Accord" (BCBS, 2001a). It is perhaps the best example of the development of a set of highly successful financial standards during the recent period (Barth *et al.*,

2001; Powell, 2003). Although designed for the internationally active banks in the G-10 economies, by early 2003 more than a hundred countries claimed adherence to the New Basel Capital Accord. Some central banks apply these standards to all banks. The first set of proposals under the Basel New Accord was published in January 2001, and the final version was published in July 2002 for implementation by 2005 (BCBS, 2002). The new set of proposals made considerable advances "in linking risk and regulatory capital for internationally active banks, especially for their corporate loan book." The implementation of this accord in the G-10 economies would indeed affect the cost of capital in the emerging market economies. The accord essentially takes an internal rating-based (IRB) approach. Indubitably the IRB approach should lead to significant changes in capital requirements and spreads for the banks that lend to the emerging market economies. The accord has proposed that for the purpose of sovereign lending, internationally-active banks should develop internal ratings according to an S&P or Moody's scale and capital charges should be levied according to the corresponding weights assigned by the standard approach.

Impact of large traders on market dynamics

The category of large traders or market agents includes proprietary desks of commercial and investment banks, and highly leveraged institutions (HLIs) like the Hedge Funds (HFs). The experiences of the 1990s demonstrated that these large traders played a palpable role in precipitating and propagating a crisis. They wield enormous market power because of their sheer size and reputation, and the metaphor of elephants bathing in small ponds instead of in large lakes is often used to describe the operations of large traders in the emerging markets. Furthermore, their enormous leveraging ability gives large traders a unique ability to influence market dynamics, usually with destabilizing consequences. Many of these large traders are too big for the relatively small financial markets of individual emerging market economies, and they have been blamed for directly creating crisis situations in these economies that are not justified by the macroeconomic fundamentals of the economies. They have been blamed not only for creating volatility in currency and asset markets in the emerging markets, but also for creating a larger systemic risk to the global financial system.[8]

Many analysts believe that the very presence of large market agents makes emerging markets vulnerable to a crisis. Their portfolio strategies are characterized by a short-term focus, which encourages speculative behavior. Small investors, in an environment of information asymmetry, tend to behave like the large market players. Phenomena like herding, momentum trading, noise trading, and bandwagon effects commonly occur in financial markets even if all the agents are small, and the presence of large traders aggravates these tendencies (Corsetti *et al.*, 2000a). During the Asian crisis of 1997–1998, the aggressive and manipulative practices of large traders were decried by financial authorities in the Asian emerging market economies. The Prime Minister of Malaysia, Dr. Mahatir Mohammed, was the most trenchant critic of the role of the large traders. He blamed them for destabilizing the Asian economies, and appealed for global control of their activities.

To assess the veracity of these allegations the HLI Working Group of the Financial Stability Forum (FSF) was convened in April 1999.[9] The objective of the FSF was to promote global financial stability through information exchange and global co-operation in financial supervision and surveillance. A Study Group on Market Dynamics in Small- and Medium-Sized Economies conducted a study of the 1998 market turmoil and the role played by the HLIs in six countries, namely Australia, Hong Kong SAR, Malaysia, New Zealand, Singapore, and South Africa. Although the Study Group could not reach consensus regarding the allegations of creating instability in the emerging market economies, it did find circumstantial evidence of aggressive trading practices. These practices followed by the HLIs resulted in crises in some emerging market economies (FSF, 2000). However, another study by the IMF (1998b), focusing only on the Asian crisis and the role of the HFs, found that they did not play a significant role in the early market turbulence in Asia.

Notwithstanding the lack of consensus in the FSF (2000) Study Group, it arrived at several noteworthy inferences. For one, it found evidence that HLIs do not threaten the stability of an emerging market economy under normal conditions. However, along with other market players, HLIs can play an active and important role in translating views about fundamentals into prices. They are faced by the same set of incentives as other market participants in avoiding outsized positions. Also, higher liquidity in the emerging market is an important benefit of the presence of HLIs. The ability and willingness to take leveraged positions makes HLIs a font of market liquidity, which contributes positively to financial market development in the host economy. The Study Group found that HLIs do establish large and concentrated positions in the emerging markets and other economies. Whenever they do so, HLIs have the potential materially to influence market dynamics. Herding behavior amplifies the size and duration of the effects on the financial market. Whether the large positions taken by the HLIs tend to destabilize can only be judged by studying each case of instability and crisis. Some members of the Study Group were of the view that HLIs' positions and tactics often represented a significant independent source of pressure in the financial market. This is where the disagreement lay. Other members opined that the evidence of this effect was feeble.

In the light of these inconclusive results, Corsetti *et al.* (2001b) conducted an extensive empirical and theoretical study. They analyzed the evidence on the correlation between exchange rate movements and major market participants' net currency positions. They next focused on the available case studies, crisis-related reporting in the financial press, and academic writings on a large number of recent episodes of market turbulence. They concluded that large HLIs and HFs played a decisive "role in several episodes of market distress in the 1990s." This included the creation of, or contribution to, financial market instability during the ERM crisis of 1992–1993,[10] the 1994 US bond market turbulence, the 1994 Mexican peso crisis, the speculative attack on the Thai baht in 1997, the depreciation of the Korean won in 1997, the Malaysian ringgit crisis in 1997–1998, the so-called "double play" on the stock and foreign exchange markets in Hong Kong SAR, the repeated pressures on Australian dollar in 1998, the rally of the yen in 1998, and the Russian and Brazilian contagion of 1998. With the help of this large sample of episodes of financial market destability, Corsetti *et al.* (2001b) concluded that there was circumstantial evidence of aggressive trading practices by the HLIs and HFs, which in turn contributed to destability in the financial markets. Thus, their results were more in agreement with the FSF (2000) study and they disagreed with the IMF (1998b) findings.

There are three important premises regarding the role of large traders in crisis episodes, which lighten their burden of blame. First, their size and market power cannot be directly related to the value of their asset holdings or their market share. Two large trades of virtually the same size can have different impacts on the emerging market they are operating in. Their ability to influence the portfolio strategies of other market players varies considerably, depending upon their access to superior information and their reputation as forecasters. Large traders are reputed to devote larger resources to data collection and analysis than do the small market players, and they are therefore more likely to have superior market information. That being said, they need not be better informed in all circumstances. Besides, if small market participants can exploit information asymmetries and market inefficiencies better than the large traders, the impact of large traders can be limited. Second, although Corsetti *et al.* (2001b) found that herding or "electronic herding" exacerbated swings in capital flows, currency value movements, or asset prices, it was a large set of investors of all genres that did it. They were small, large, domestic, foreign, highly-leveraged, and not leveraged. They coalesced to contribute to the episodes of volatility in the 1990s. Third, analysis of many episodes of market turbulence during this period demonstrated that crises unfolded in the backdrop of deteriorating market fundamentals, policy uncertainties, and structural infirmities (Corsetti *et al.*, 2001b).

The flip side of this coin is that large traders are not only better informed (or perceived to be so) but they are also able to build sizable short positions through leverage. Based on their ability to analyze and assess financial markets and weaknesses in economic fundamentals, they take the market initiative in making market moves. Smaller traders, who are considered prone to herding behavior, monitor the market moves of large traders. Together they often follow aggressive trading practices. However, the role of large players in the global financial markets has undergone a radical transformation in the early 2000s. Some of the largest macro-HFs and other HLIs have either been closed down or have retrenched their operations.[11] Over a thousand medium- and small-sized HFs either became illiquid, or incurred large losses. Thus, a large number of them ran out of business. This has partly caused worries about lack of liquidity in the financial markets, which may lead to asset price volatility. Further to the considerably reduced operations of the HFs, the official sector has seriously started addressing the market dynamics-related issues in the HLI Working Group of the FSF. This group considered both the implications of HLIs for systemic risk in the global financial markets and the role of HLIs in the emerging market economies (Corsetti *et al.*, 2001b).

6   Exchange rate policies and financial globalization

The choice of an exchange-rate regime is vital in determining the stability of an economy in an open globalized financial market. As textbooks report, the Mundellian trilemma or "impossible trinity" has three policy strands – (1) free capital mobility; (2) a fixed or stable nominal exchange rate; and (3) an autonomous monetary policy – only two of which can co-exist.[12] During the Bretton-Woods period (1945–1971), the economic and political environment was not conducive to rapid trans-border capital flows. The large economies of Europe were engrossed in post-War reconstruction with the help of the US, and they needed the autonomy of monetary policy to achieve their domestic reconstruction objectives. As capital flows did not start taking place until quite late in this period, the other policy strand that came to these economies, as a residual, was adoption of stability in exchange rates. However, the strategic priorities of the post-Bretton-Woods era were different. Of the three Mundellian conditions, autonomous monetary policy to achieve domestic objectives and free capital mobility were the choice of this period. Exchange rate stability was given up in favor of capital mobility. As capital mobility received affirmation from the policy-makers, financial globalization progressed during the post-Bretton-Woods era.

The process of financial globalization created many exchange-rate related problems for the emerging market economies.[13] Many of these were based on the fact that financial markets, both domestic and international, in general are far from perfect. Financial market imperfections include incomplete markets, asymmetric information, noise trading, bubbles, herding, multiple equilibria, moral hazard, and contagion. Problems such as incomplete markets apply more to the domestic financial markets, while those like asymmetric information plague the international financial system.

While the post-Bretton-Woods pursuance of autonomy in domestic monetary policy and free capital mobility worked reasonably well for the industrial economies, the emerging markets faced torrid conditions in this arena. They tried adopting a range of exchange-rate arrangements, but in many cases this was with only limited success and these economies were bruised by crises. Their range covered arrangements like soft pegging, hard pegging, crawls, stationary bands, moving banks, flexible exchange-rate systems, currency boards, and dollarization.[14] Of late, several emerging market economies have demonstrated a preference for the flexible exchange-rate system. Although the popularity of this arrangement has been on the rise, the emerging market economies that adopted it have displayed an overly cautious attitude in practicing it. These economies have shown that even after opting for a flexible exchange rate, they want to restrict the currency value movements in practice. Consequently they are not able to benefit from an autonomous monetary policy (Larrain and Velasco, 2001; Calvo and Reinhart, 2002).

The emerging market economies not only failed to benefit from all the possible advantages of financial globalization, but were also bruised by currency, banking and debt crises, or the so-called triple crises. The recent (2002–2003) crises in Ecuador and Argentina had all three elements (Bordo *et al.*, 2001). Global market financial flows into these economies were far from steady. They were not able to follow counter-cyclical monetary policy, and could not take advantage of consumption smoothening, deepening, and diversification of their domestic financial markets, discernible reduction in the cost of capital, and significant augmentation of capital and domestic investment. Thus, the benefits of financial globalization to emerging markets have so far been far from optimal (Mishkin, 2001b).

Eichengreen (2003) believed that in a rapidly globalizing economy, pursuing a flexible exchange-rate policy is helpful for an emerging market economy. This regime encourages banks and corporates not to rely excessively on short-term unhedged foreign debts. In a flexible exchange rate regime, economic agents remain eager to hedge their foreign currency exposures. Conversely, a pegged exchange rate provides an incentive to economic agents to accumulate unhedged foreign currency debts. To defend the peg, the central bank is forced to carry on the drum beat that the *status quo* will be maintained and the peg will not change. Given this background, hedging becomes an expensive and redundant measure. As opposed to this, when the exchange rate is flexible and financial transactions involving foreign currency are hedged, large and unexpected variations in exchange rates do not create financial havoc for the banks and corporates by increasing the cost of servicing of short-term debts. A sharp currency depreciation will not become a financial crash, as it did for some of the Asian economies during the Asian crisis.

De la Torre *et al.* (2002) have taken this argument a step farther than Eichengreen (2003), positing that in the contemporary era of financial globalization, emerging market economies need the "blessed trinity" to ward off the triple crises. Their concept of the blessed trinity includes: (1) a strong international currency; (2) flexible exchange rate; and (3) sound institutions. If the "blessed trinity" is achieved, the economies can integrate well with the global capital markets and take advantage of all the potential benefits. The reverse of the "blessed trinity" apparently is having a weak currency, an overly cautious floating system, and weak institutions. When this combination exists, economies are not only able to integrate well with the global financial markets but also become vulnerable to the triple crises.

Of the three characteristics of the blessed trinity, the first is the most onerous and time-consuming to achieve. While a flexible exchange rate with a credible float and sound institutions are achievable in a relatively short period by a set of knowledgeable policy-makers who know their job, the process of creating a strong currency which has an international stature – one that is accepted as a store of value both at home and abroad – takes time and constant endeavor. Credible macroeconomic policies contribute to and support the international stature of a currency. In particular, the fiscal policy of the currency-issuing country has to be balanced and devoid of any shade of profligacy, so that the solvency of the issuer is never called into question. An emerging market that has succeeded in achieving the blessed trinity can integrate successfully into imperfect financial markets without difficulties because "the components of the trinity interact in virtuous ways to control the risks of financial globalization while maximizing its benefits."

7   Summary and conclusions

It was Robert Rubin who coined the expression "international financial architecture." The academic and policy-making community enthusiastically adopted the inapt metaphor he used. While there is no widely agreed and tersely stated definition of what precisely constitutes global financial architecture, it refers broadly to the framework and set of institutions, structures, and measures that can help prevent crises or, when faced with one, help to manage it better in the more integrated international financial environment.

Over the last half-century, since the creation of the Bretton-Woods system, the principal characteristics of the global financial system have undergone radical, albeit somewhat gradual, transformation. There has been an inevitable and desirable evolution in it. The global financial system has been transformed from an administered or government-led system to a decentralized or market-led system. With the passage of time, the former revealed its weaknesses and began to show its irrelevance in some areas.

Under the new market-led system, the financial markets acted swiftly and imaginatively in creating a new and progressively wide range of instruments. This was their contribution to the completeness of the financial markets, without making them fully complete. Market disequilibria and volatility have been and continue to be inherent to the functioning of global financial markets. Information asymmetries frequently give rise to overshooting, sharp market corrections, and crises. With the rapid globalization of capital flows and portfolios, the sophistication and dynamism of the financial world has increased enormously.

The global financial system is an organic whole, and global financial architecture is a global public good. Hence any reform plan requires collective action at the level of global participants. There is a pressing need fundamentally and comprehensively to reform the various facets of it. There is no shortage of proposals and novel ideas for reforms; they have come thick and fast from both public and private sources. Reform in the global financial architecture has been the focus of attention of policy mandarins and academics alike.

The IMF can play several salutary roles, both pre- and post-crisis, in reforming the global financial architecture. Institutionally, the IMF plays the role of "one part wealthy benefactor, one part stern schoolmarm and one part global firefighter. It lectures countries on economic orthodoxy, proffers financing in return for approved behavior and rides dramatically to rescue when countries fall prey to financial crises." It has come to acquire a pivotal role in the global financial system. When a crisis situation does develop in an emerging market economy that is otherwise following sound economic policies but is suffering from a short-term loss of investor confidence, the IMF can arrange for short-term financial resources to tide it over the turbulent period. To this end, the IMF needs skillfully to manage international liquidity. If the IMF manages international liquidity in such a manner that crises and contagions can be prevented, this will lead to success in reducing the adverse economic and social effects of the crises in the emerging market economies. Another uniquely positioned institution is the World Bank, which has also attempted to strengthen partnerships with the relevant standard setting bodies and other institutions in the areas of corporate governance, accounting and auditing, and insolvency regimes to forge a consensus and catalyze concerted actions.

In a financially globalized world, a consensus on international codes of conduct in financial areas is indispensable. These international codes and standards cover corporate governance, accounting standards, and financial supervision and regulation. Dissemination and transparency of financial information and data on financial affairs of governments, banks, and corporates are equally important for strengthening market discipline. Capital account liberalization is another important feature which has a bearing on the global financial architecture. When it occurs abruptly and in a premature manner, without sufficiently reforming and strengthening the financial system, it can lead an emerging market economy to a crisis and have a contagious effect. It is now widely recognized that having a strong domestic financial system, including an efficient regulatory and supervision network, is a precondition for successful capital account liberalization.

As portfolio investment and short-term capital flows are characterized by instability, strong institutions and fundamentals are sometimes not enough to ward off a crisis when the maturity structure of the borrowing emerging market economies is skewed toward the short term. Sequencing capital account liberalization, liberalizing short-term flows last, and, even after liberalizing, avoiding excessive short-term capital inflows must be policy objectives of the central bankers in the emerging market economies. Faced with the potentially destabilizing effects of financial globalization, the emerging market economies have been trying to strengthen as well as harmonize their financial regulatory infrastructure in a concerted manner. Standstill provision is a post-crisis measure. In the past, once a crisis situation had precipitated in an emerging market, it helplessly faced financial chaos including capital flight, sharp exchange-rate depreciation, and steep interest-rate hikes. The standstill provision can provide a respite from these highly destabilizing features and give time to plan for proper crisis alleviation measures.

The category of large traders or market agents includes the proprietary desks of commercial and investment banks, and highly leveraged institutions (HLIs) like the Hedge Funds (HFs). The experiences of the 1990s demonstrated that these large traders played a palpable role in precipitating and propagating a crisis. It was believed by many that they affected the dynamics of financial markets and created serious instability, although there is no consensus on this issue. A great deal of the attention of the global financial community has been focused on the activities of the large traders and containing their deleterious global and economy-specific ramifications. During the early 2000s, some of the largest HFs collapsed and many smaller ones were closed down. The official sector has seriously started addressing the market dynamics-related issues in the HLI Working Group of the FSF. This group considered both the implications of HLIs for systemic risk in the global financial markets, and the role of HLIs in the emerging market economies.

The choice of an exchange-rate regime is vital in determining the stability of an economy in an open globalized financial market. Of late, several emerging market economies have demonstrated a preference for the flexible exchange-rate system. Although the popularity of this arrangement has been on the rise, the emerging market economies that adopted it have displayed an overly cautious attitude in practicing it. These economies have shown that even after opting for a flexible exchange rate, they want to restrict the currency value movements in practice. To be sure, in a rapidly globalizing economy, pursuing a flexible exchange-rate policy is helpful for an emerging market economy. One important built-in feature of this regime is that it encourages banks and corporates not to rely excessively on short-term unhedged foreign debts. However, in the contemporary era of financial globalization, emerging market economies need the "blessed trinity" to ward off the triple crises. The concept of the blessed trinity includes: (1) a strong international currency; (2) a flexible exchange rate; and (3) sound institutions. If the "blessed trinity" is achieved, the emerging market economies can integrate well with the global capital markets and potentially take advantage of all the benefits of global capital flows.

Notes

1 The emergence of emerging market economies

1 Horst Kohler, Managing Director of the International Monetary Fund, 2002.
2 The financial crisis in Thailand began on 2 July 1997.
3 See, for instance, Gilpin (2001) and Kolodko (2002).
4 Including Korea and Turkey, the Organization for Economic Cooperation and Development (OECD) has 30 members. While 28 of its members are industrial market economies, Korea and Turkey do not qualify for this status.
5 Chile, Hong Kong SAR, Korea (Republic of), Singapore, and Taiwan. Hong Kong is a special administrative region (or SAR) of the People's Republic of China (or China).
6 Once again clarity eludes us. This definition is not free of disagreement. Hong Kong SAR, Israel, Korea (Republic of), Singapore, and Taiwan have been classified as "advanced economies" by the International Monetary Fund (IMF) and the World Bank since 1997, while the investment banks still classify them as emerging market economies.
7 In 2003, the Institute of International Finance (IIF) had 28 countries on its list of emerging market economies. It included five economies from Africa and the Middle East (Algeria, Egypt, Morocco, South Africa, Tunisia), seven from Asia-Pacific (China, India, Indonesia, Malaysia, Philippines, Korea, Thailand), seven from Europe (Bulgaria, Czech Republic, Hungary, Poland, Romania, Russian Federation, Slovakia), and nine from Latin America (Argentina, Brazil, Chile, Colombia, Ecuador, Mexico, Peru, Uruguay, Venezuela).
8 Refer to International Monetary Fund, 1997, Chapter 3, p. 61, footnote 1.
9 These 20 countries are: one in Africa (South Africa); ten in Asia (China, Hong Kong SAR, India, Indonesia, Korea (Republic of), Malaysia, the Philippines, Singapore, Taiwan, and Thailand); three in Europe (the Czech Republic, Hungary, and Poland); and five in the Western hemisphere (Argentina, Brazil, Chile, Mexico, Venezuela). Israel is the only Middle Eastern country included in the IMF list.
10 According to *The Economist*, 2003a. These 25 economies are: ten Asian economies (China, Hong Kong, India, Indonesia, Malaysia, the Philippines, Singapore, South Korea, Taiwan, and Thailand); seven Western hemisphere economies (Argentina, Brazil, Chile, Colombia, Mexico, Peru, and Venezuela); four Middle Eastern and African economies (Egypt, Israel, South Africa, and Turkey); four East European economies (the Czech Republic, Hungary, Poland, and the Russian Federation).
11 The three case studies by Sylla (1999) convincingly establish this fact.
12 In the latter half of 1997, a financial crisis struck Indonesia, Korea, Malaysia,

the Philippines, and Thailand. Other Asian economies, including Hong Kong SAR and Singapore, were also adversely affected by the crisis.

13 This study was a joint endeavor between the Confederation of Indian Industries and the World Bank. It was based on the survey of 1,000 Indian firms in 10 states, and was completed in 2001. It provides a wealth of information and data on firm characteristics, and the impact of government policies and the business environment on firm performance. The study was designed as a prototype for similar studies in other large developing economies. It is available in processed form from the World Bank (see Dollar *et al.*, 2001).

14 Guillermo Ortiz, Governor, Bank of Mexico, in his 2002 Per Jacobsson Lecture (delivered on 7 July in the City Hall, Basel, Switzerland) gave a lot of importance to the role of "market sentiment" in recent emerging market crises. See pages 36–8 of his lecture, published by the Per Jacobsson Foundation, Washington DC.

15 "Herding" implies buying or selling an asset contemporaneously because other market participants are doing so.

16 When market participants buy an asset as its price rises and sell when it falls, it is called momentum trading.

17 In the international finance literature these are also known as the ERM (or exchange rate mechanism) crises of 1992–1993. It needs to be clarified that the ERM crises had little to do with capital flows, although speculators had an active role in these crises.

18 During the Russian crisis the ruble nearly collapsed.

19 In mid-2002 Turkey was the largest borrower from the International Monetary Fund, and its financial crisis had not yet ended.

20 LTCM (Long-Term Capital Management) was a large US Hedge Fund, having high market standing.

21 The Brazilian stock market crashed on 13 January 1999; it fell by 13 percent in one day.

22 See IMF (2002a), Chapter 1.

23 These results are supported by both the studies, by Bosworth and Collins (1999) and by Mody and Murshid (2002).

24 Refer to *Global Development Finance* (2002), published by the World Bank, for these statistics.

2 Global capital flows to emerging market economies

1 See various issues of *International Banking and Financial Market Developments: International Banking Statistics,* Bank for International Settlements, Basel, Switzerland.

2 The annual average for the 1983–1989 period was $11.6 billion (we are only considering net private capital flows to the emerging market economies).

3 The source of these statistics is the *World Economic Outlook* database of the International Monetary Fund.

4 Statistics come from various IMF sources, in particular from IMF (1997) and various issues of the *World Economic Outlook* (WEO).

5 Brady bonds were not considered part of the normal bond issuance activity, and were not included in bond issuance statistics because they represent repackaged bank loans. However, when emerging markets started buying back Brady bonds and issuing global bonds in their place, the new bonds were included in the bond issuance statistics (refer to Chapter 4, Section 3).

6 Technically speaking this is not arbitrage, because arbitrage is considered to be riskless.

7 Non-performing loans are those that are in default or close to being in default – that is, typically past due for 90 days or more. In December 2002 the non-performing loans of Japanese banks were estimated at $384 billion. See the *Financial Times*, 2002a. The financial system was long overdue for a thorough overhaul.

8 Refer to *BIS Quarterly Review,* various issues.

9 Hong Kong is the special administrative region of the Republic of China, and is referred to as Hong Kong SAR.

10 See Razin and Sadka (2001) and Calvo *et al.* (2002) for a theoretical treatment of these arguments.

11 As textbooks report, the Mundellian trilemma or "impossible trinity" has three policy strands – (1) free capital mobility, (2) a fixed or stable nominal exchange rate, and (3) an autonomous monetary policy – only two of which can co-exist.

12 John Williamson's original definition of the Washington consensus involved ten different aspects of economic policy. One may, however, roughly summarize this consensus, at least as it influenced the beliefs of markets and governments, more simply: liberalize trade, privatize state-owned enterprises, balance the budget, peg the exchange rate, and one will have laid the foundations of an economic take-off. Find a country that has done these things, and one may confidently expect to realize high returns on investments.

13 Not all the 30 members of the OECD can be considered to be matured industrial economies; the economic structure and institutions of Korea and Turkey are far from matured.

14 For instance see Calvo *et al.*, 1996; Das, 1996b; Fernandez-Arias, 1996; Goldberg, 2001; World Bank, 2001a; Jeanneau and Micu, 2002.

15 Hedge funds are private sector investment pools, and are often resident offshore for tax and regulatory purposes. These funds face few restrictions on their portfolios and transactions, with the benefit that they are free to use a wide variety of investment techniques. To raise returns and cushion themselves they use instruments like short positions, transactions in derivatives, and leverage. Their transactions were characterized by high risk in the recent period; therefore, a number of them collapsed.

16 This observation applies most to firms in Thailand that had taken on a great deal of short-term debt.

17 What is stated here is a generalization. After the near collapse of the Long-Term Capital Management (LTCM), New York, in the last quarter of 1998, it became known that while the base funds of LTCM were $5 billion, the leveraged funds were of the order of $1,000 billion.

18 In a seminal study, Shiller (1989) analyzed the herding behavior of investors during the 1987 stock market crash. The only reason consistently given by those selling stocks for their actions was the fact that prices were plummeting.

19 This statement has been made in the current context. A polemist may question it by stating that the Bretton-Woods period was not known for speculative attacks on currencies.

20 ERM stands for the exchange rate mechanism. Along with the Ecu (or European Currency Unit), the exchange rate mechanism was one of the foundation stones of economic and monetary union of the European Economic Communities (EEC). It gave currencies a central exchange rate against the Ecu. That in turn gave them central cross-rates against one another. It was hoped that the mechanism would help to stabilize exchange rates in the EEC economies, encourage trade within Europe, and control inflation. The ERM gave national currencies an upper and lower limit on either side of this central rate within which they could fluctuate. In 1992 the ERM was wrenched apart when a

number of currencies could no longer keep within these limits. On what became known as Black Wednesday, the British pound was forced to leave the system. The Italian lira also left, and the Spanish peseta was devalued. As Economic and Monetary Union progressed, a currency's ability to stay within its margins became one of the convergence criteria in deciding its suitability to join the single currency and complete monetary union. The original ERM became obsolete when the euro was launched. In September 1998, the ERM II was created for the members of the European Union that were not participating in the euro.

21 Bank for International Settlements, is based in Basel, Switzerland.

22 Revised statistics issued by the US government on 31 July 2002 showed that the US economy grew much more slowly than expected in the second quarter of 2002 – by only 1.1 percent at an annualized rate. The revised statistics also indicated that the 2001 recession was significantly worse than previously estimated, and growth in the first quarter of 2002 a bit less impressive than earlier statistics had indicated. The backward changes implied a necessary downward revision to America's spectacular productivity figures, and cast doubt on the "miracle" of the new economy.

23 In August 2002, the Dow Jones Industrial Average, and the FTSE 100 index, after slipping for months, came close to a mini-crash and created volatility in all the important stock markets around the globe. The WorldCom accounting scandal and bankruptcy followed the Enron and Andersen debacles. Andersen, the legendary accounting and consulting colossus, was convicted of obstruction of justice in the biggest accounting scandal in US corporate history. By August 2002, the debacle had cost investors more than $300 billion and put tens of thousands out of work. Insular and inbred, Andersen was unable to respond swiftly to crises. Its collapse represented an unimaginable failure of leadership and governance (*Business Week*, 2002). WorldCom sought Chapter 11 protection on 22 July 2002. With more than $107 billion in assets, this was the largest US insolvency ever – twice as large as Enron's record bankruptcy filing a few weeks before. Revelations of one major accounting scandal after another in the US drove the global stock markets to the edge of a precipice.

24 Published by the International Monetary Fund in December 2002 (IMF, 2002b).

25 Source: IMF (2002b), Table 3.1.

26 In particular, refer to Chapter 3 for greater details and complete statistics. At the beginning of this paragraph it was mentioned that the statistics used here are gross, and are therefore not comparable to those in Table 2.1.

27 The EU Accession Treaty was signed by the following ten countries in mid-April 2003, in Athens: Cyprus, the Czech Republic, Estonia, Hungary, Latvia, Lithuania, Malta, Poland, Slovakia, and Slovenia. These countries will be members of the EU in May 2004.

28 Oil prices had reached their peak of nearly $40 a barrel in March 2003.

29 Domestic demand in Germany was weak, and the recent appreciation of the euro against the dollar curbed export demand as well. Most economists agree that interest rates were too high for Germany during this period, but the objective of the European Central Bank (ECB) was to set monetary policy in the interests of the Euro zone as a whole. While the monetary loosening Germany needed was proving elusive, fiscal policy provided no relief either. Thanks to the stability and growth pact, which set strict budget-deficit limits, the government found itself tightening fiscal policy to try to bring its budget deficit back within the permitted range. The European Central Bank should consider raising its inflation target, which was 0.2 percent at that time. The International Monetary Fund (IMF) stressed that the circumstances warranted

relaxing of monetary policy in the European Union, but on 12 April 2003, the ECB president, Wim Duisenberg, argued that European interest rates were at the right level.

3 Financial liberalization in the emerging market economies: growth, volatility, or both?

1 The G-7 group of countries comprises Canada, France, Germany, Italy, Japan, the UK, and the US.
2 Williamson and Mahar (1998) provide a detailed survey of financial liberalization endeavors.
3 Rajan and Zingales (1998) and Eichengreen (2002) provide a literature survey of the empirical studies that attempt to quantify the growth impact of capital account liberalization.
4 This was a common weakness of empirical studies, although Kaminsky and Schmukler (2001) did manage to develop a homogeneous dataset for several dimensions of financial liberalization.
5 Several recent studies provide evidence of these static and dynamic effects. For instance, refer to Klenow and Rodriguez-Clare, 1997; Bekaert and Harvey, 2001; Henry, 2000a, 2000b; Bekaert *et al.*, 2002.
6 Some of the recent studies that bring out this point are Claessens *et al.*, 2001a; Galindo *et al.*, 2001; Moel, 2001; Mishkin, 2001a.
7 See Hellman *et al.* (2000).
8 Refer to studies by the World Bank (1989) and Roubini and Sala-I-Martin (1991).
9 Results of several empirical studies can be cited for this purpose. For instance, refer to Ghani (1992), King and Levine (1993a), Levine *et al.* (1999); Loayza and Beck (1999); Beck *et al.* (2000).
10 Paul Krugman strongly supported Malaysia's adoption of capital controls in 1998. Other economists who proposed limiting capital flows included Rodrik (1998).
11 Until the end of 1999, the IFC published these data series. In January 2000, Standard and Poor's took over the ownership of the IFC's price indexes.

4 Evolving financial market structure in the emerging market economies

1 In 2003, the following 11 countries were the members of the Group of Ten (or G-10): Belgium, Canada, France, Germany, Italy, Japan, the Netherlands, Sweden, Switzerland, the United Kingdom (UK), and the United States of America (USA).
2 The following report published by the Group of Ten (G-10) Report on Consolidation of the Financial Sector, in Basel, focuses on the consolidation process in a comprehensive manner. Refer to Chapters 2 and 6 in particular for a generalized picture of causes behind consolidation of the banking and financial sector.
3 For a detailed treatment of these and related issues refer to Berger *et al.* (1999); Focarelli *et al.* (1999), Walter and Boot (1999).
4 Panzar and Rosse (1987) showed that the sum of the elasticities of a firm's revenues with respect to a firm's input prices, the so-called H statistics, could be used to identify the nature of the market structure in which the firm operates.
5 The Herfindahl–Hirshman (HH) index is a standard measure of consolidation in any industry, and is defined as the sum of squared deposit market shares of all the banks in the market. The index is so constructed that the HH index has an upper value of 10,000 in the case of a monopolized firm with a 100 percent

share of the market, while it tends to be zero in the case of a large number of firms with very small market shares.

6 The five Asian crisis economies were Indonesia, Korea, Malaysia, the Philippines, and Thailand.

7 According to the BIS and International Monetary Fund (IMF) statistics, in 2000 in the US bond market the total bonds outstanding were 165 percent of the GDP, in Japan they were 130 percent, in Germany 116 percent, and in the United Kingdom 113 percent.

8 Mihaljek (1998) has provided a historical account of the creation of bond markets in the US since 1776, when the US was a small underdeveloped economy.

9 It was entitled *A New Approach to Sovereign Debt Restructuring*, written by Anne O. Kruger.

10 These 21 emerging market economies are: (1) China, (2) Hong Kong SAR, (3) India, (4) Indonesia, (5) Korea, (6) Malaysia, (7) the Philippines, (8) Singapore, and (9) Thailand in Asia; (1) Argentina, (2) Brazil, (3) Chile, (4) Colombia, (5) Mexico, and (6) Peru in Latin America; and (1) the Czech Republic, (2) Hungary, (3) Poland, and (4) the Russian Federation in Central and Eastern Europe; plus (1) Israel and (2) South Africa.

11 The Bank for International Settlements (BIS) statistics do not include Brady bonds, because they are repackaged bank loans.

12 Statistical data in this section have been taken from Mihaljek *et al.*, 2002. They in turn gleaned them from the International Monetary Fund and the World Bank joint publication entitled *Developing Government Bond Markets: A Handbook* (Washington, DC, 2001) and the Bank for International Settlements (BIS).

13 Fifteen European sovereign nations institutionalized an economic union called the European Union. A sub-set of these economies, 12 of 15, voluntarily surrendered their monetary sovereignty and elected to adopt a common currency called the euro, which is managed by a common central bank, the European Central Bank, based in Frankfurt.

14 See IMF (2003b), Chapter 4, in particular Box 4.1.

15 For a detailed historical account, refer to Caprio and Vittas (1997).

16 This expectation was articulated by TNCs in a survey undertaken by G-10 (2001). See Chapter II of the G-10 (2001) study for the results of this survey.

17 See Hawkins and Mihaljek (2001), Table 8, for the relevant statistical data.

18 For instance, see Barajas *et al.* (2000) for Colombia, Kiraly *et al.* (2000) for Hungary, and Honohan (2000) for Greece and Portugal.

19 The source of these statistics is the Standard & Poors' Emerging Market Database (2001), published by the International Finance Corporation.

20 Stock markets in Korea and Taiwan are known for very high trading volumes.

21 This has become a much-researched area lately, and several studies have tracked the recent growth of bourses and stock markets in the emerging market economies. The noteworthy pieces of research among them are Levine and Zrvos (1998), Catalan *et al.* (2000), Beck *et al.* (2001), Demirguc-Kunt and Levine (2001), Kaminsky and Schmukler (2001), Karolyi (2001), Hargis (2001), Pagano *et al.* (2001), and Claessens *et al.* (2002).

22 Griffin *et al.* (2003) had data for three more economies, but they were not used.

23 The practice of cross-listing of stocks on other global exchanges was begun by the European corporations to globalize their financial reach. Depository receipts (DRs) were frequently used by the emerging market economies to attain the same objective during the 1990s. They are negotiable claims against

ordinary shares in the home market of a firm created by the US or global depositary banks that trade over-the-counter on major stock exchanges. Two kinds of DRs are in popular use, namely American Depositary Receipts (ADRs) and Global Depositary Receipts (GDRs). These are foreign currency denominated derivative instruments issued by large global or foreign banks like Citibank, HSBC, ING Baring, and Bank of New York. These banks represent home securities held with a local custodian.

24 Source: Claessens *et al.* (2002).
25 These statistics were compiled and cited by Karolyi (2003).
26 See, for instance, recent works such as those by Jorion and Goetzmann (1999) and Longin and Solnik (2001).

5 Financial and macroeconomic instability in the emerging market economies

1 Bekaert and Harvey (2001); Bekaert *et al.* (2001), and Chari and Henry (2002b) reached this conclusion.
2 Refer to Edwards (2001) and McKenzie (2001) for such a conclusion. Arteta *et al.* (2001) found a conditional positive link; that is, that global capital flows do influence domestic investment and growth but only in the absence of macroeconomic imbalances.
3 Herding implies buying or selling an asset contemporaneously because other market participants are doing so.
4 ERM stands for the exchange rate mechanism. Along with the Ecu (or European Currency Unit), the Exchange Rate Mechanism was one of the foundation stones of economic and monetary union of the European Economic Community (EEC). It gave currencies a central exchange rate against the Ecu, which in turn gave them central cross-rates against one another. It was hoped that the mechanism would help to stabilize exchange rates in the EEC economies, encourage trade within Europe, and control inflation. The ERM gave national currencies an upper and lower limit on either side of this central rate within which they could fluctuate. In 1992 the ERM was wrenched apart when a number of currencies could no longer keep within these limits. On what became known as Black Wednesday, the British pound was forced to leave the system. The Italian lira also left, and the Spanish peseta was devalued. As Economic and Monetary Union progressed, a currency's ability to stay within its margins became one of the convergence criteria deciding its suitability to join the single currency and complete monetary union. The original ERM became obsolete when the euro was launched. In September 1998, the ERM II was created for the members of the European Union that were not participating in the euro.
5 Recent examples of currency collapse include the Russian ruble and the Brazilian real.
6 China shared this characteristic with the other economies of the so-called Greater China, namely Hong Kong SAR and Taiwan, both of whom had accumulated large foreign currency reserves.
7 Cited in *The Economist* (2003b).
8 Some of the contagions were regional (as in case of the Asian crisis in 1997–1998), while others were global (as in the case of the Russian crisis of 1998).
9 IMF's programs for Indonesia, Korea, and Thailand fall under these categories.
10 As Professor Joe Stiglitz would have us believe.
11 This section draws on World Bank (2002), Chapter 2, in particular pp. 40–5.
12 Refer to BIS (1997) for a more detailed treatment of this issue.

13 During the decade of the 1990s, Venezuela, the Nordic countries, Japan, and the United States all had similar experiences.

14 Das (2001c) provides a detailed treatment of this kind of exploitation in the crisis-affected emerging market economies of Asia.

15 Korea and the Philippines, during and in the aftermath of the Asian crisis, revealed the largest number of instances of this kind.

16 Feldstein (2000), Frankel (2000), Schmulkler and Zoido-Lobaton (2001), and Kaminsky and Reinhart (2003) provide an excellent analysis of this issue.

17 "Herding" implies buying or selling an asset contemporaneously because other market participants are doing so.

18 Momentum trading refers to buying an asset when its price rises and selling when its prices fall.

19 A long-term history of financial crises has been provided by Kindleberger (1996).

20 Please note that this is a large issue and it has been dealt with in a more deservingly detailed manner elsewhere by the author. One suggested reference is Das (2003b).

21 The 1997–1998 crisis in Thailand is particularly revealing in this respect. Policy-makers were remiss and had made several of these errors; consequently, Thailand acquired the dubious distinction of becoming the Asian economy that launched the Asian crisis.

22 During the Asian crisis, China and Taiwan accumulated large currency reserves and succeeded in keeping the contagion at bay.

23 See, for instance, Guiditti (1999) and Greenspan (1999).

24 For instance, refer to Caves *et al.*, 2002, pp. 520–6.

6 Financial globalization and the contagion effect

1 On 17 August 1998, the Russian Federation announced a *de facto* devaluation by widening the trading band of the ruble. It also announced its intention to restructure all official domestic currency debt falling due to the end of 1999, and imposed a 90-day moratorium on the repayment of private external debt. The period in the lead-up to these events and declarations held evidence of substantial stress.

2 Long-Term Capital Management (LTCM) was a large US hedge fund. Although at this point LTCM did not go bankrupt, it came close to a collapse and had to be bailed out by the Federal Reserve Bank of New York (FRBNY). On 23 September 1998, the FRBNY organized a bail-out by encouraging 14 banks to invest in the hedge fund for a stake in the firm to save it from default. The LTCM crisis turned out to be relatively short, spanning only a few weeks. One of the possible reasons why the LTCM crisis lasted for such a short period was Federal Reserve's aggressive easing of monetary policy during this period (Jorion, 2000).

3 One key characteristic of the crisis in the Russian Federation and near-collapse of the LTCM was that the risk of default was mainly on tradable securities. As opposed to this, in other recent crises, like that in Asia, the trigger was the risk of default on bank loans. The BIS (1999) adjudged the Russian bond default and the subsequent near-collapse of the LTCM as the "worst crisis" in the recent period.

4 See for instance Claessens and Forbes (2001) and Claessens *et al.* (2001b), which are two excellent survey articles. Some of the other noteworthy works are Glick and Rose, 1999; Chang and Velasco, 2001; Forbes and Rigobon, 2001, 2002; Forbes, 2002.

5 Stock markets in Hong Kong SAR plunged 25 percent in four days, starting 20 October 1997. Asset prices continued to fall until the end of November, influencing returns in several other emerging market and industrial economies.

6 The two related papers by Corsetti *et al.* (2000b, 2001a) provide a theoretical appraisal of studies on contagion and interdependence.

7 Forbes (2000b) provides a discussion of numerous channels responsible for the creation of a contagion effect. Seekers of greater detail than provided in this chapter should refer to this paper.

8 LIBOR is a benchmark interest rate, and stands for London Inter-Bank Offer Rate.

9 The definitions of herding behavior and momentum trading were provided earlier in Chapter 1, Section 5. The former implies buying or selling an asset contemporaneously because other market participants are doing so. Momentum trading refers to buying an asset when its prices are rising, and selling when its prices are falling.

10 This definition was provided by Forbes and Rigobon (2000).

11 The fundamental in this case is the change in competitiveness of exports in the third-country market.

12 See, for instance, Pericoli and Sbracia (2001); Corsetti *et al.* (2000b, 2001a); Claessens *et al.* (2001b).

13 This section draws on Kaminski and Reinhart (2003a).

14 See the seminal analyses by Millar (1998).

15 During this period, the Philippines had large exposure to the US banks.

16 For an overview of this literature and empirical evidence at the industry level, see Forbes (2000b, 2002), and Glick and Rose (1999).

17 The abbreviation ERM stands for the exchange rate mechanism. Along with the Ecu (or European Currency Unit), the Exchange Rate Mechanism was one of the foundation stones of economic and monetary union of the European Economic Community (EEC). It gave currencies a central exchange rate against the Ecu. That, in turn, gave them central cross-rates against one another. It was hoped that the mechanism would help stabilize exchange rates in the EEC economies, encourage trade within Europe and control inflation. The ERM gave national currencies an upper and lower limit on either side of this central rate within which they could fluctuate. In 1992, the ERM was wrenched apart when a number of currencies could no longer keep within these limits. On what became known as Black Wednesday, the British pound was forced to leave the system. The Italian lira also left, and the Spanish peseta was devalued. As Economic and Monetary Union progressed, a currency's ability to stay within its margins became one of the convergence criteria deciding its suitability to join the single currency and complete monetary union. The original ERM became obsolete when the euro was launched. In September 1998, the ERM II was created for the members of the European Union that were not participating in the euro.

18 Its full name is Mercado Comun del Sur, or the common market of the south. Its membership includes Argentina, Brazil, Paraguay, and Uruguay.

19 The four ANIEs are Hong Kong SAR, Korea, Taiwan, and Thailand.

20 Glick and Rose (1999) were the first to use the expression "ground-zero country."

21 For instance, see Radelet and Sachs (1998a, 1998b), Stiglitz (1998a), Krugman (1999), Kawai *et al.* (2001).

22 Some of the recent studies providing evidence of this include Glick and Rose (1999) and Wolf (1997).

23 They have been dealt with in a cursory manner here. For a detailed discussion, refer to Kaminsky and Reinhart (2003b).
24 Some of the recent studies providing evidence of this include Glick and Rose (1999) and Wolf (1997).

7 Global financial architecture and financial and regulatory infrastructure

1 Refer to Crockett (2003) for complete details of the two types of systems and the transformation process.
2 Refer to Chapter III through Chapter VIII of the Article of Agreement of the International Monetary Fund.
3 Group of 22 (or G-22) was a mixed *ad hoc* group, created by the US in April 1998, and had its first meeting in Washington, DC. It was originally created to study the fallout from the Asian crisis and plan a "new international economic architecture." Its members are the G-7 economies plus Argentina, Australia, Brazil, China, Hong Kong (SAR), India, Indonesia, Malaysia, Mexico, Poland, Russia, Singapore, South Africa, Korea (Republic of), and Thailand. The Bretton-Woods institutions were given observer status.
4 This was jointly made by Lord John Eatwell and Lane Taylor.
5 Refer to Jordan and Majnoni (2002) and Jordan and Lubrano (2002) for more detailed discussion of these issues.
6 The English Common Law system is one of the best examples of this kind of legal arrangement.
7 For a thorough discussion see Giovanoli (2001).
8 For a detailed treatment of this issue, readers are referred to an excellent unpublished paper by Corsetti *et al.* (2001b).
9 The Forum brings together on a regular basis the national authorities responsible for financial stability in significant international financial centers, international financial institutions, sector-specific international groupings of regulators and supervisors, and committees of central bank experts. The FSF seeks to co-ordinate the efforts of these various bodies in order to promote international financial stability, improve the functioning of markets, and reduce systemic risk.
10 The abbreviation ERM stands for the exchange rate mechanism. Along with the Ecu (or European Currency Unit), the exchange rate mechanism was one of the foundation stones of economic and monetary union of the European Economic Community (EEC). It gave currencies a central exchange rate against the Ecu. That, in turn, gave them central cross-rates against one another. It was hoped that the mechanism would help stabilize exchange rates in the EEC economies, encourage trade within Europe and control inflation. The ERM gave national currencies an upper and lower limit on either side of this central rate within which they could fluctuate. In 1992 the ERM was wrenched apart when a number of currencies could no longer keep within these limits. On what became known as Black Wednesday, the British pound was forced to leave the system. The Italian lira also left and the Spanish peseta was devalued. As Economic and Monetary Union progressed, a currency's ability to stay within its margins became one of the convergence criteria deciding its suitability to join the single currency and complete monetary union. The original ERM became obsolete when the euro was launched. In September 1998, the ERM II was created for the members of the European Union that were not participating in the euro.
11 Some of the largest HFs in the world, such as Long-Term Capital Management (LTCM), the Tiger Group of Funds, and the Quantum Group of Funds, no longer exist.

12 Obstfeld and Taylor (2002) have tried to interpret the various periods of globalization in terms of the Mundellian "impossible trinity."
13 See, for instance, Chang and Velasco (2000); Bordo *et al.* (2001); Aghion *et al.* (2001); Calvo (2002); Calvo and Reinhart (2002).
14 Dollarization refers to the widespread domestic use of another country's currency (typically the US dollar) to perform the standard function of money – that of unit of account, medium of exchange, and store f value.

References and bibliography

Abheysinghe, T. and Forbes, K.J. (2003) Trade Linkages and Output-multiplier Effects: a VAR Approach with a Focus on Asia, Cambridge, MA: National Bureau of Economic Research and the University of Chicago. NBER Working Paper No. 8600.

Abreu, M. (1996) "Trade in manufactures: the outcome of the Uruguay Round and developing country interests," in W. Martin and L.A. Winters (eds) *The Uruguay Round and the Developing Economies*, Cambridge: Cambridge University Press.

Abu-Lughod, J. (1989) *Before European Hegemony: The World System AD 1250–1350*, New York: Oxford University Press.

Agenor, P.R. (2002) Benefits and Costs of International Financial Integration: Theory and Facts, Washington, DC: The World Bank Policy Research Working Paper No. 2788. February.

Agenor, P.R. (2003) Does Globalization Hurt the Poor? January 7 (unpublished paper).

Aghion, P., Bachetta, P. and Banergee, A. (2001) "Currency crises and monetary policy in an economy with credit constraints," *European Economic Review* 45: 7, 1121–50.

Alejandro, C.D.F. (1983) "Stories of the 1930s for the 1980s," in P. Aspe, R. Dornbusch and M. Obstfeld (eds) *Financial Policies and the World Capital Markets*, Chicago: University of Chicago Press.

Anderson, J.E. and van Wincoop, E. (2001) Gravity with Gravitas: a Solution to the Border Puzzle, Cambridge, MA: National Bureau of Economic Research. Working Paper No. 8079. Revised version available at www.virginia.edu./~econ/vanwincoopx.htm.

Anderson, K., Francois, J., Hertel, T., Hoekman, B. and Martin, W. (2001) *Potential Gains from Trade Reforms in the New Millennium*, Washington, DC: The World Bank.

Andrea, G. and Court, J. (2002) Inequality, Growth and Poverty in the Era of Liberalization and Globalization, Helsinki, Finland: United Nations University, World Institute for Development Economic Research. Policy Brief, No. 4.

Arteta, C., Eichengreen, B. and Wyplosz, C. (2001) When Does Capital Account Liberalization Help More than it Hurts? London: Centre for Economic Policy Research. Discussion Paper No. 2910. December.

Bachatta, P. and van Wincoop, E. (2000) "Capital flows to emerging markets: liberalization, overshooting, and volatility," in S. Edwards (ed.) *Capital Flows and*

Emerging Economies, Cambridge, MA: National Bureau of Economic Research and the University of Chicago.

Baig, T. and Goldfajn, I. (1999) "Financial market contagion in the Asian crisis," *IMF Staff Papers* 46: 1, 167–95.

Bakker, A.F.P. (1996) *The Liberalization of Capital Movements in Europe 1958–94*, Dordrecht: Kluwer Academic Publishers.

Baldwin, R.E. and Martin, P. (1999) Two Waves of Globalization: Superficial Similarities, Fundamental Differences, Cambridge, MA: National Bureau of Economic Research. NBER Working Paper No. 6904.

Baldwin, R.E. and Venables, A.J. (1995) "Regional economic integration," in G. Grossman and K. Rogoff (eds) *Handbook of International Economics*, Amsterdam: Elsevier Science, pp. 1597–634.

Ball, L. (2000) Policy Rules and External Shocks, Cambridge, MA: National Bureau of Economic Research. Working Paper No. 7910.

Bank for International Settlements (BIS) (1997) *Financial Stability in Emerging Market Economies*, Basel: BIS.

Bank for International Settlements (BIS) (1999) *A Review of Financial Market Events in Autumn 1998*, Basel: Committee on Global Financial Systems, BIS.

Bank for International Settlements (BIS) (2002) Determinants of International Bank Lendings to Emerging Market Countries, Basel: BIS Working Paper No. 112.

Barajas, A., Steiner, R. and Salazar, N. (2000) "Foreign investment in Colombia's financial sector," in S. Claessens and M. Jansen (eds) *The Internationalization of Financial Services*, Boston, MA: Kluwer Academic Press, pp. 134–68.

Barro, R.J. (1991) "Economic growth in cross-section of countries," *Quarterly Journal of Economics* 56: 2, 407–43.

Barth, J.R., Caprio, G. and Levine, R. (2001) The Regulation and Supervision of Banks Around the World: A New Database, Washington, DC: World Bank.

Bartolini, L. and Drazen, A. (1997) "When liberal policies reflect external shocks, what do we learn?" *Journal of International Economics* 42: 249–73.

Basel Committee on Banking Supervision (BCBS) (2001a) The New Basel Capital Accord Basel: Bank for International Supervision.

Basel Committee on Banking Supervision (BCBS) (2001b) Consultative Document: the New Basel Capital Accord, Basel: Bank for International Supervision.

Basel Committee on Banking Supervision (BCBS) (2002) An Overview of the New Basel Capital Accord, Basel: Bank for International Supervision.

Beck, T., Demirguc-Kunt, A., Levine, R. and Maksimovic, V. (2001) "Financial structure and economic development: firm, industry and country evidence," in A. Demirguc-Kunt and R. Levine (eds) *Financial Structure and Economic Growth*, Cambridge, MA: MIT Press, pp. 12–46.

Beck, T., Levine, R. and Loayza, N. (2000) "Finance and sources of growth," *Journal of Financial Economics* 58: 1, 261–300.

Bekaert, G. and Harvey, C. (2001) "Foreign speculators and emerging equity markets," *Journal of Finance* 55: 2, 565–613.

Bekaert G., Harvey, C. and Lundblad, R. (2001) Does Financial Liberalization Spur Growth? Cambridge, MA: National Bureau of Economic Research Working Paper No. 7724.

Bekaert G., Harvey, C.R. and Lundblad, C. (2002) Does Financial Liberalization Spur Growth? Paper presented at the Joint Conference between the World Bank and George Washington, University on *Financial Globalization: A Blessing or A Curse?*, 30–31 May, Washington, DC.

Berger, A.N., Demsetz, R.S. and Strahan, P.E. (1999) "The consolidation of financial services industry: causes, consequences and implications for the future," *Journal of Banking and Finance* 23: 1, 135–94.

Blinder, A.S. (2003) "A new global financial order: the art of the possible," in D.K. Das (ed.) *An International Finance Reader*, London and New York: Routledge, pp. 104–13.

Bordo, M., Eichengreen, B. and Irwin, D.A. (1999) Is Globalization Today Really Different than Globalization a Hundred Years Ago? Cambridge, MA: National Bureau of Economic Research Working Paper No. 6195.

Bordo, M., Eichengreen, B., Klingebiel, D. and Martinez-Paria, M.S. (2001) Financial crises: lessons from the past 120 years," *Economic Policy* 45: 4, 110–36.

Bordo, M.D. (1993) "The Bretton Woods International Monetary System: a historical overview," in M.D. Bordo and B.J. Eichengreen (eds) *A Retrospective on the Bretton Woods System: Lessons for International Monetary Reforms*, Chicago: University of Chicago Press, pp. 160–95.

Bordo, M.D. and Eichengreen, B.J. (1998) "Implication of the Great Depression for the development of the international monetary system," in M.D. Bordo, C. Goldin and E.N. White (eds) *The Defining Moment: The Great Depression and the American Economy in the Twentieth Century*, Chicago: University of Chicago Press, pp. 212–42.

Bordo, M.D., Edelstein, M. and Rockoff, H. (1999) Was Adherence to Gold Standard a 'Good Housekeeping Seal of Approval' During the Interwar Period? Cambridge, MA: National Bureau of Economic Research. Working Paper No. 7186. June.

Borensztein, E., De Gregorio, J. and Lee, J.W. (1998) "How does foreign direct investment affect growth?" *Journal of International Economics* 45: 1, 115–35.

Bosworth, B. and Collins, S.M. (1999) "Capital flows to developing economies: implications for savings and investment," *Brookings Papers on Economic Activity*, 1: 143–69.

Bourguignon, F. and Morrisson, C. (2001) Inequality Among World Citizens: 1820–1992, Paris: THEMA et DELTA. Working Paper No. 2001-25.

Brash, D.T. (2000) How Should Monetary Policy Makers Respond to the New Challenges of Global Economic Integration? Paper presented at the symposium on *Global Economic Integration: Opportunities and Challenges*, sponsored by the Federal Reserve Bank of Kansas, at Jackson Hole, Wyoming, on August 24–26.

Brooks, R. and Del Negro, M. (2002). The Rise in Co-movements Across National Stock Markets: Market Integration or Global Bubble? Washington, DC: International Monetary Fund. Working Paper No. WP/02/147. September.

Buch, C.M. (2000) "Why do banks go abroad: evidence from German data," *Financial Markets, Institutions and Instruments* 9: 1, 33–67.

Buiter, W.H. (2000) The New Economy and Old Monetary Economics, London: Bank of England. Discussion Paper.

Burnside, C., Eichenbaum, M. and Rebelo, S. (2001). "Hedging and financial fragility in fixed exchange rate regimes," *European Economic Review* 45: 6, 1151–93.

Business Week (2002) Fall from Grace, 2 August, pp. 45–6.

Bussiere, M. and Mulder, C. (1999). External Vulnerability in Emerging Market

Economies, Washington, DC: International Monetary Fund. Working Paper No. WP/99/98.

Calomiris, C.W. and Karceski, J. (1998) Is the Bank Merger Wave of the 1990s Efficient? New York: Columbia University Department of Economics Working Paper No. 98-0022.

Calvo, G.A. (2002) Globalization Hazard and Weak Government in Emerging Markets, Washington, DC: Inter-American Development Bank Working Paper.

Calvo, G.A., Izquierdo, A. and Talvi, E. (2002) Sudden Stops, the Real Exchange Rate and Fiscal Stability: Lessons from Argentina, Washington, DC: Inter-American Development Bank Working Paper No. 469.

Calvo, G.A., Leiderman, L. and Reinhart, C.M. (1996) "Inflows of capital to developing countries in the 1990s," *Journal of Economic Perspective* 10: 123–39.

Calvo, G.A. and Mendoza, E. (1998) *Rational Herd Behavior and the Globalization of Securities Markets*, College Park, MD: University of Maryland.

Calvo, G.A. and Mendoza, E. (2000) "Capital market crises and economic collapse in emerging markets: an informational-frictions approach," *American Economic Review*, Papers and Proceedings 90: 59–70.

Calvo, G.A. and Reinhart, C. (1999) When Capital and Inflows Come to a Sudden Stop: Consequences and Policy Options, Baltimore, MD: University of Maryland. Available at http://www.puaf.umd.edu/faculty/papers/reinhart/imfbook.pdf.

Calvo, G.A. and Reinhart, C. (2002) "Fear of floating," *Quarterly Journal of Economics* 117: 2, 112–40.

Cameron, R.E. (1993) *A Concise Economic History of the World*, New York: Oxford University Press.

Cannadine, D. (1990) *Decline and Fall of the British Aristocracy*, New Haven, CT: Yale University Press.

Caprio, G. and Vittas, D. (1997) *Reforming Financial Systems: Historical Implications for Policy*, Washington, DC: World Bank.

Catalan, M., Impavido, G. and Musalem, A.R. (2000) "Contractual Savings of Stock Market Developments: Which Leads? Washington, DC: World Bank Policy Research Working Paper No. 2421.

Caves, R., Frankell, J.A. and Jones, R. (2002) *World Trade and Payments*, 9th edn, Boston, MA: Addison Wesley Longman.

Centre for International Economics (CIE) (2001) *Globalization and Poverty: Turning the Corner*, Canberra: CIE.

Chang, R. and Velasco, A. (2000) "Exchange rate policy in developing countries," *American Economic Review: Papers and Proceedings* 90: 5, 71–5.

Chang, R. and Velasco, A. (2001) "A model of financial crises in emerging markets," *Quarterly Journal of Economics* 116: 3, 489–517.

Chari, A. and Henry, P.B. (2001) "Stock market liberalization and the repricing of systemic risk," Cambridge, MA: National Bureau of Economic Research Working Paper No. 8265.

Chari, A. and Henry, P.B. (2002a) "Capital account liberalization: allocative efficiency or animal spirit? Paper presented at the Joint Conference between the World Bank and George Washington, University on *Financial Globalization: A Blessing or A Curse?*, 30–31 May, Washington, DC.

Chari, A. and Henry, P. (2002b) Capital Account Liberalization: Allocative Efficiency or Animal Spirits? Cambridge, MA: National Bureau of Economic Research Working Paper No. 8908.

Chen, Z. and Khan, M.S. (2003) "Patterns of capital flows to emerging market economies," in D.K. Das (ed.) *An International Finance Reader*, London and New York: Routledge, pp. 341–54.

Citrin, D. and Fischer, S. (2000) "Meeting the challenges of globalization in the advanced economies," in H. Wagner (ed.) *Globalization and Unemployment*, Berlin: Springer, pp. 19–35.

Claessens, S., Demirguc-Kunt, A. and Huizinga, H. (2000) "The role of foreign banks in domestic banking systems," in S. Claessens and M. Jansen (eds) *The Internationalization of Financial Services: Issues and Lessons for Developing Countries*, Boston, MA: Kluwer Academic Press.

Claessens, S., Demirguc-Kunt, A. and Huizinga, H. (2001a) "How does foreign entry affect domestic banking markets?" *Journal of Banking and Finance* 25: 4, 891–911.

Claessens, S., Dooley, M.P. and Warner, A. (1995) "Portfolio capital flows: hot or cold?" *World Bank Economic Review* 9: 1, 153–74.

Claessens, S., Dornbusch, R. and Park, Y.C. (2001b) "Contagion: why crises spread and how," in S. Claessens and K.J. Forbes (eds) *International Financial Contagion*, Boston, MA: Kluwer Academic Publishers, pp. 19–41.

Claessens, S., Klingebiel, D. and Schmukler, S. (2001c) *The Future of Stock Markets in Emerging Economies*, Washington, DC: The World Bank.

Claessens, S., Klingebiel, D. and Schmukler, S. (2002) Explaining the Migration of Stocks from Exchanges in Emerging Economies to International Centers, London: Centre for Economic Policy Research Discussion Paper No. 3301.

Claessens, S. and Forbes, K.J. (2001) "International financial contagion: an overview," in S. Claessens and K.J. Forbes (eds) *International Financial Contagion*, Boston, MA: Kluwer Academic Publishers, pp. 3–17.

Clarida, R., Gali, J. and Gertler, M. (1999) "The science of monetary policy: a new Keynesian perspective," *Journal of Economic Literature* 37: 2, 1661–707.

Clark, X., Dollar, D. and Kraay, A. (2001) *Decomposing Global Inequality, 1960–99*, Washington, DC: The World Bank.

Clarke, G., Cull, R., Paria, M.S.M. and Sanchez, S.M. (2001) Foreign Bank Entry: Experience, Implications for Developing Countries, and Agenda for Further Research. Background paper for the *World Development Report 2002*.

Coe, T.D., Subramanian, A. and Tamirisa, N.T. (2002) The Missing Globalization Puzzle, Washington, DC: IMF Working Paper. WP/02/171.

Collier, P. and Gunning, J.W. (1999) "Explaining African economic performance," *Journal of Economic Literature* 37: 2, 64–111.

Cordell, T. and Grilo, I. (1998) Globalization and Relocation in a Vertically Differentiated Industry, Washington, DC: IMF Working Paper No. WP/98/48. April.

Corsetti, G., Dasgupta, A., Morris, S. and Shin, H.S. (2000a) Does One Soros Make a Difference? The Role of a Large Trader in Currency Crises, New Haven, CT: Yale University. Cowles Foundation Discussion Paper No. 1273.

Corsetti, G., Pericoli, M. and Sbracia, M. (2000b) *The Transmission of Financial Shocks*, Rome: Bank of Italy.

Corsetti, G., Pericoli, M. and Sbracia, M. (2001a) "Correlation analysis of financial contagion: what one should know before running a test," *Temi di Discussione* 408, Rome: Bank of Italy.

Corsetti, G., Pesenti, P. and Roubini, N. (2001b) The Role of Large Players in Currency Crises. Paper presented at the NBER Conference on *Currency Crises Prevention*, 15 January, Cambridge, MA.

Crafts, N.F.R. (1985) *British Economic Growth During the Industrial Revolution,* Oxford: Clarendon Press.

Crafts, N.F.R. (2000) "Globalization and Growth in the Twentieth Century," Washington, DC: IMF Working Paper No. WP/00/44. March.

Crockett, A. (2000) "How should financial market regulators respond to the new challenges of global economic integration?" in *Global Economic Integration: Opportunities and Challenges,* Kansas City: The Federal Reserve Bank of Kansas City, pp. 130–65.

Crockett, A. (2003) "Strengthening the international financial architecture," in D.K. Das (ed.) *An International Finance Reader,* London and New York: Routledge, pp. 87–103.

Crosby, A. (1972) *The Columbian Exchange: Biological and Cultural Consequences of 1492,* London: Greenwood Press.

Dahlquist, M. and Robertsson, G. (2001) "Direct foreign ownership, institutional investors, and firm characteristics," *Journal of Financial and Quantitative Analysis* 59: 2, 413–40.

Daianu, D. (2002) Is Catching-up Possible in Europe? Warsaw: The Leon Kozminski Academy of Entrepreneurship and Management. Transformation Integration and Globalization Economic Research (TIGER). Working Paper Series No. 19. May.

Daly, M. and Kuwahara, H. (1998) "The impact of the Uruguay Round on tariff and non-tariff barriers to trade in the Quad," *The World Economy* 21: 2, 207–34.

Das, D.K. (1986) *Migration of Financial Resources to Developing Countries,* London: Macmillan Press Ltd.

Das, D.K. (1989) "Brady plan and the international banks: a cautious reception," *The Business Standard,* Bombay, August 24, p. 6.

Das, D.K. (1990) *International Trade Policy,* London: Macmillan Press Ltd.

Das, D.K. (1991a) *Korean Economic Dynamism,* London: Macmillan Press Ltd.

Das, D.K. (1991b) *Import Canalisation,* London: Sage Publications.

Das, D.K. (1996a) *The Asia-Pacific Economy,* London: Macmillan Press Ltd.

Das, D.K. (1996b) "Emerging markets and macroeconomic stabilization," *Journal of the Asia Pacific Economy* 1: 3, 319–46.

Das, D.K. (2000a) Asian Crisis: Distilling Critical Lessons, United Nations Conference on Trade and Development (UNCTAD), Geneva, Discussion Paper No. 152.

Das, D.K. (2000b) "Portfolio investment in emerging market economies: trends, dimensions and issues," *Journal of Asset Management* 3: 3, 144–82. September.

Das, D.K. (2001a) "Stimulants to capital inflows into emerging markets and the recent role of speculators," *Journal of International Development* 27: 2, 130–74.

Das, D.K. (2001b) "Liberalization efforts in China and accession to the World Trade Organization," *The Journal of World Investment,* London, pp. 130–65. December.

Das, D.K. (2001c) "Corporate governance and restructuring: a post-crisis Asian perspective," *The Asia Pacific Journal of Economics and Business,* June: 140–85.

Das, D.K. (2001d) China's Accession to the World Trade Organization: Issues and Implications, Australian National University, Asia Pacific School of Economics and Management, Canberra. Working Paper No. EA01-1. Available at http://ncdsnet.anu.edu.au.

Das, D.K. (2001e) *Global Trading System at the Crossroads: A Post Seattle Perspective*, London and New York: Routledge.

Das, D.K. (2002) "Managing financial markets and exchange rate volatility arising from globalization," *Global Business and Economic Review* 4: 2, 296–324.

Das, D.K. (2003a) "Globalization in the world of finance," in D.K. Das (ed.) *An International Finance Reader*, London and New York: Routledge, pp. 12–26.

Das, D.K. (2003b) "Managing globalization: macroeconomic, financial sector and exchange rate volatility," in D.K. Das (ed.) *An International Finance Reader*, London and New York: Routledge, pp. 27–45.

Das, D.K. (2003c) *Financial Globalization and Emerging Market Economies*, London and New York: Routledge.

Das, D.K. (2003d) *The Economic Dimensions of Globalization*, Basingstoke: Palgrave Macmillan Ltd.

Davidson, C. and Matusz, S. (2001) Globalization, Employment and Income: Analyzing the Adjustment Process," Nottingham, The University of Nottingham: Leverhulme Centre for Research on Globalization and Economic Policy. Research Paper 2001/04.

Davis, L.E. and Gallman, R.E. (2001) *Evolving Financial Markets and Capital Flows: Britain, the Americas and Australia, 1870–1914*. The Japan–US Center. Sanwa Monograph on International Financial Markets. Cambridge: Cambridge University Press.

De Gregorio, J. and Guidotti, P. (1993) *Financial Development and Economic Growth*, Washington, DC: International Monetary Fund.

De Gregorio, J. and Valdes, R.O. (2001) "Crisis transmission: evidence from the debt, tequila and Asian flu crises." *World Bank Economic Review* 15: 2, 289–314.

De la Torre, A., Yeyati, E.L. and Schmukler, S.L. (2002) Financial Globalization: Unequal Blessings, Washington, DC: World Bank Policy Research Working Paper No. 2903.

Demirguc-Kunt, A. and Detriagiache, E. (1998) Financial Liberalization and Financial Fragility, Washington, DC: International Monetary Fund Working Paper No. WP 98/83.

Demirguc-Kunt, A. and Levine, R. (2001) *Financial Structure and Economic Growth*, Cambridge, MA: MIT Press.

Demirguc-Kunt, A., Levine, R. and Min, H. (1998) *Foreign Banks: Issues of Efficiency, Fragility and Growth*, Washington, DC: World Bank.

Dollar, D. and Kraay, A. (2001) Trade, Growth and Poverty, Washington, DC: The World Bank Policy Research Working Paper No. 2199.

Dollar, D., Hallward-Driemeier, M., Mengistae, T., Goswami, O., Shrivastava, G.G. and Arun, A.K. (2001) *Investment Climate and Firm Productivity in India: 2000–2001*, Washington, DC: The World Bank.

Domowitz, I., Glenn, J. and Madhavan, A. (2001) "Liquidity, volatility and equity trading costs across countries and over time," *International Finance* 4: 2, 221–55.

Dooley, M.P., Mathieson, D.J. and Rojas-Suarez, L. (1996) Capital Mobility and Exchange Market Intervention in Developing Countries, WP/96/131, Washington, DC: International Monetary Fund.

Dornbusch, R. and Park, Y.C. (2001) "Defining contagion," *International Economics Update*, December. Available at http://www.internationaleconomics.net.

Dungey, M., Fry, R., Gonzalez-Hermosillo, B. and Martin, V. (2002) International Contagion Effects from the Russian Crisis and the LTCM Near-collapse, Washington, DC: IMF Working Paper No. WP/02/74.

Dungey, M., Martin, V.L. and Pagan, A.R. (2000) "A multivariate latent factor decomposition of international bond yield spreads," *Journal of Applied Econometrics* 15: 3, 697–715.

Easterly, W. (2000) *The Lost Decades and the Coming Boom? Policies, Shocks, and Developing Countries' Stagnation 1980–1998*, Washington, DC: World Bank.

Easterly, W. and Kraay, A. (1999) Small States, Small Problems, Washington, DC: World Bank Policy Research Working Paper No. 2139.

The Economist (1998) "Scared of heights?" 28 March, pp. 16–18.

The Economist. (2001) "Enter the dragon," 10 March, pp. 21–4.

The Economist (2002a) "In the balance," 22 July, p. 19.

The Economist (2002b) "Survey on e-commerce: shopping around the web," February 26.

The Economist (2003a) "Emerging market indicators," 25 January, p. 102.

The Economist (2003b) "Banking on growth," 20 January, pp. 67–8.

The Economist (2003c) "The emerging market scapegoat," Available at http://www.economist.com/agenda/displaystory.cfm?story_id=1544907.

The Economist (2003d) "Economic focus: a better way to go bust," 1 February, p. 64.

Edison, H.J. and Warnock, F.E. (2001) A Simple Measure of the Intensity of Capital Controls, Washington, DC: International Monetary Fund Working Paper No. WP/01.180.

Edison, H.J. and Warnock, F.E. (2003) US Investor's Emerging Market Equity Portfolio: a Security-level Analysis. Paper presented at the *Global Linkage Conference*, organized by the International Monetary Fund, 30–31 January, Washington, DC.

Edwards, S. (2000) *Capital Flows and Economic Performance: Are Emerging Markets Different?* Los Angeles: University of California.

Edwards, S. (2001) Capital Mobility and Economic Performance: Are Emerging Economies Different? University of California: Working Paper.

Eichengreen, B. (2002) "Capital account liberalization: what do the cross-country studies tell us?" *World Bank Economic Review* 22: 2, 177–208.

Eichengreen, B. (2003) "Strengthening the international financial architecture," in D.K. Das (ed.) *An International Finance Reader*, London and New York: Routledge, pp. 65–86.

Eichengreen, B. and Mody, A. (1998) What Explains Changing Spreads on Emerging Market Debt? Cambridge, MA: National Bureau of Economic Research Working paper No. 6408.

Eichengreen, B., Hausman, R. and Panizza, U. (2002) "Original sin: the pain, the mystery, and the road to redemption." Paper presented at the Inter-American Development Bank Conference on *Currency and Maturity Matchmaking: Redeeming Debt from Original Sin*, 11 November, Washington, DC.

Eichengreen, B., Rose, A. and Wyplosz, C. (1996) "Speculative attacks on pegged exchange rates," in M. Canzoneri, P. Masson and V. Grilli (eds) *Transatlantic Economic Issues*, Cambridge: Cambridge University Press.

Eichengreen, B., Rose, A. and Wyplosz, C. (1997) "Contagious currency crises," *Scandinavian Economic Review* 32: 6, 1120–51.

Eichengreen, B.J. (1992a) *Golden Fetters: The Gold Standard and the Great Depression*, Oxford: Oxford University Press.

Eichengreen, B.J. (1992b) "Trends and cycles in foreign lending," in H. Siebert (ed.) *Capital Flows in the World Economy*, Tubingen: J.C.B. Mohr Publisher.

Engel, C. and Rogers, J.H. (2001) "Deviations from purchasing power parity: causes and welfare costs," *Journal of International Economics* 55: 10, 29–57.

Environics (2001) "Poll findings suggest trouble ahead for global agenda: survey of 20,000." Available at http://environicsinternational.com.

Faini, R., de Melo, J. and Zimmermann, K. (1999) *Migration: The Controversies and the Evidence*, Cambridge: Cambridge University Press.

Favero, C.A. and Giavazzi, F. (2002) Looking for Contagion: Evidence from the ERM. Cambridge, MA: National Bureau of Economic Research Working Paper No. 7797.

Feenstra, R.C. (1998) "Integration of trade and disintegration of production in the global economy," *Journal of Economic Perspective* 12: 4, 31–50.

Feldstein, M. (2000) Aspects of Global Economic Integration: Outlook for the Future, Cambridge, MA: National Bureau of Economic Research Working Paper No. 7899.

Feldstein, M. and Horioka, C. (1980) "Domestic savings and international capital flows," *The Economic Journal* 90: 2, 314–29.

Fernandez, R. and Ports, J. (1998) "Returns to regionalism: an analysis of non-traditional gains from regional trade agreements," *World Bank Economic Review* 12: 2, 197–200.

Fernandez-Arias, E. (1996) "The new wave of private capital flows: push or pull?" *Journal of Development Economics* 48: 389–418.

Fernandez-Arias, E. and Montiel, P.J. (1996) "The surge of capital inflows to developing countries: an analytical overview," *World Bank Economic Review* 10: 1, 51–77.

Fiess, N. (2003) Capital Flows, Country Risk and Contagion, Washington, DC: World Bank. World Bank Policy Research Working Paper No. 2943.

Finance and Development (*F&D*) (1997) "Capital flow sustainability and speculative currency attacks," December, pp. 8–11.

Financial Stability Forum (FSF) (2000) "Report of the market dynamics study group of the FSF working group on highly leveraged institutions." Available at http://www.fsforum.org/Reports/RepHLI.html.

Financial Times (2002a) "Japanese banks given deadline over debt," 30 November/1 December.

Financial Times. (2002b) "Middle classes in China's long march to prosperity," London, 29 December, p. 3.

Findlay, R. (1996) The Emergence of the World Economy: Towards a Historical Perspective, New York, Columbia University, Columbia University Economics Discussion Paper No. 9596.

Findlay, R. and O'Rourke, K.H. (2001) Commodity Market Integration, 1500–2000. Paper presented at the NBER Conference on *Globalization in Historical Perspective*, Santa Barbara, CA, May 2002.

Fischer, S. (1998) "Capital account liberalization and the role of the IMF," *Essays in International Finance*, No. 207. Princeton, NJ: Princeton University Press, 1–10.

Fischer, S. (1999) "Reforming the international financial system," *Economic Journal* 109: 3, 557–76.

Fletcher, M.E. (1958) "The Suez Canal and the world of shipping; 1869–1914," *Journal of Economic History* 18: 3, 556–73.

Flynn, D.O. and Giraldez, A. (1995) "Born with a silver spoon: the origin of world trade in 1571," *Journal of World History* 18: 3, 556–73.

Focarelli, F., Panetta, F. and Salleo, C. (1999) "Why do banks merge?" *Temi di Discaussione del Servizio Studi 361*, Rome: Bank of Italy.

Focarelli, F. and Pozzolo, A. (2000) The Determinants of Cross-border Shareholdings: An Analysis with Bank-level Data from OECD Countries. Paper presented at a conference organized by the Federal Reserve Bank of Chicago on *Structure of Bank*, 20 May, Chicago.

Forbes, K.J. (2000) The Asian Flu and the Russian Virus: Firm Level Evidence on How Crises are Transmitted Internationally, Cambridge, MA: National Bureau of Economic Research Working Paper No. 7807.

Forbes, K.J. (2002) "Are trade linkages important determinants of country vulnerability to crises?" in S. Edwards and S. Frankel (eds) *Preventing Currency Crises in Emerging Markets*, Chicago: University of Chicago Press, pp. 77–124.

Forbes, K.J. (2003) "The Asian flu and Russian virus: firm level evidence on how crises are transmitted internationally," Cambridge, MA: Sloan School of Management. Available at http://mit.edu/kjforbes/www.

Forbes, K.J. and Rigobon, R. (2000) Contagion in Latin America: Definitions, Measurement and Policy Implications, Cambridge, MA: National Bureau of Economic Research Working Paper No. W7885.

Forbes, K.J. and Rigobon, R. (2001) "Measuring contagion: conceptual and empirical issues," in S. Claessens and K.J. Forbes (eds), *International Financial Contagion*, Boston, MA: Kluwer Academic Publishers, pp. 43–66.

Forbes, K.J. and Rigobon, R. (2002) "No contagion, only interdependence: measuring stock comovements," *Journal of Finance* 57: 7, 2223–61.

Frankel, J.A. (1997) *Regional Trading Blocs in the World Economic System*, Washington, DC: Institute of International Economics.

Frankel, J.A. (2000) Globalization of the Economy, Cambridge, MA: National Bureau of Economic Research Working Paper No. 7858.

Frankel, J.A. (2001) "Globalization and the economy," in J. Nye and J. Donahue (eds) *Governance in a Globalizing World*, Washington, DC: The Brookings Institution Press, pp. 132–58.

Frankel, J.A. (2003) "Coping with crises in emerging markets: adjustment versus financing," in D.K. Das (ed.) *An International Finance Reader*, London and New York: Routledge.

Frankel, J.A. and Romer, D. (1999) "Does trade cause growth?" *American Economic Review* 89: 2, 379–99.

Frankel, J.A. and Rose, A. (1996) "Currency crashes in the emerging markets: an empirical treatment," *Journal of International Economics* 41: 3, 351–66.

Friedman, T.L. (1999a) *The Lexus and The Olive Tree*, New York: Farrar Straus Giroux.

Friedman, T.L. (1999b) "Dueling globalization: a debate between Thomas Friedman and Ignacio Ramonet," *Foreign Policy*, Fall, 110–19.

Fujita, M., Krugman, P.R. and Venables, A.J. (1999) *The Spatial Economy: Cities, Regional and International Trade*, Cambridge, MA: MIT Press.

Galindo, A., Micco, A. and Ordonez, G. (2002) Financial Liberalization and Growth: Empirical Evidence. Paper presented at the Joint Conference between the World Bank and George Washington, University on *Financial Globalization: A Blessing or A Curse?*, 30–31 May, Washington, DC.

Galindo, A., Schiantarelli, F. and Weiss, A. (2001) *Does Financial Liberalization Improve the Allocation of Investment?* Washington, DC: Inter-American Development Bank.

Gamber, E.N. and Hung, J.H. (2001) "Has the rise in globalization reduced US inflation in the 1990s?" *Economic Enquiry* 39: 1, 58–73.

Gelos, R.G. and Roldos, J. (2002) Consolidation and Market Structure in Emerging Markets Banking System. Paper presented at the Joint Conference between the World Bank and George Washington University on *Financial Globalization: A Blessing or A Curse?*, 30–31 May, Washington, DC.

Ghani, E. (1992) How Financial Markets Affect Long-term Growth: A Cross-Country Study, Washington, DC: World Bank Policy Research Working Paper No. WPS 843.

Giannini, C. (2001) *Broad in Scope, Soft in Method: International Cooperation and the Quest for Financial Stability in Emerging Markets*, Rome: Bank of Italy.

Gilchrist, S. and Himmelberg, C. (1998) *Investment Fundamentals and Finance*, NBER Macroeconomic Annual, Cambridge, MA: MIT Press.

Gilpin, R. (2001) *Global Political Economy: Understanding the International Economic Order*, Princeton, NJ: Princeton University Press.

Giovanoli, M. (2001) A New Architecture for the Global Financial Market: Legal Aspects of International Financial Standard Setting, Basel: International Monetary Law Association.

Glick, R. and Rose, A. (1999) "Contagion and trade: why are currency crises regional?" *Journal of International Money and Finance* 18: 3, 603–17.

Goetzmann, W.N., Li, L. and Geert Rouwenhorst, K. (2003) Long-term Global Market Correlations. Paper presented at the *Global Linkage Conference* organized by the International Monetary Fund, 30–31 January, Washington, DC.

Goklany, I.M. (2002) The Globalization of Human Well-being, Washington, DC: Cato Institute. Policy Analysis Paper No. 447. August 22.

Goldberg, L. (2001) When is US Bank Lending to Emerging Markets Volatile? Cambridge, MA: National Bureau of Economic Research Working Paper No. 8209.

Goldsmith, R. (1969) *Financial Structure and Development*, New Haven, CT: Yale University Press.

Greenspan, A. (1999) Remarks by the Chairman of the Federal Reserve Board of Governors of the Federal Reserve System before the World Bank Conference on Recent Trends in Reserve Management, 29 April, Washington, DC.

Greenspan, A. (2000) Global Challenges, Keynote lecture at a conference on *The Financial Crises* organized by the Council on Foreign Relations, 12 July, New York.

Griffin, J.M., Nardari, F. and Stulz, R.M. (2003) Are Daily Cross-border Equity Flows Pushed or Pulled? Paper presented at the *Global Linkage Conference*, organized by the International Monetary Fund, 30–31 January, Washington, DC.

Group of Ten (G-10) (2001) *Report on Consolidation of the Financial Sector*, Basel.

Grubel, H.G. (2000) "The merit of a Canada–US monetary union," *North American Journal of Economics and Finance* 11: 19–40.

Guiditti, P. (1999) Currency Reserves and Debt. Paper presented at the World Bank Conference on Recent Trends in Reserve Management, 29 April, Washington, DC.

Guillaumont, P., Jeanneney, S.G. and Bern, J.F. (1999) "How instability lowers African growth," *Journal of African Economics* 8: 1, 87–108.

Hargis, K. (2001) "International cross-listing and stock market developments in emerging economies," *International Review of Economics and Finance* 55: 2, 101–22.

Hatton, T. and Williamson, J.G. (1998) *The Age of Mass Migration: Causes and Economic Impact*, Oxford: Oxford University Press.

Hatton, T. and Williamson, J.G. (2001) Demographic and Economic Pressure on Immigration out of Africa, Cambridge, MA: National Bureau of Economic Research. Working Paper No. 8124.

Hawkins, J. (2002) "Bond markets and banks in emerging market economies," in *The Development of Bond Markets in the Emerging Market Economies?* Basel: Bank for International Settlements, pp. 42–8.

Hawkins, J. and Mihaljek, D. (2001) The Banking Industry in Emerging Market Economies, Basel: Banks for International Settlements, BIS Paper No. 4.

Held, D., McGrew, A.G., Goldblatt, D. and Perraton, J. (1999) *Global Transformations: Politics, Economics and Culture*, Stanford, CA: Stanford University Press, p. 16.

Hellman, T., Murdock, K. and Stiglitz, J. (2000) "Liberalization, moral hazard in banking, and prudential regulation: are capital requirements enough?" *American Economic Review* 90: 1, 147–65.

Henry, P.B. (2000a) "Stock market liberalization, economic reforms and emerging market equity prices," *Journal of Finance* 58: 1–2, 301–34.

Henry, P.B. (2000b) "Does market liberalization cause investment booms?" *Journal of Finance and Economics* 55: 2, 529–63.

Hernandez, L.F. and Valdes, R.O. (2001) What Drives Contagion: Trade, Neighborhood, or Financial Links? Washington, DC: International Monetary Fund Working Paper No. WP/01/29.

Hertel, T. and Martin, W. (2001) "Liberalizing agriculture and manufactures in a millennium round: implications for developing countries," in B. Hoekman and W. Martin (eds) *Developing Countries and the WTO: A Pro-Active Agenda*, Oxford: Basil Blackwell, pp. 110–42.

Hicks, J. (1959) *Essays in World Economy*, Oxford: Clarendon Press.

Hoekman, B.M. and Kostecki, M.M. (2001) *The Political Economy of the World Trading System*, Oxford: Oxford University Press.

Honohan, P. (2000) "Consequences for Greece and Portugal of the opening up of the European banking markets," in S. Claessens and M. Jansen (eds) *The Internationalization of Financial Services*, Boston, MA: Kluwer Academic Press, pp. 169–99.

Horsefield, J.K. (1969) *The International Monetary Fund, 1945–65*, Vol. 3. Washington, DC: International Monetary Fund.

Hubbard, G. (1998) "Capital market imperfections and investment," *Journal of Economic Literature* 36: 3, 193–225.

Hufbauer, G., Wada, E. and Warren, T. (2002) *The Benefits of Price Convergence: Speculative Calculations*, Policy Analysis in Economics. Paper No. 65. Washington, DC: Institute for International Economics.

Hummels, D. (1999) Have International Transportation Costs Declined? Chicago: University of Chicago (mimeo).

Institute of International Finance (IIF) (1999) *Capital Flows to Emerging Market Economies*, Washington, DC: IIF.

Institute of International Finance (IIF) (2003) *Capital Flows to Emerging Market Economies*, Washington, DC: IIF.

Inter-American Development Bank (IDB) (1995) *Overcoming Volatility: Economic and Social Progress in Latin America*, Washington, DC: Inter-American development Bank.

International Monetary Fund (IMF) (1995) *International Capital Markets: Developments, Prospects and Policy Issues*, Washington, DC: IMF.

International Monetary Fund (IMF) (1997) *International Capital Markets: Developments and Prospects*, Washington, DC: IMF.

International Monetary Fund (IMF) (1998a) *World Economic Outlook and International Financial Markets*, Washington, DC: IMF.

International Monetary Fund (IMF) (1998b) Hedge Funds and Financial Market Dynamics, Washington, DC: IMF Occasional Paper No. 166.

International Monetary Fund (IMF) (1999) *World Economic Outlook*, Washington, DC: IMF.

International Monetary Fund (IMF) (2000) *International Capital Markets: Developments, Prospects and Key Policy Issues*, Washington, DC: IMF.

International Monetary Fund (IMF) (2001) *International Capital Markets: Developments, Prospects and Key Policy Issues*, Washington, DC: IMF.

International Monetary Fund (IMF) (2002a) *World Economic Outlook*, Washington, DC: IMF.

International Monetary Fund (IMF) (2002b) *Global Financial Stability Report*, Washington, DC: IMF.

International Monetary Fund (IMF) (2003a) *World Economic Outlook, 2003*, Washington, DC: IMF.

International Monetary Fund (IMF) (2003b) *Global Financial Stability Report*, Washington, DC: IMF.

International Monetary Fund and the World Bank (2001) *Developing Government Bond Markets: A Handbook*, Washington, DC: IMF.

Irwin, D.A. (1998) "From Smoot-Hawley to reciprocal trade agreements: changing the course of US trade policy in the 1930s," in M.D. Boro, C. Goldin and E. White (eds) *The Defining Moment: The Great Depression and the American Economy in the Twentieth Century*, Chicago: University of Chicago Press.

Jalilian, H. and Kirkpatrick, C. (2002) "Financial development and poverty reduction," *International Journal of Finance and Economics* 7: 1, 97–108.

Jayaratna, J. and Strahan, P.E. (1996) "The finance–growth nexus: evidence from bank branch deregulation." *Quarterly Journal of Economics* 111: 3, 639–70.

Jeanneau, S. and Micu, M. (2002) Determinants of International Bank Lending to Emerging Market Countries, Basel, Switzerland: Bank for International Settlements. BIS Working Paper No. 112.

Jiang, G., Tang, N. and Law, E. (2001) "Cost benefit analysis of developing debt markets," *Hong Kong Monetary Authority Quarterly Bulletin* 29: 1–18.

Johnson, S., Boone, P., Breach, A. and Friedman, E. (2000). "Corporate governance in the Asian financial crisis," *Journal of Financial Economics* 58: 141–86.

Jordan, C. and Lubrano, M. (2002) "How effective are capital markets in exerting governance on corporations?" in *Financial Sector Governance*, Washington, DC: The Brookings Institution Press.

Jordan, C. and Majnoni, G. (2002) Financial Regulatory Harmonization and the Globalization of Finance, Washington, DC: World Bank Policy Research Working Paper No. 2919. October.

Jorion, P. (2000) "Risk management lessons from long term capital management," *European Financial Management* 6: 9, 277–300.

Jorion, P. and Goetzmann, W.N. (1999) "Global stock markets in the twentieth century," *Journal of Finance* 54: 3, 953–80.

Kalaitzidakis, P. (2001) "Measures of human capital and nonlinearities in economic growth," *Journal of Economic Growth* 6: 3, 229–54.

Kaminsky, G. and Reinhart, C. (1999) "The twin crises: causes of banking and balance of payments problems," *American Economic Review* 89: 6, 122–40.

Kaminsky, G. and Reinhart, C. (2003a) "On crisis, contagion and confusion," in D.K. Das (ed.) *An International Finance Reader*, London and New York: Routledge, pp. 359–80.

Kaminsky, G. and Reinhart, C. (2003b) The Center and the Periphery: the Globalization of the Financial Turmoil. Paper presented at *Global Linkage Conference* organized by the International Monetary Fund, 30–31 January, Washington, DC.

Kaminsky, G.L. and Schmukler, S.L. (2001) On Booms and Crashes: Financial Liberalization and Stock Market Cycles, Washington, DC: World Bank Policy Working Paper No. 2565.

Kaminsky, G.L. and Schmukler, S.L. (2002) Short-run Pain, Long-term Gain: The Effects of Financial Liberalization. Paper presented at the Joint Conference between the World Bank and George Washington, University on *Financial Globalization: A Blessing or A Curse?*, 30–31 May, Washington, DC.

Karolyi, G.A. (2001) "DaimlerChrysler AG: the first truly global shares," Columbus: Ohio State University.

Karolyi, G.A. (2003) The Role of ADRs in the Development and Integration of Emerging Equity Markets." Paper presented at the *Global Linkage Conference*, organized by the International Monetary Fund, 30–31 January, Washington, DC.

Karolyi, G.A. and Stulz, R.M. (2003) "Are financial assets priced locally or globally?" in G. Constantinides, M. Harris and R. Stulz (eds) *Handbook of the Economics of Finance*, Amsterdam: North-Holland Publishers, pp. 140–86.

Kawai, M., Newfarmer, R. and Schmukler, S. (2001) Crisis and Contagions in East Asia: Nine Lessons, Washington, DC: The World Bank Policy Research Working Paper No. 2610. October.

Kehoe, P. and Chari, S. (1996) Contagious currency crises. Mimeo.

Kenwood, A.G. and Lougheed, A.L. (1983) *The Growth of International Economy 1820–1980: An Introductory Text*, 2nd edn, London: Unwin Hyman.

Keohane, R.O. and Nye, J.S. (2001) "Introduction," in R.O. Keohane and J.S. Nye (eds) *Governance in a Globalizing World*, Washington, DC: Brookings Institution Press, pp. 1–41.

Keynes, J.M. (1919) *Economic Consequences of the Peace*. Available at http://www.socsci.mcmaster.ca/~econ/ugcm/3ll3/keynes/peace.htm.

Keynes, J.M. (1982) "Shaping the post-war world: the clearing union," in D. Moggridge (ed.) *The Collected Writings of John Maynard Keynes*, Vol. 25, London: Macmillan Press Ltd.

Khan, A.R. and Riskin, C. (1998) "Income inequality in China: composition, distribution, and growth of household income, 1988–1995," *China Quarterly* 31: 2, 221–53.

Khan, A.R. and Riskin, C. (2001) *Inequality and Poverty in China in the Age of Globalization*, New York: Oxford University Press.

Kindleberger, C.P. (1989) "Commercial policy between the wars," in P. Mathias and S. Pollard (eds) *The Cambridge Economic History of Europe*, Vol. III, Cambridge: Cambridge University Press.

Kindleberger, C.P. (1996) *Mania, Panics and Crashes*, New York: Wiley & Sons.

King, M. (1999) "Challenges for monetary policy: new and old," in *New Challenges for Monetary Policy*, Kansas City: Federal Reserve Bank of Kansas City.

King, M. (2001) "Who triggered the Asian financial crisis?" *Review of International Political Economy* 8: 2, 438–66.

King, R. and Levine, R. (1993a) "Finance and growth: Schumpter might be right," *Quarterly Journal of Economics* 109: 3, 717–37.

King, R.G. and Levine, R. (1993b) "Finance, entrepreneurship and growth: theory and evidence," *Journal of Monetary Economics* 32: 3, 513–42.

Kiraly, J., Majer, B., Matyas, L., Ocsi, B., Sugar, A. and Verhegyi, E. (2000) "Experience with internationalization of financial services: case study: Hungary," in S. Claessens and M. Jansen (eds) *The Internationalization of Financial Services*, Boston, MA: Kluwer Academic Press, pp. 230–63.

Klenow, P. and Rodriguez-Clare, A. (1997) "Economic growth: a review essay," *Journal of Monetary Economics* 40: 3, 597–617.

Kohler, H. (2002) "Strengthening the framework for the global economy," speech given at the Award Ceremony of the Konrad Adenauer Foundation, Berlin, 15 November. Available at http://www.imf.org/external/np/speeches/2002/111502.htm.

Kolodko, G.W. (2000) *From Shock to Therapy: The Political Economy of Post-Socialist Transformation,"* Oxford: Oxford University Press.

Kolodko, G.W. (2001) "Globalization and transformation: illusions and reality," Paris: OECD Development Center. Technical Paper No. 176.

Kolodko, G.W. (2002) Globalization and Catching-up in Emerging Market Economies, Helsinki, Finland: United Nations University. World Institute for Development Economics Research Discussion Paper. WDP 2002/51.

Krueger, A.O. (1980) "Trade policy as an input to development," *The American Economic Review* 70: 2, 288–92.

Krueger, A.O. (2000) "Factors affecting export growth and performance," in D.K. Das (ed.) *Asian Exports*, Oxford: Oxford University Press, pp. 25–74.

Krueger, A.O. (2002) *A New Approach to Sovereign Debt Restructuring*, Washington, DC: International Monetary Fund.

Krueger, A.O. (2003) "Promoting international financial stability: sovereign debt restructuring," in D.K. Das (ed.) *An International Finance Reader*, London and New York: Routledge, pp. 114–41.

Krugman, P. (1995) "Dutch tulips and emerging markets," *Foreign Affairs* July/August: 25–44.

Krugman, P. (1997a) Currency Crises. Paper presented at the NBER Conference, 17 October 1997, Chicago, Illinois.

Krugman, P. (1997b) "What should trade negotiators negotiate about?" *Journal of Economic Literature* 35: March, pp. 113–20.

Krugman, P. (1998) "Saving Asia: it's time to get radical," *Fortune* 7 September: 74–80.

Krugman, P. (1999) *Balance Sheets, the Transfer Problem and Financial Crises,* Cambridge, MA: Massachusetts Institute of Technology.

Laeven, L. (2000) Does Financial Liberalization Reduce Financial Constraints? Washington, DC: World Bank Policy Research Working Paper No. 2435.

Laird, S. (2002a) "Multilateral market access negotiations in goods and services," in C. Milner and R. Read (eds) *Trade Liberalization, Competition and the WTO,* Cheltenham: Edward Elgar, pp. 23–58.

Laird, S. (2002b) "The WTO agenda and the developing countries," in C. Milner and R. Read (eds) *Trade Liberalization, Competition and the WTO,* Cheltenham: Edward Elgar, pp. 227–52.

Lamartine Yates, P. (1959) *Forty Years of Foreign Trade,* New York: Macmillan Press Ltd.

Lane, P.R. (1997) "Inflation in open economies," *Journal of International Economics* 42: 2, 327–47.

Lane, T., Ghosh, A., Human, J., Phillips, S., Schulze-Ghatta, M. and Tsikata, T. (1999) *IMF Supported Programs in Indonesia, Korea, and Thailand,* Washington, DC: International Monetary Fund.

Langois, J.D. (1981) *China Under Mongol Rule,* Princeton: Princeton University Press.

Lardy, N.R. (2001) Foreign Financial Firms in Asia. Paper presented at a conference on *Open Doors: Foreign Participation in Financial Systems in Developing Countries,* jointly organized by the Brookings Institutions, the World Bank and the International Monetary Fund, Washington, DC. 15 April.

Larrain, P. and Velasco, A. (2001) "Exchange rate policies in emerging market economies: the case for floating," *Essays in International Economics,* No. 224, Princeton, NJ: Princeton University.

Lejour, A.M. and Tang, P.J.G. (1999) Globalization and Wage Inequality, Rotterdam: CPB Netherlands Bureau of Economic Policy and Analysis (mimeo).

Levine, R. (1999) Foreign Bank Entry and Capital Control Liberalization: Effects on Growth and Stability, Minnesota: Department of Finance, University of Minnesota, (mimeo).

Levine, R., Loayza, N. and Beck, T. (1999) Financial Intermediation and Growth: Causality and Causes, Washington, DC: World Bank Policy Research Working Paper No. 2400.

Levine, R. and Zrvos, S. (1998) "Stock markets, banks and economic growth," *American Economic Review* 88: 3, 538–58.

Limao, N. and Venables, A.J. (2000) *Infrastructure, Geographical Disadvantage, and Transport Costs,* Washington, DC: The World Bank.

Lindert, P. and Williamson, J. (2001a) Does Globalization Make the World More Equal, Cambridge, MA: National Bureau of Economic Research. NBER Working Paper 8228.

Lindert, P. and Williamson, J. (2001b) Globalization: a Long History. Paper presented at the Annual Bank Conference on Development Economics – Europe Conference. Barcelona, World Bank, June 25–27.

Lindgren, C., Garcia, G. and Saal, M.I. (1996) *Bank Soundness and Macroeconomic Policy,* Washington, DC: International Monetary Fund.

Lindsey, B. (2000) "Globalization in the streets again," Washington, DC, Cato Institute, Center for Trade Policy Studies, 27 May. Available at freetrade.org/pubs/articles/bl-4-15-00.html.

Lipsey, R.E. (1999) The Role of Foreign Direct Investment in International Capital Flows, Cambridge, MA: National Bureau of Economic Research. NBER Working Paper No. 7094.

Loisel, O. and Martin, P. (2001) "Coordination, co-operation, contagion, and currency crises," *Journal of International Economics* 53: 2, 399–419.

Longin, F. and Solnik, B. (2001) "Extreme correlation of international equity markets," *Journal of Finance* 56: 2, 649–75.

Maddison, A. (1995) *Monitoring the World Economy 1820–1992*, Paris: Organization for Economic Co-operation and Development.

Maddison, A. (2001) *The World Economy: A Millennial Perspective*, Paris: Organization for Economic Development and Cooperation.

Marshall, R. (1993) *Storm from the East: From Genghis Khan to Khubilai Khan*, Los Angeles: University of California Press.

Martin, P. and Rey, H. (2002) Financial Globalization and Emerging Markets: With or Without Crash? Paper presented at the Joint Conference between the World Bank and George Washington University on *Financial Globalization: A Blessing or A Curse?*, 30–31 May, Washington, DC.

Martin, W. (2001) *Trade Policies, Developing Countries and Globalization*, Washington, DC: The World Bank.

Martin, W. and Winters, L.A. (1996) "The Uruguay Round: a milestone for the developing countries," in W. Martin and L.A. Winters (eds) *The Uruguay Round and the Developing Countries*, Cambridge: Cambridge University Press, pp. 1–29.

Masson, P. (1999) "Contagion: monsoonal effects, spillovers, and jumps between multiple equilibria," in P.R. Agenor, M. Millar, D. Vines and A. Weber (eds) *The Asian Financial Crisis: Causes, Contagions and Consequences*, Cambridge: Cambridge University Press, pp. 134–65.

Mathieson, D. and Roldos, J. (2001) The Role of Foreign Banks in Emerging Markets. Paper presented at the third Annual World Bank, International Monetary Fund, Brookings Institution *Financial Markets and Development Conference*, 12–13 April, New York.

Matusz, S.J. and Tarr, D. (2000) "Adjusting to trade policy reforms," in A.O. Krueger (ed.) *Economic Policy Reform: The Second Stage*, Chicago: University of Chicago Press, pp. 130–64.

Mauro, P., Sussman, N. and Yafeh, Y. (2000) Emerging Market Spreads: Then Versus Now, Washington, DC: International Monetary Fund Working Paper No. WP/00/190.

McKenzie, D. (2001) "The impact of capital controls on growth convergence," *Journal of Economic Development* 26: 1, 857–80.

McKinnon, R.I. (1973) *Money and Capital in Economic Development*, Washington, DC: The Brookings Institution.

McKinnon, R.I. and Pill, H. (1999) "Credible economic liberalization and overborrowing," *American Economic Review* 89: 2, 187–93.

Melchior, A., Telle, K. and Wiig, H. (2000) Globalization and Inequality: World Income Distribution and Living Standards 1960–98, Norway: The Royal Norwegian Ministry of Foreign Affairs. Report No. 68.

Meyer, L.H. (2000) "Structural changes and monetary policy," presentation made before the Joint Conference of Federal Bank of San Francisco and the Stanford Institute of Economic Policy Research, San Francisco, California, on 3 March. Available at http://www.frbsf.org/economics/conferences/000303/agenda/html.

Micklethwaite, J. and Wooldridge, A. (2000) *A Future Perfect*, New York: Random House.

Mihaljek, D. (1998) "Theory and practice of confederate finances," in P. Sorensen (ed.) *Public Finance in a Changing World*, London: Macmillan Press Ltd.

Mihaljek, D., Scatigna, M. and Villar, A. (2002) "Recent trends in bond markets," in *The Development of Bond Markets in the Emerging Market Economies?* Basel: The Bank for International Settlements, pp. 13–48.

Milanovic, B. (2002) Can We Discern the Effects of Globalization on Income Distribution? Washington, DC: The World Bank Policy Research Working Paper No. 2876. April.

Miller, S.R. and Parkhe, A. (1998) "Patterns in the expansion of U.S. Banks' foreign operations," *Journal of International Business Studies* 29: 2, 359–90.

Miller, V. (1998) "The double drain with a cross-border twist: more on the relationship between banking and currency crises," *American Economic Review: Papers and Proceedings* 88: 2, 439–43.

Milner, C. and Read, R. (2002) "Introduction: the GATT Uruguay Round, trade liberalization and the WTO," in C. Milner and R. Read (eds) *Trade Liberalization, Competition and the WTO*, Cheltenham: Edward Elgar, pp. 1–22.

Mishkin, F. (2001a) Financial Policies and the Prevention of Financial Crises in Emerging Market Countries, Cambridge, MA: National Bureau of Economic Research Working Paper No. W8087.

Mishkin, F. (2001b) "Financial policies and prevention of financial crises," in M. Feldstein (ed.) *Economic and Financial Crises in Emerging Market Countries*, Chicago: University of Chicago Press, pp. 134–60.

Mody, A. and Murshid, A.P. (2002) Growing Up with Capital Flows, Washington, DC: International Monetary Fund Working Paper No. WP/02/75.

Moel, A. (2001) "On American depository receipts and emerging markets," *Economica* 2: 1, 209–73.

Mote, F.W. (1999) *Imperial China: 900–1800*, Boston, MA: Harvard University Press.

Mundell, R. (2000) "A reconsideration of the twentieth century," *American Economic Review* 90: 3, 327–40.

Mussa, M. (1998) "Trade liberalization," in Z. Iqbal and M.S. Khan (eds) *Trade Reform and Regional Integration in Africa*, Washington, DC: International Monetary Fund, pp. 19–65.

Neal, L. (1990) *The Rise of Financial Capitalism: International Capital Markets in the Age of Reason*, Cambridge: Cambridge University Press.

Needham, J. (1954) *Science and Civilization in China*, Vol. I, Cambridge: Cambridge University Press.

O'Rourke, K.H. and Williamson, J.G. (2000) When Did Globalization Begin? Cambridge, MA: National Bureau of Economic Research. NBER Working Paper 7632. April.

Obstfeld, M. (1995) "International capital mobility in the 1990s," in P.B. Kenan (ed.) *Understanding Interdependence: The Macroeconomics of Open Economy*, Princeton: Princeton University Press.

Obstfeld, M. (2000) "Globalization and macroeconomics," *NBER Reporter*, Fall, 18–23.

Obstfeld, M. and Rogoff, K. (2001) The Six Major Puzzles in International Macroeconomics: Is There a Common Cause? Cambridge, MA: National Bureau of Economic Research. Working Paper No. 7777.

Obstfeld, M. and Taylor, A.M. (1997) "The great depression as a watershed: international capital mobility over the long run." NBER Working Paper No. 5960.

Obstfeld, M. and Taylor, A.M. (1998) "The great depression as a watershed: international capital mobility over the long run," in M.D. Bordo, C. Goldin and N. White (eds) *The Defining Moment: The Great Depression and the American Economy in the Twentieth Century*, Chicago: University of Chicago Press, pp. 353–402.

Obstfeld, M. and Taylor, A. (2002) Globalization and Capital Markets, Cambridge, MA: NBER Working Paper No. 8846.

Okina, O., Shirakawa, M. and Shiratsuka, S. (1999) "Financial market globalization: present and future," *Monetary and Economic Studies* 17: 3, 48–82.

Organization for Economic Cooperation and Development (OECD) (1997) *Economic Globalization and the Environment*, Paris: OECD.

Organization for Economic Cooperation and Development (OECD) (2002) *Revenue Statistics*, Paris: OECD.

Ortiz, G. (2002) "Recent emerging market crises: what have we learned?" Per Jacobsson Lecture, delivered in the City Hall, Basel, Switzerland, on 7 July.

Pagano, M., Randal, O., Roell, A. and Zechner, J. (2001) "What makes stock exchanges succeed? Evidence from cross-listing decisions," *European Economic Review* 45: 4, 770–82.

Panzar, J.C. and Rosse, J.N. (1987) "Testing for 'methodology' equilibrium," *The Journal of International Economics* 35: 4, 443–56.

Parsley, D.C. and Wei, S.J. (2001) Limiting Currency Volatility to Stimulate Goods Market Integration: A Price-based Approach, Cambridge, MA: National Bureau of Economic Research. NBER Working Paper No. 8468.

Peek, J. and Rosengren, E.S. (2000) "Implications of the globalization of banking sector: the Latin American experience," *New England Economic Review* 22: 2, 45–62.

Pericoli, M. and Sbracia, M. (2001) "A primer on financial contagion," *Temi di discussione*, No. 407, Rome: Bank of Italy.

Perrault, J.F. (2002) "Private capital flows to emerging market economies," *Bank of Canada Review* Spring: 33–43.

Phillips, E.D. (1969) *The Mongols*, New York: Frederick A. Praeger Publishers.

Powell, A. (2003) "A capital accord for emerging economies?" Available at http://econ.worldbank.org/files/13169_wps2808.pdf.

Powell, J. (1990) "The evolving international debt strategy," *Bank of Canada Review* Fall: 3–25.

Quinn, D. (1997) "The correlates of changes in international financial regulations," *American Political Science Review* 91: 3, 531–51.

Radelet, S. and Sachs, J.D. (1998a) "The East Asian financial crisis: diagnosis, remedies, prospects," *Brookings Papers on Economic Activity* 1: 1–90.

Radelet, S. and Sachs, J.D. (1998b) The Onset of the East Asian Financial Crises, Cambridge, MA: NBER Working Paper No. 6680.

Rajan, R. and Zingales, L. (1998) "Financial dependance and growth," *American Economic Review* 88: 3, 559–86.

Rapopori, H. (2001) Who is Afraid of Brain Drain? Human Capital Flight and Growth in Developing Countries, Stanford, CA: Stanford University, Stanford Institute for Economic Policy Research. Economic Policy Brief. November.

Razin, A. and Sadka, E. (eds) (1999) *The Economics of Globalization*, Cambridge: Cambridge University Press.

Razin, A. and Sadka, E. (2001) Country Risk and Capital Flow Reversals, Cambridge, MA: NBER Working Paper No. 8171.

Reinhard, C.M. and Tokatlidid, I. (2002) Paper presented at the Joint Conference between the World Bank and George Washington University on *Financial Globalization: A Blessing or A Curse?*, 30–31 May, Washington, DC.

Robertson, R. (2000) "Trade liberalization and wage inequality: lessons from Mexican experience," *The World Economy* 23: 6, June, 827–49.

Rodrik, D. (1997) *Has Globalization Gone Too Far?* Washington, DC: Institute of International Economics.

Rodrik, D. (1998) "Who needs capital account convertibility?" *Princeton Essays in International Finance*, No. 207, Princeton, NJ: Princeton University Press, pp. 55–65.

Rogers, J.H. (2002) Price Level Convergence, Relative Prices, and Inflation in Europe, Washington, DC: Board of Governors of the Federal Reserve System. International Finance Discussion Paper No. 699.

Rogoff, K. (1999) "Economic institutions for reducing global financial instability," *Journal of Economic Perspectives* 13: 1, 21–42.

Rose, A.K. (2002) *Estimating Protectionism from the Gravity Model*, Washington, DC: International Monetary Fund.

Rossabi, M. (1983) *Khubilai Khan: His Life and Times*, Los Angeles: University of California Press.

Roubini, N. and Sala-I-Martin, X. (1991) Financial Development, the Trade Regime and Economic Growth, Cambridge, MA: NBER Working Paper No. 3876.

Rousseau, P.L. and Sylla, R. (2001) Financial Systems, Economic Growth, and Globalization, Cambridge, MA: National Bureau of Economic Research. Working Paper No. 8323. June.

Rugman, A.M. (2002) "New rules for international investment: the case for a multilateral agreement on investment (MAI) at the WTO," in C. Milner and R. Read (eds) *Trade Liberalization, Competition and the WTO*, Cheltenham: Edward Elgar, pp. 176–89.

Sab, R. and Smith, S.C. (2001) Human Capital Convergence: International Evidence, Washington, DC: International Monetary Fund. Working Paper No. WP/01/32.

Sachs, J. (1997) Alternative Approaches to Financial Crises in Emerging Markets. Discussion Paper No. 568. Cambridge, MA: Harvard Institute for International Development.

Sachs, J., Tornell, A. and Velasco, A. (1996) "Financial crisis in emerging markets: the lessons from 1995," *Brookings Papers on Economic Activity* 1: 15–54.

Sachs, J.D. and Warner, A.M. (1995) "Fundamental sources of long-run growth," *American Economic Review, Papers and Proceedings*, Vol. 85, pp. 122–34.

Sampson, G.P. (2000) *Trade, Environment and the WTO: The Post-Seattle Agenda*, Baltimore, MD: Johns Hopkins University Press.

Sarkissian, S. and Schill, M. (2001) "The overseas listing decisions: new evidence of proximity preference. Social Science Research Network. Available at http://papers.ssrn.com/sol3/papers.cfm?/abstract_id:267103.

Sbracia, M. and Zaghini, A. (2001a) *The Role of the Banking System in the International Transmission of Shocks*, Rome: The Bank of Italy.

Sbracia, M. and Zaghini, A. (2001b) "Crisis and contagion: the role of the banking system," in *Macro- and Micro-Prudential Dimensions of Financial Stability.* Basel: Bank for International Settlements, pp. 241–60.

Schmulkler, S.L. and Zoido-Lobaton, P. (2001) *Financial Globalization: Opportunities and Challenges for Developing Countries,* Washington, DC: World Bank.

Schulze, G.G. and Ursprung, H.W. (1999) "Globalization of economy and nation state," *The World Economy* 22: 2, 295–352.

Shaw, E. (1973) *Financial Deepening in Economic Development,* New York: Oxford University Press.

Shiller, R. (1989) *Market Volatility,* Cambridge, MA: MIT Press.

Shirai, S. (2001) Searching for New Regulatory Framework for the Intermediate Financial Market in Post-crisis Asia," Tokyo: Asian Development Bank Institute Working Paper No. 24.

Shleifer, A. (2003) "Will the sovereign debt market survive?" *American Economic Review* 92: 5, 170–4.

Slaughter, M. (1999) "Globalization and wages: a tale of two perspectives," *The World Economy* 22: 3, 609–29.

Solimano, A. (2001) International Migration and the Global Economic Order: An Overview, Washington, DC: The World Bank Policy Research Working Paper No. 2720. November.

Srinivasan, T.N. (2002) Globalization: Is It Good or Bad? Stanford, CA: Stanford Institute for Economic Policy Research. Economic Policy Brief, December 23.

Standard & Poor's (S&P) (2000) *The S&P Emerging Market Indices: Methodology, Definitions, and Practices,* New York: S&P.

Stiglitz, J. (1994) "The role of state in financial markets," in M. Bruno and B. Pleskovic (eds) *Proceedings of the World Bank Annual Bank Conference on Development Economics 1993,* Washington, DC: World Bank, pp. 19–52.

Stiglitz, J. (1998a) "Knowledge for development: economic science, economic policy, and economic advice," in M. Bruno and B. Pleskovic (eds) *Proceedings of the World Bank Annual Bank Conference on Development Economics 1993,* Washington, DC: World Bank, pp. 19–52.

Stiglitz, J. (1998b) "Towards a new paradigm for development: strategies, policies, and processes," Raul Prebisch Lecture. Delivered at the UNCTAD Secretariat, Geneva, 19 October.

Stiglitz, J. (1999) "Bleak growth for the developing world," *International Herald Tribune* 10–11 April: 6.

Stiglitz, J. (2000a) "Capital market liberalization, economic growth and instability," *World Development* 28: 7, 1075–86.

Stiglitz, J. (2000b) "What I learned at the world economic crisis," *The New Republic* 17 April: 56–60.

Stulz, R.M. (1999a) "Globalization of equity markets and the cost of capital." Paper presented at the conference on *Global Equity Markets,* organized by New York Stock Exchange and Bourse de Paris, 19 February, Paris.

Stulz, R.M. (1999b) "International portfolio flows and security markets," in M. Feldstein (ed.) *International Capital Flows,* Chicago: University of Chicago Press.

Summers, L. (2000) "International financial crises: causes, preventions and cures," *American Economic Review: Papers and Proceedings* 90: 5, 1–16.

Sutton, J. (2000) Rich Trade, Scarce Capabilities: Industrial Development Revisited, Discussion Paper No. E1/28. London: London School of Economics and Political Science. September.

Sylla, R. (1999) "Emerging markets in history: United States, Japan and Argentina," in R. Sato (ed.) *Global Competition and Integration*, Boston: Kluwer Academic Publishers, pp. 427–44.

Sylla, R., Wilson, J.W. and Wright, R.E. (2002) Trans-Atlantic Capital Market Integration: 1790–1845. Paper presented at the High-Level Seminar on *Globalization in Historical Perspective*, organized by the International Monetary Fund, on 12–14 August, in Washington, DC.

Tanzi, V. (2000) Globalization, Technological Developments, and the Work of Fiscal Termites, Washington, DC: International Monetary Fund. Working Paper No. WP/00/181.

Taylor, A.M. (1996) International Capital Mobility in History: Purchasing Power Parity in the Long-run. NBER Working Paper No. 5742. Cambridge, MA: National Bureau of Economic Research. August.

Taylor, A.M. (1998) "International capital mobility in history: the saving–investment relationship," *Journal of Development Economics* 57: 1, 147–84.

Taylor, M.P. and Sarno, L. (1997) "Capital flows to developing countries: long- and short-term determinants," *World Bank Economic Review* 11: 3, 451–70.

Tesar, L. and Werner, I. (1998) "Internalization of securities markets since the 1987 crash," in R.E. Litan and A. Santomero (eds) *Brookings-Wharton Papers on Financial Services*, Washington, DC: Brookings Institution Press, pp. 281–372.

Tschoegl, A.E. (1985) "Ideology and changes in regulations: the case of foreign bank branches over the period 1920–1980," in T.L. Brewer (ed.) *Political Risks in International Business*, New York: Praeger, pp. 95–114.

Tschoegl, A.E. (2000) "International banking centers: geography and foreign banks," *Financial Markets, Institutions and Instruments* 9: 1, 1–32.

Ulan, M.K. (2000) "Is a Chilean-style tax on short-term capital inflows stabilizing?" *Open Economies Review* 11: 1, 149–77.

United Nations Conference on Trade and Development (UNCTAD) (2002) *World Investment Report 2001*, Geneva.

United States Senate (USS) (1990) "Implementation of the Brady plan." Hearing before the Subcommittee on International Debt of the Committee on Finance, 2 March.

Volcker, P. (1999) "A perspective on financial crisis," in J.S. Little and G. Olivei (eds) *Rethinking the International Monetary System*, Boston: The Federal Reserve Bank of Boston.

Wagner, H. (2000a) "Which exchange rate regime in an era of high capital mobility?" *The North American Journal of Economics and Finance* 11: 1, 191–203.

Wagner, H. (2000b) "Globalization and inflation," in H. Wagner (ed.) *Globalization and Unemployment*, Berlin: Springer, pp. 345–90.

Wagner, H. (2001) Implications of Globalization for Monetary Policy, Washington, DC: International Monetary Fund. Working Paper No. WP/01/184. November.

Walker, E. (2002) "The Chilean experience with completing markets with financial indexation," in P. Le-Fort and E.R. Schmidt-Hebbel (eds) *Inflation and Monetary Policy*, Santiago: Central Bank of Chile, pp. 122–42.

Walter, I. and Boot, A. (1999) "The future of banking: two essays on consolidation in the financial sector," Amsterdam: Amsterdam Center for Corporate Finance.

Wei, S.J. and Wu, Y. (2002) *Globalization and Inequality in Without Differences in Data Definition, Legal System, and Other Institution*, Washington, DC: The Brookings Institution.

Williamson, J. and Mahar, M. (1998) "A survey of financial liberalization," *Essays in International Finance* No. 211, Princeton, NJ: Princeton University Press.

Williamson, J.G. (1996) "Globalization, convergence and history," *Journal of Economic History* 56: 2, 277–306.

Winters, L.A. (2002) "Trade policies for poverty alleviation," in B. Hoekman, A. Mattoo and P. English (eds) *Trade, Development, and the WTO*, Washington, DC: The World Bank.

Wolf, H.C. (1997) Regional Contagion Effects in Emerging Markets. Working Paper in International Economics. No. G-97-03, Princeton, NJ: Princeton University.

World Bank (1997a) *Private Capital Flows to Developing Countries: The Road to Financial Integration*, New York: Oxford University Press.

World Bank (1997b) *Sharing Rising Incomes: Disparities in China*, Washington, DC: Oxford University Press.

World Bank (1998) *Assessing Aid: What Works? What Doesn't and Why?* New York: Oxford University Press.

World Bank (2000) *Global Economic Prospects and Developing Countries*, Washington, DC: Oxford University Press.

World Bank (2001a) *Global Development Finance: Building Coalitions for Effective Development Finance*, Washington, DC: World Bank.

World Bank (2001b) *World Development Report 2000/2001*, New York. Oxford University Press.

World Bank (2001c) *World Development Indicators*, Washington, DC: Oxford University Press.

World Bank (2001d) *Global Economic Prospects and the Developing Economies*, Washington, DC: Oxford University Press.

World Bank. (2001e) *Finance for Growth: Policy Choices in a Volatile World.* Washington, DC: Policy Research Report.

World Bank (2002a) *Global Economic Prospects*, Washington, DC: World Bank.

World Bank (2002b) *Globalization, Growth and Poverty*, New York: Oxford University Press.

World Bank (2002c) *Global Development Finance*, Washington, DC: World Bank.

World Development Report (WDR) (2000) Washington, DC: Oxford University Press.

World Trade Organization (WTO) (1994) "Developing countries and the Uruguay Round: an overview," Geneva. Committee on Trade and Development, Seventy-Seventh Session, 25 November.

World Trade Organization (WTO) (1998) "Tariffs: more binding and closer to zero." Available at http://www.wto.org/about/agmnts2.htm.

World Trade Organization (WTO) (1999) *The Legal Texts: the Results of the Uruguay Round of Multilateral Trade Negotiations*, Cambridge: Cambridge University Press.

World Trade Organization (WTO) (2001) "Doha WTO ministerial: briefing notes: 52 years of GATT/WTO," Geneva. Available at http://www-heva.wto-ministerial.org/english/the wto_e/minist_e/min01_e/brief_e/brief21_e.htm.

Wyplosz, C. (2001) How Risky is Financial Liberalization in the Developing Countries? London: Centre for Economic Policy Research. Discussion Paper No. 2724.

Yamori, N. (1998) "A note on location choice of multinational banks: the case of Japanese financial institutions," *Journal of Banking and Finance* 32: 1, 109–20.

Zeira, J. (1999) "International overshooting, booms and crashes," *Journal of Monetary Economics* 43: 2, 237–57.

Ziegler, D. (2003) "The weakest link: a survey of Asian finance," *The Economist* 8 February 2003.

Index